THE RIGHT SIDE OF HISTORY

THE RIGHT SIDE
OF HISTORY

How Reason and Moral

Purpose Made the West Great

—

BEN SHAPIRO

BROADSIDE BOOKS
An Imprint of HarperCollinsPublishers

To my parents, who taught me life has a reason.
To my wife, who taught me life has meaning.
To my children, who taught me life has a purpose.

CONTENTS

INTRODUCTION xi

CHAPTER 1: THE PURSUIT OF HAPPINESS 1

CHAPTER 2: FROM THE MOUNTAINTOP. 19

CHAPTER 3: FROM THE DUST 39

CHAPTER 4: COMING TOGETHER 55

CHAPTER 5: ENDOWED BY THEIR CREATORS 73

CHAPTER 6: KILLING PURPOSE, KILLING CAPACITY 97

CHAPTER 7: THE REMAKING OF THE WORLD 121

CHAPTER 8: AFTER THE FIRE 159

CHAPTER 9: THE RETURN TO PAGANISM 183

CONCLUSION: HOW TO BUILD 211

ACKNOWLEDGMENTS 219

NOTES 223

INDEX. 243

INTRODUCTION

This book is about two mysteries.

The first mystery: Why are things so good?

The second mystery: Why are we blowing it?

Human beings spent tens of thousands of years living in dire poverty, under subsistence conditions, in constant threat of physical danger both from nature and from other human beings. For nearly all of human history, life has been nasty, brutish, and short. In 1900, some 10 percent of all infants died before reaching their first birthday in the United States; in other countries, the number was far higher. Approximately one in every one hundred mothers could expect to die in childbirth.

Yet we now live in an era in which mothers can expect to survive pregnancy and childbirth (the mortality rate among pregnant women has dropped 99 percent).[1] Babies can be expected to survive infancy and then live another eight decades; we live in an era in which the vast majority of the American population lives in climate-controlled spaces with plenty of food, a car, and at least one television. We can speak with each other across thousands of miles instantaneously, find and collate information with the touch of a few keys, send money seamlessly whirring around the globe, and buy products manufactured in dozens of different places for cents on the dollar without leaving our homes.

Then there are our freedoms. We can expect that a baby born in the United States will never be enslaved, murdered, or tortured; an adult in the United States can go about his or her daily business with the expectation that she will not be arrested for espousing an unpopular viewpoint or worshipping the wrong god or no god at all. There are no restrictions barring particular races or genders from particular jobs, no governmental rules designed to privilege one particular biological or religious in-group at the expense of any other out-group. We can live with whom we choose, have as many or as few children as we want, and open any business we see fit. We can expect to die richer than we were born.

We don't live in a perfect world, but we do live in the best world that has ever existed. So, the first mystery is this: How did all of this happen? What changed?

Then there's the second, more important question: Why are we throwing it away?

We are killing ourselves at the highest rates in decades. Rates of depression have skyrocketed. Drug overdoses are now responsible for more deaths than car crashes. Marriage rates have declined, as have childbearing rates. We're spending more money on luxuries, and enjoying everything less. Conspiracies have replaced reason and subjective perceptions have replaced objective observation. Facts have been buried to make way for feelings; a society of essential oils and self-esteem has replaced a society of logic.

We're more divided than at any time in the recent past. The exit polls show that on the day of the 2016 election, just 43 percent of voters had a favorable opinion of Hillary Clinton; 38 percent of voters had a favorable opinion of Donald Trump. Only 36 percent of voters thought Hillary was honest and trustworthy; 33 percent of voters thought Trump was. Fully 53 percent of Americans said they would feel concerned or scared if Clinton won; 57 percent of Americans felt that way if Trump won. Never have two more unpopular candidates run against each other.[2]

They still both earned millions of votes in support. Not just that—people who were uncomfortable with their candidate vitriolically attacked anyone who voted for the other; they broke off friendships with those who voted differently. In July 2017, Pew Research found that 47 percent of self-described liberal Democrats said they'd have a tough time staying friends with those who voted for Trump; 13 percent of conservatives said the same, but it's difficult to say whether that number might have been reversed if Trump had lost. It's also worth noting that fully 47 percent of Clinton voters said they didn't have a single close friend who voted for Trump. A more telling statistic: 68 percent of Democrats said it was "stressful and frustrating" to talk to political opponents; 52 percent of Republicans agreed.[3]

Something deeper than political differences is going on here. Virtually all of our trust in key institutions has vanished. Gallup polls show that our average trust in fourteen key institutions is just 32 percent. Just 27 percent of Americans trust banks; just

20 percent of Americans trust newspapers; just 41 percent of Americans say they trust organized religion; that number is 19 percent for the federal government overall, and 39 percent for the health care system.[4] Only 30 percent of Americans trust the public schools, 18 percent trust big business, and 9 percent trust Congress.[5] We still trust our police, but those numbers have dropped over the past decade, particularly among Democrats.[6] The only thing we still seem to trust is the military—which makes sense, since it provides for our common defense.[7]

We don't trust each other, either. As of 2015, just 52 percent of Americans said they trusted all or most of their neighbors; just 31 percent of blacks and 27 percent of Hispanics say they can trust their neighbors. Just 46 percent of Americans say they spend an evening with neighbors even once per month, compared to 61 percent of Americans who did in 1974.[8] Another 2016 survey showed that just 31 percent of Americans thought "most people can be trusted."

As for our democracy, fewer and fewer people like it. An October 2016 poll showed that 40 percent of Americans said they had "lost faith in American democracy," with another 6 percent stating that they never had faith to begin with. No wonder only 31 percent of those polled said they would "definitely" accept the results of the election if their candidate lost. And 80 percent of Americans said America was more divided today than ever—*ever*.[9] Just a reminder: we've had a full-scale civil war in this country, as well as Jim Crow and the domestic terrorism of the 1960s.

Brutal division has infused every aspect of our social fabric: we can't watch a football game together without debating the merits of protesting during the National Anthem or watch a television show without falling into debates over representation of women or go to church without arguing over our vote. We fight harder and more viciously over smaller and smaller matters—the more frivolous the topic, the harsher the battles.

What in the world happened?

There are some trendy answers.

Some blame our current political and social disintegration on heightened economic divides. Many commentators and politicians argue that income inequality has generated unprecedented conflict in American life. They say that too many Americans feel left behind by the new, globalized economy, and that either mild protectionism or redistributionism will heal those ills. They argue that the 1 percent have outpaced the 99 percent, that urbanites have outpaced rural Americans, that white-collar jobs have outpaced blue-collar jobs.

Such economic reductionism seems misplaced. The upper middle class in the United States grew from 12 percent of Americans in 1979 to 30 percent as of 2014.[10] Income mobility hasn't changed significantly in the United States since the 1970s.[11] America has seen far worse economic times—as of this writing, we're living at 4 percent unemployment, with record stock market gains. The Great Depression didn't tear us apart the way we're torn apart today—and our economy has indeed grown steadily since 2009. Economic change has been a constant force in American life, with a long-term upward trend for all demographics. The difference is our social divide, not our wallets.

How about race? In this view, our political conflicts are a proxy for deeper racial wounds, which have reopened in recent years. This argument is made most passionately by Ta-Nehisi Coates, who suggested that Barack Obama was black America's best and final hope ("a champion of black imagination, of black dreams and black possibilities"[12]), and that Donald Trump's presidency represents the revenge of white America. "To Trump, whiteness is neither notional nor symbolic but is the very core of his power," Coates recently wrote. "In this, Trump is not singular. But whereas his forebears carried whiteness like an ancestral talisman, Trump cracked the glowing amulet open, releasing its eldritch energies."[13] Black Americans, Coates argued, "have been cast into a race in which the wind is always at your face and the hounds are always at your heels. . . . The plunder of black life was drilled into this country in its infancy and reinforced across its history, so that plunder has become an heirloom, an intelligence, a sentience, a default setting to which, likely to the end of our days, we must invariably return."[14]

The photo negative of Coates's perspective comes courtesy of the racist alt-right movement, which accepts Coates's characterization of American politics but sees things in reverse: an America overrun by identity politics of racial minorities. The alt-right *loves* Coates's characterization of white America as all-powerful; as Richard Spencer told *New York Times Magazine* contributing writer Thomas Chatterton Williams, "This is why I'm actually very confident, because maybe those leftists will be the easiest ones to flip."[15] More than that, the alt-right also sees the world in terms of a race war—one they hope one day to finally win.

However, racial divides can't explain our current crisis. Racial conflagrationists have always existed in the United States. This is still the country that endured slavery and Jim Crow. Have things really gotten worse since then in terms of race?

In truth, we're more racially equal than ever before in our history—more equal than any other society in human history. In 1958, just 4 percent of Americans approved of black-white intermarriage; as of 2013, that statistic was 87 percent.[16] In that year, 72 percent of white Americans thought race relations were good, and so did 66 percent of black Americans; that statistic had remained relatively stable from 2001 through 2013. And yet our racial battles are now bloody and brutal, with renewed tribalism raging on all sides; by July 2016, just 53 percent of Americans said race relations were good, while 46 percent said they were bad.[17] Something is indeed falling apart, but it's hard to attribute that collapse to a resurgence of racist sentiment.

A third popular argument explaining our national disintegration suggests technology as the culprit. Social media, we hear, is dividing us more than ever. We are hunkering down in our bubbles, speaking only to those who agree with us. We only follow those we like on social media; we're engaging in social situations less and less frequently. If we all sit in our living rooms and avoid one another, interacting only to prop up our preconceived notions, we're less likely to see those who disagree as brothers and sisters. Mostafa El-Bermawy of Wired.com suggests, "From your Facebook feed to your Google Search, as your experience online grows increasingly personalized, the internet's islands keep getting more segregated and sound proofed. . . . Without realizing it, we develop tunnel vision."[18]

This is an attractive theory. But according to researchers, there's not much evidence to support it. According to economics professors at Stanford and Brown, political polarization is taking place more for "demographic groups least likely to use the internet and social media."[19] Polarization seems to cross demographic boundaries, without reference to level of technological use.[20]

Finally, there's the most basic argument of all: for whatever reason, human nature has kicked back in. We're naturally tribal, naturally possessive, naturally angry. For a while, we suppressed those instincts; we called that the "Enlightenment." Jonah Goldberg, in his masterful *Suicide of the West*, calls that overthrow of human instinct "The Miracle."[21] Steven Pinker, author of *Enlightenment Now*, makes a similar case: he says that the Enlightenment changed everything—that it brought about science and humanism, reason and progress. Enlightenment thinking substituted rationality for irrationality, and the effect was the creation of the modern world.[22] Goldberg, arguing that Enlightenment ideals are unnatural, says that our current dissolution looks like a reversion to our tribal, reactionary nature. Pinker agrees.

But this answer doesn't explain why, precisely, modernity ever should have burst forth in the first place—if human nature cuts against the liberalism and capitalism and humanism and science, then what caused them to bloom? More important, this answer doesn't explain why we're tearing down these powerful forces *now*, as opposed to any time in the past two centuries.

I believe these two questions are intimately related. This book argues that Western civilization, including our modern notions of values and reason and science, was built on deep foundations. And this book argues that we're tossing away what's best about our civilization because we've forgotten that those foundations even exist.

So, where did this book come from? It came from my sense—widely reflected, I think—that we're tearing each other apart. That realization hit me on a precise date: February 25, 2016.

Late in 2015, I'd started a speaking tour on college campuses, heading first to the University of Missouri. That campus exploded into the national news after Black Lives Matter protests against the administration; the football team vowed not to take the field for a scheduled game, despite the administration's over-zealous response to vague reports of isolated racist incidents, some of which were completely unsubstantiated. Student protesters declared a hunger strike, formed an encampment, and refused access to journalists. One professor, Melissa Click, infamously asked for someone to physically manhandle a student reporter seeking to cover the event.

I gave a speech to students on campus, viewed half a million times online within a week; I posited that all people of good heart wanted to fight racism, but that vague charges of institutional racism and white privilege obscured individual evil—and slandered the country more broadly. I attended the speech without security. Everything went well despite an attempt to pull the fire alarm, and students lined up for a broad-based question-and-answer session, too.

Just three months later came the rude awakening.

I was scheduled to give a speech to the Young America's Foundation group at California State University at Los Angeles. Two weeks in advance of the speech, we began hearing rumblings about protests; the week before the speech, the president of the university announced that the event had been canceled outright. I refused to accede to that clear breach of First Amendment rights—my taxpayer dollars had gone to the California State University system, after all—and I announced that I would show up anyway.

My business partner, Jeremy Boreing, insisted I bring a security team, but I was pretty skeptical. After all, I'd never needed security for any event. This wasn't Fallujah. This was a major college campus in the middle of my home city.

Just to be safe, Jeremy hired security anyway.

Thank God I listened.

On the day of the scheduled event, our security team began hearing rumors that violence was in the offing. An hour before the event, the president of the university announced that he would back down, and that police would protect the speech.

As we approached the campus, we could see helicopters swirling overhead.

We pulled into a parking lot behind the auditorium, and dozens of armed, uniformed police quickly formed a cordon and rushed me through the back door. I was puzzled more than anything else.

The security precautions didn't end there. Backstage were another dozen cops.

Hundreds of student protesters had filled the hallway outside the auditorium, and they had blocked off all the entrances.

A few rioters were physically assaulting students who wanted to enter; the police set up a back-door route but could only sneak students in two at a time. I put my ear to the auditorium door; it sounded like a zombie apocalypse outside. Members of the police department said that the administration had told them to stand down and allow the protesters to do whatever they pleased.

The police offered us a choice: we could wait for two hours while they filled the room, or we could go ahead with the speech.

We decided to go ahead, despite the mostly empty auditorium, and despite the near riot happening just outside the door.

As the speech progressed, students pulled the fire alarm; the lights went out and the alarm began beeping loudly. Students continued pounding the doors outside. I spoke through the discord, announcing that the disrupters wouldn't stop us from exercising our free speech rights.

As I finished, I turned to those in the audience—I was more than a bit amped up by this point—and asked if they wanted to go outside and mingle with the protesters. They responded in the affirmative—at which point my security team and the police pulled me backstage. "If you go outside," one of the officers warned me, "we can protect you from the first guy who throws a punch, and the second guy, but not the third guy. Also, we won't be able to protect all the students here if they walk out with you. You should leave the campus, and we'll keep all the students inside until the crowd disperses."

Duly chastened, I acquiesced to being escorted from campus. The moving cordon of police officers sneaked me out of the forum through back hallways and kitchens, ushered me into a tinted-window black van, and guided me from the campus with a police escort flashing their lights.

So, what went wrong?

I found out later that a professor on campus had been telling her students that I was a white supremacist, that I was akin to a Ku Klux Klan member, that I was a Nazi (I'm just wearing the yarmulke as deep cover, apparently). The students had believed their professors, and they had reacted accordingly. The value of speech had been overthrown in favor of a subjective rage that had nothing to do with facts.

This, of course, was just the beginning. At the University of Wisconsin, my speech was nearly shut down by protesters who flooded the front of the stage. At Penn State, protesters gathered outside my speech and pounded on the doors. At DePaul University, the administration threatened to arrest me if I came to campus and called out a Cook County sheriff to do the honors. At Berkeley, the administration called out hundreds of police officers to protect law-abiding citizens from the rage of violent rioters.

That wasn't the end of the 2016 circus, however.

During the election cycle, I was highly critical of both candidates. As a conservative, I'd been a lifelong critic of Hillary Clinton. But I was also highly critical of Donald Trump. Thanks to my criticisms of Trump—and thanks to my very public break with Breitbart News, an outlet I believed had become a propaganda tool for the Trump campaign—I quickly found myself targeted by a new breed of radical. In late March, the execrable Milo Yiannopoulos penned a story at Breitbart openly praising the alt-right, including odes to racist cretins like Richard Spencer. Egging on his alt-right followers, cheering on their "jolly trollery," Milo sent me a picture of a black baby on the day of my son's birth that May—the point being that I was a "cuck."

Over the course of the 2016 campaign, I would become the top recipient of anti-Semitism among Jewish journalists on the internet. By a huge margin. According to the Anti-Defamation League, approximately 19,253 anti-Semitic tweets were directed at journalists during the August 2015 through July 2016 period. I received 7,400 of those tweets, or 38 percent of the total.[23]

I went through most of my adult life involved in public political conversations with others without threat of violence or racist slur. Now, I required hundreds of police officers to protect me while speaking at a variety of campuses, and my Twitter feed was flooded with images straight from the pages of *Der Stürmer*.

Something, obviously, had changed.

Something *has* changed.

We've lost something.

This book is my attempt to determine what we've lost and how we can find it.

To find what we've lost, we're going to need to retrace our steps. This book is filled with old ideas—ideas from people we may dimly remember from our days in high school and college and Sunday school, but whose central importance we've essentially forgotten.

Those ideas, I'll argue, are crucial. We must learn them anew.

This doesn't mean that I believe philosophers changed history on their own. I don't think Adam Smith invented capitalism any

more than Immanuel Kant invented morality. But these philosophers and thinkers offer a window into the most important ideas
of their time. Tolstoy famously asks in *War and Peace* what moves
history, and concludes that history is merely the progression of
all of the various forces at play in the universe, channeled into
action in a particular moment. There's truth to that, of course. But
ideas matter, and important ideas—as best articulated by great
thinkers—represent the motivational road along which humanity
journeys. We act because we believe.

In order to fix ourselves, then, we must reexamine what we
believe.

We believe freedom is built upon the twin notions that God
created every human in His image, and that human beings are
capable of investigating and exploring God's world. Those notions were born in Jerusalem and Athens, respectively.

Those twin notions—those diamonds of spiritual genius—
built our civilization, and built us as individuals. If you believe
that life is more than materialistic pleasures and pain avoidance,
you are a product of Jerusalem and Athens. If you believe that
the government has no right to intrude upon the exercise of your
individual will, and that you are bound by moral duty to pursue virtue, you are a product of Jerusalem and Athens. If you
believe that human beings are capable of bettering our world
through use of our reason, and are bound by higher purpose to
do so, you are a product of Jerusalem and Athens.

Jerusalem and Athens built science. The twin ideals of Judeo-
Christian values and Greek natural law reasoning built human
rights. They built prosperity, peace, and artistic beauty. Jerusalem
and Athens built America, ended slavery, defeated the Nazis and

the Communists, lifted billions from poverty, and gave billions spiritual purpose. Jerusalem and Athens were the foundations of the Magna Carta and the Treaty of Westphalia; they were the foundations of the Declaration of Independence, Abraham Lincoln's Emancipation Proclamation, and Martin Luther King Jr.'s Letter from Birmingham Jail.

Civilizations that rejected Jerusalem and Athens, and the tension between them, have collapsed into dust. The USSR rejected Judeo-Christian values and Greek natural law, substituting the values of the collective and a new utopian vision of "social justice"—and they starved and slaughtered tens of millions of human beings. The Nazis rejected Judeo-Christian values and Greek natural law, and they shoved children into gas chambers. Venezuela rejects Judeo-Christian values and Greek natural law, and citizens of their oil-rich nation have been reduced to eating dogs.

In America, especially, with our unique history and success, we have long seen progress and prosperity as our birthright. The conflicts that tear apart other nations are not for us; we certainly don't need to worry about revolution or collapse. We're America. We're different.

That sanguine view is utterly wrong. The fight against entropy is never over. Our way of life is never more than one generation away from the precipice. We have already begun to see a huge number of our citizens lose faith in free speech, in democracy, in economic freedom, in the idea of a shared morality or cause. That turn away from our values began when we lost faith in the path that brought us here in the first place.

We are in the process of abandoning Judeo-Christian values

and Greek natural law, favoring moral subjectivism and the rule of passion. And we are watching our civilization collapse into age-old tribalism, individualistic hedonism, and moral subjectivism. Make no mistake: we are still living off the prosperity of the world built by Jerusalem and Athens. We believe we can reject Judeo-Christian values and Greek natural law and satisfy ourselves with intersectionality, or scientific materialism, or progressive politics, or authoritarian governance, or nationalistic solidarity. We can't. We've spent the last two centuries carving ourselves off from the roots of our civilization. Our civilization could survive and thrive—for a time. Then it began to die, from the inside out. Our civilization is riddled with internal contradictions, communities bereft of values, and individuals bereft of meaning.

The economies of the West aren't going to die overnight; stacking socialist programs atop capitalist infrastructures won't immediately collapse the West. But we flatter ourselves to believe that we can abandon the values of the past and somehow survive indefinitely. Philosophically, the West has been running on fumes for generations. We are viewing birth rates plummet and government spending skyrocket across the West—and we are watching large swaths of immigrants unfamiliar with Western values imported to fill the gap, resulting in polarizing backlash. We are watching European politics devolve into a battle between far-left socialists who promise utopia and far-right nationalists who promise national restoration. Both are bound to fail. And though America lags behind, America is following the European path. The ties that bind us together are fraying.

Those ties were forged through fire and water, reason and

prayer. The journey to modernity was a long road. That road wasn't always pretty—often, it was violent. The tension between Jerusalem and Athens is real. But removing the tension by abandoning either Jerusalem or Athens collapses the bridge built between the two.

To strengthen our civilization, then, we must examine how the bridge was built. It took Western civilization three thousand years to get here—we can lose it all in one generation, unless we begin shoring up our foundations. We must stop chipping away, and we must start retrofitting. That task requires us to reexamine those foundations, brick by brick.

In this book, we'll reexamine those foundations. We'll be moving through thousands of years of philosophy and history, which means we'll inevitably be giving great philosophers shorter shrift than they deserve, and simplifying issues for the sake of brevity. This book won't tell you all you need to know about any of these ideas and philosophers—not even close. That means you should pursue further the specific ideas that interest you, with people more expert than I, in more detail (and for my part, I've tried to restrict my philosophical synopses to points upon which there seems to be general agreement). But this book *does* represent my attempt to dive into those ideas in the most user-friendly way in pursuit of wisdom about the essential questions of our civilization.

So, let us begin at the beginning.

CHAPTER 1

THE PURSUIT OF HAPPINESS

A re you happy?"

It's a question my wife asked me one day, a few years ago. We were going through a stressful period—my wife is a doctor, and she was working brutal hours; our youngest child, Gabriel, was waking us up at all hours of the night; our eldest, Leeya, was going through a stretch in which she'd burst into tears at the tiniest provocation. And work was trying, too: my business partners and I were working to get our website, The Daily Wire, functioning at top level; we were building out my podcast; I was traveling to various campuses, each a security challenge and a test of wills with sometimes violent students and obstructive administrators.

"Sure," I said. "Of course I am."

Like a lot of other people who answer that question from a spouse, I knew there was a correct answer; you never want to say no, lest your spouse think it's his or her fault.

But this question *is* the most crucial one.

So, was I happy?

Or, more precisely, when was I *most* happy?

Formulated like that, the question became easy: on Sabbath.

Every week, I drop everything for twenty-five hours. As an Orthodox Jew, I celebrate the Sabbath, which means that my phone and television are off-limits. No work. No computer. No news. No politics. A full day, plus an hour, to spend with my wife and children and parents, with my community. The outside world disappears. It's the high point of my life. There is no greater happiness than sitting with my wife, watching the kids play with (and occasionally fight with) each other, a book open on my lap.

I'm not alone. Sabbath is the high point of many Jews' weeks. There's an old saying in the Jewish community: the Jews didn't keep the Sabbath, the Sabbath kept the Jews. It certainly kept us sane.

Now, I cover politics for a living. And I'm happy doing it— it's purposeful and important, and working to understand and convey ideas can be thrilling. But politics isn't the root of happiness for me. Politics is about working to build the framework for the *pursuit* of happiness, not the achievement of it; politics helps us establish the preconditions necessary for happiness, but can't provide happiness in and of itself. The Founding Fathers knew that. That's why Thomas Jefferson didn't write that the government was granted power to grant you happiness: it was there to protect your pursuit of happiness. The government existed to protect your rights, to prevent those rights from being infringed upon. The government was there to stop someone from stealing your horse, from butchering you in your sleep, from letting his cow graze on your land.

At no point did Jefferson suggest that government could achieve happiness. None of the Founders thought it could.

Yet more and more Americans are investing their happiness in politics. Instead of looking inward to find ways to better their lives, we've decided that the chief obstacle to our happiness is outside forces, even in the freest, richest country in the history of the world. This desire to silence—or subdue—those who disagree with us has been reaching new, terrifying heights.

To take a minor example, in September 2017, Republicans and Democrats clubbed each other savagely over the *exact same policy*: President Obama had issued an executive amnesty for certain children of illegal immigrants, the so-called DREAMers; President Trump had revoked that amnesty, but called on Congress to pass a legislative version that would protect the DREAMers. Democrats called Republicans cruel, inhumane; one congressman called Trump "Pontius Pilate." Meanwhile, Republicans called Democrats lawless and irresponsible.

Over the *exact same policy*.

And it's getting uglier. We seem dedicated to the proposition that if only we can change the political landscape—or at least attribute nasty motives to our political opponents—then we can achieve the happiness we crave. Instead of leaving each other alone, we seek to control one another—if only Bob would do what I want, I'd be happy! And if I elect the right guy, *he'll* make Bob do what I want him to do!

Our politicians know that we seek happiness through them, and they capitalize off that misguided quest. In 2008, Michelle Obama said that Americans should back her husband because he could help us "fix our souls." How, exactly? She explained:

"Barack Obama . . . is going to demand that you shed your cynicism. That you put down your divisions. . . . That you push yourselves to be better. And that you engage. Barack will never allow you go to back to your lives as usual, uninvolved, uninformed."[1] In May 2016, then candidate Trump openly stated, "I will give you everything. I will give you what you've been looking for for 50 years. I'm the only one."[2]

We're fools to believe them. And what's more, we *know* we're fools to believe them. Polls show that we don't trust our politicians. We think they're lying to us, and we're right. They pander to us. They fib to us. They tell us promises specifically designed to garner our support, then make excuses to break those promises. And yet we eagerly invest them with more and more authority, and browbeat those who oppose our favorite candidates.

Why have we invested so much meaning, so much time, so much effort in brutal policy fights over seemingly minor matters, when none of it brings us closer to happiness? Why, overall, do the American people seem to be less and less optimistic? Why, by polling data, do nearly three-quarters of Americans say they aren't confident "life for our children's generation will be better than it has been for us"—the lowest number in decades?[3] Why are a huge plurality of young Americans themselves more fearful than hopeful about the future?[4] Why are suicide rates rising dramatically among some of the most materially prosperous segments of society, to rates not seen in thirty years?[5]

Perhaps the problem is that what we're pursuing isn't happiness anymore. We're instead pursuing other priorities: physical pleasure, emotional catharsis, monetary stability. All these things are important, of course, but they don't bring lasting happiness. At best, they're means necessary to the pursuit of happiness. But we've mixed up the means with the end. And in doing so, we've left our souls in desperate need of sustenance.

HAPPINESS IS MORAL PURPOSE

Pleasure can be gained from a variety of activities: golf, fishing, playing with your children, sex. Amoral activities can bring us pleasure—that temporary high, that feeling of forgetting our cares. However, that pleasure is never enough. Lasting happiness can only be achieved through cultivation of soul and mind. And cultivating our souls and minds requires us to live with moral purpose.

This has been clear since the dawn of Western civilization. The very terminology for happiness is imbued with such meaning in both the Judeo-Christian and the Greek context. The Hebrew Bible calls happiness *simcha*; Aristotle called happiness *eudaimonia*. What does the Bible mean by *simcha*? It means right action in accordance with God's will. In Ecclesiastes, Solomon laments, "I said to myself: 'Come now, I will mix [wine] with joy and experience pleasure,' and behold, this too was vanity."[6] The Bible doesn't seem to care very much about what we want. Instead, God *commands* us to live in *simcha*. How can He command an emotion? He can't—he can only command our enthusiastic pursuit of an ideal He sets forth for us. If we do not pursue that purpose, we pay a price: we serve foreign gods, which cannot provide us any sort of true fulfillment.

> Because you did not serve the Lord your God joyfully and gladly in the time of prosperity, therefore in hunger and thirst, in nakedness and dire poverty, you will serve the enemies the Lord sends against you. He will put an iron yoke on your neck until he has destroyed you.[7]

We might not think of binge-watching *Stranger Things* as an iron yoke on our neck, but if television is our best reason to live, we're not really living. Rejoice in the purpose God gives you. Here's Solomon again: "There is nothing better for a person than to rejoice in his work, because that is his lot."[8] He's not talking about finding your "why" at a software start-up. He means the work of serving God and following Him. As Rabbi Tarfon says in Ethics of the Fathers, "The day is short, the work is great, the workers are lazy, but the reward is great, and the Master of the house is knocking at your door." And what if you don't want to work? Well, tough: "It is not upon you to finish the work, but neither are you free to desist from it."[9]

Aristotelian *eudaimonia* similarly relies on living in accordance with moral purpose. Like the Bible, Aristotle didn't define happiness as temporary joy. He saw happiness in a life well-lived. How could we live a good life? First, by determining what "good" means; second, by pursuing it. To Aristotle, "good" wasn't a subjective term, something for each of us to define for ourselves; "good" was a statement of objective fact.

Something was "good" if it fulfilled its purpose. A good watch tells time; a good dog defends its master. What does a good human being do? Acts in accordance with right reason. What makes human beings unique, says Aristotle, is our capacity to reason, and to use that reason to investigate the nature of the world and our purpose in it:

> What, then, prevents one from calling happy someone who is active in accord with complete virtue and who is adequately equipped with external goods, not for any chance time but in a complete life?[10]

Act well, and in accordance with your value as a rational being, and you will be happy. We find moral purpose in cultivating our reason, and using that reason to act virtuously; pursuing moral purpose makes us "great-souled."

So, in the end, the Bible and the Philosopher come to the same conclusion from opposite directions: the Bible commands us to serve God with happiness and identifies that moral purpose with happiness; Aristotle suggests that it is impossible to achieve happiness without virtue, which means acting in accordance with a moral purpose that rational human beings can discern from the nature of the universe—a universe Aristotle traced back to an Unmoved Mover. George Washington puts the synthesis well in his letter to the Protestant Episcopal Church on August 19, 1789: "the consideration that human happiness and moral duty are inseparably connected, will always continue to prompt me to promote the progress of the former, by inculcating the practice of the latter."[11]

If all this sounds like a more restrictive version of happiness than we're used to, that's because it is. Happiness isn't rolling around in the mud at Woodstock, nor is it a nice golf game after a rough week at work. Happiness is the pursuit of purpose in our lives. If we have lived with moral purpose, even death becomes less painful. When *Washington Post* columnist Charles Krauthammer knew that his death was imminent, he wrote a letter in anticipation of his passing. Here's what that great-souled man wrote: "I believe that the pursuit of truth and right ideas through honest debate and rigorous argument is a noble undertaking. . . . I leave this life with no regrets." Only living with moral purpose can grant profound happiness.[12]

As Austrian psychiatrist Viktor Frankl wrote in his stirring memoir about surviving the Holocaust, *Man's Search for Meaning*, "Woe to him who saw no more sense in his life, no aim, no purpose, and therefore no point in carrying on. He was soon lost. . . . We had to learn ourselves and, furthermore, we had to teach the despairing men, that *it did not really matter what we expected from life, but rather what life expected from us.*"[13]

Frankl's feeling isn't anecdotal. According to a fourteen-year longitudinal study from the University of Carleton in Canada, those who reported strong purpose in life at the outset of the study were 15 percent more likely to still be alive than those who did not. That statistic held true for every age group. Another similar study from the University College London found that for those above retirement age, a sense of purpose correlated with a 30 percent decrease in chances of death over an eight-and-a-half-year period. Overall, as Professor Steve Taylor of Leeds Beckett University states, "Those who reported the highest level of fulfillment lived, on average, two years longer."[14] A study of 951 patients with dementia found that those who said they felt a sense of purpose were 2.4 times less likely to develop Alzheimer's than others. Cancer patients given "meaning-centered" therapy rather than "support-focused" therapy were more motivated to keep living—and even felt better than their colleagues. A study of teenagers found that those who increased their empathy and altruism most also saw the greatest drop in cardiovascular risk. As Dr. Dhruv Khullar, researcher at the Weill Cornell Department of Healthcare Policy and Research writes in the *New York Times*, "Only about a quarter of Americans strongly endorse having a clear sense of purpose and of what makes their lives meaningful, while nearly 40 percent either feel neutral or say they don't. This is both a social and public health problem."[15]

So, what do we need to generate the moral purpose that provides the foundation for happiness?

We need, in my estimate, four elements: individual moral purpose, individual capacity to pursue that purpose, communal moral purpose, and communal capacity to pursue that purpose. These four elements are crucial; the only foundation for a successful civilization lies in a careful balance of these four elements.

THE NECESSITY FOR INDIVIDUAL MORAL PURPOSE

In the pre-Biblical era, you were invested with meaning by your place in the social structure. In the Hammurabi Code, only the king was described as created in God's image; the closer you were to the king, the more rights you had.

Not so in the Bible. The key phrase—the beginning of Western civilization—lies in Genesis 1:26: we are all made in God's image. All of us, not just kings or potentates. That means we all have inherent value, and that our mission in life is to draw close to something beyond ourselves. That individual purpose can be extended to our relationships with other people—in fact, Judeo-Christianity insists that it must be. But the root of our relationship with other people is our relationship with the Divine Creator who endowed us with our value, and who insists that we seek Him out.

We are endowed not merely with rights, but with duties. Those duties give us purpose. And those duties devolve on us as individuals, regardless of social circumstance, thanks to our innate value as creatures made just "a little lower than the angels and crowned . . . with glory and honor."[16]

Without individual moral purpose granted by a relationship to a Creator, we seek meaning instead in the collective, or we destroy ourselves on the shoals of libertinism. We live lives of amoral hedonism, in the non-disparaging sense. All of which sounds benign. But too often, it isn't. After all, to me, my interests are far more pressing than your rights, and atomistic individualism has a tendency to drift toward self-justifying oppression of others. Even the most ardent atheists have historically conceded that much; Voltaire famously stated, "I want my lawyer, my tailor, my servants, even my wife to believe in God, because it means that I shall be cheated and robbed and cuckolded less often. . . . If God did not exist, it would be necessary to invent him." Without belief in our innate individual value, we collapse into animals incapable of seeking moral purpose, even though we feel the need for it beating in our chests.

It matters how we fill that need for individual moral purpose. Yet we're continually drawn to false gods. We proselytize endlessly for everything from intersectionality to consumerism, from Instagram to organic food, from political protest to essential oils. How many of us truly feel that lifelong purpose is to be found in those transitory distractions?

THE NECESSITY FOR INDIVIDUAL CAPACITY

It's not enough to know our individual moral purpose, to know that we must seek happiness through virtuous action. In order for us to be happy, we must believe that we can *pursue* that happiness with some degree of success. We must believe that we have the capacity to cultivate and utilize a skill set—that we're free, active agents in our own lives.

All of the American founders were self-help specialists. Washington spent his formative years copying out rules of civility; as biographer Richard Brookhiser writes, "The rules address moral issues, but they address them indirectly. They seek to form the inner man (or boy) by shaping the outer."[17] Benjamin Franklin was a notorious devotee of self-betterment—he actually created a calendar of virtues, seeking to wipe out his tendency toward wrongdoing (you can actually buy copies of Franklin's calendar yourself online).[18]

We must believe that even in the direst circumstances, we

have the capacity to better ourselves. As Frankl wrote about living through the Holocaust, "Every day, every hour, offered the opportunity to make a decision, a decision which determined whether you would or would not submit to those powers which threatened to rob you of your very self, your inner freedom; which determined whether or not you would become the plaything of circumstance, renouncing freedom and dignity to become molded into the form of the typical inmate."[19]

We must also assume that we exist as meaningful individuals, not mere clusters of cells. We're not just balls of meat wandering through the universe, material agglomerations of matter changing with every moment. We are individuals with identities and responsibilities.

We must believe, too, in the power of our reason—our rational capacity. We're not just instincts and firing neurons. We have the ability to *think things through*. Scientific materialists talk constantly about the power of reason, and why reason ought to reject religion. But the very notion of reason—the notion of a logical argument that *drives my behavior*—is foreign to scientific materialism. If we are a set of firing neurons and flowing hormones and nothing more, why appeal to reason? Why appeal to arguments? Reason is just an illusion, the same way free will is. Neurons fire, which cause other neurons to fire, generating a response from another set of neurons in another human body. Of course, to deny reason would be to end all human communication, destroy our politics, to tear down what it means to be a human being at the root. It would end science itself—we can only stab through the pasteboard mask at the nature of the universe by using our cognitive abilities. We *must* believe in reason to live productive lives.

Finally, we must believe that we are pursuing *true* goals—not merely effective ones. Darwinian evolution leaves no room for the true; it only leaves room for the evolutionarily beneficial. Survival of the fittest isn't a moral principle; survival itself isn't a moral proposition. If it were beneficial to us to kill babies and eat them, that would not make it moral; if it were beneficial for us to calculate that 2+2=5, it would not make it true. But we care about both the moral and the true, and that requires a baseline assumption: that we can discover the moral and the true.

THE NECESSITY FOR COMMUNAL MORAL PURPOSE

We are social creatures, not merely individuals. That means we seek contact, and want to feel like part of something larger than ourselves. That is why we seek friends and communities in which we participate. Seneca stated, "No one can live happily who has regard to himself alone and transforms everything into a question of his own utility."[20] Solomon wrote in Ecclesiastes, "Two are better than one, because they have a good reward for their labor, for if they fall, the one will lift up his fellow, but woe to him that is alone when he falls, for he has no one to help him up."[21]

Social science agrees. Sociologist Emile Durkheim found that we can measure suicide rate by social connection; as Jonathan Haidt writes, "If you want to predict how happy someone is, or how long she will live (and if you are not allowed to ask about her genes or personality), you should find out about her social relationships. Having strong social relationships strengthens the immune system, extends life (more than does quitting smoking), speeds recovery from surgery, and reduces the risks of depression and anxiety disorders."[22] In fact, a massive longitudinal Harvard study found that the single best predictor of lifelong happiness was the presence of close relationships: satisfaction with relationships at age fifty was actually more predictive of long-term health than cholesterol level.[23]

But what binds us to each other?

Of course, there's romantic love, which grows into deeper, more companionate love; there's friendship, prized by Aristotle because it was based in virtuous appreciation for the value of the other. But we need even more than that. We need communities. We need civic vitality, engagement in that community. We need nets to fall back on, friends to rely upon, fellow citizens to defend. In Harvard political scientist Robert Putnam's terms, we need social capital to function properly as individuals: we require trust, shared norms, civic virtue.

So, what builds communities? A shared vision of what the community's moral purpose is.[24] Like Aristotle, the founders believed in social organizations fostering virtue: a country without such social ties could not survive in freedom. They also agreed that the Judeo-Christian tradition had to provide a basis for sound values for individuals living in a free community: as John Adams stated in a letter to the Massachusetts militia, "We have no Government armed with Power capable of contending with human Passions unbridled by . . . morality and Religion. Avarice, Ambition, Revenge or Gallantry, would break the strongest Cords of our Constitution as a Whale goes through a Net. Our Constitution was made only for a moral and religious People. It is wholly inadequate to the government of any other."[25]

The best countries—and the best societies—are those where citizens are virtuous enough to sacrifice for the common good but unwilling to be *forced* to sacrifice for the "greater" good. Flourishing societies require a functional social fabric, created by citizens working together—and yes, separately— toward a meaningful life.

THE NECESSITY FOR COMMUNAL CAPACITY

The pursuit of individually and communally virtuous goals can only be effectuated when strong social institutions thrive— institutions like churches and synagogues and social clubs and charity organizations—and when government is both strong enough to protect against anarchy and limited enough to check its tendency toward tyranny. This is a delicate balance. We need social institutions to provide us the safety to take risks, institutions that help pick us up when we fall; we also need governmental structures that leave us free to take those risks. We need social organizations promoting civic virtue in order to instill individual virtue; we need government to protect individuals' free right to choose. Society is not the government; government is not society.

It's easy to upset this delicate balance. We tend toward tribalism and group loyalty; we cease worrying about how we can improve ourselves, and we begin reshaping and remolding the society around us, using the power of the collective to crush individuals. We crack eggs to make omelets, as Stalin's then right hand Lazar Kaganovich (an egg Stalin would later crack himself) told *Time* in 1932.

In the past, we've conflated communal capacity with powerful government. After all, big governments build big things. In 2012, the Democratic National Convention featured a video with the slogan, "Government's the only thing we all belong to." That belief has been the defining feature of tyrannies the world over: the utopian notion that if we all pull our oars in the same direction, at the behest of a centralized government, we'll be able to accomplish more together.

That's dangerous stuff. It's tempting to mobilize our ardor for collective mobilization and use it as a state-wielded club to *force* individual virtue, or to *force* large-scale change. Tyranny rarely begins with jackboots; it usually begins with ardent wishes for a better future, combined with an unfailing faith in the power of mass mobilization.

Alternatively, we've discounted the value of communal capacity altogether. We've worshipped at the altar of radical individualism, suggesting that community standards stifle creativity and destroy individuality. The image of repressive small-town Puritans preventing Kevin Bacon from dancing his heart out still resonates with many Americans. Fulfillment, in this vision, is to be found by looking within, by ignoring what your community demands of you.

So, what does positive communal capacity look like? It looks like a governmental system capable of mobilizing to stop external threats, but unable to threaten individual liberties; it looks like a social fabric powerful enough to support community members, confident enough to avoid the tools of governmental compulsion. Few governments in human history have met that standard.

Communal capacity must somehow make room for us to pursue our individual moral purposes and exercise our individual capacity while also providing us the means to work together toward communal moral goals.

In the end, communal capacity requires two things: active social communities promoting virtue, and a state nonrestrictive enough to provide a forum for our free choice.

THE INGREDIENTS FOR HAPPINESS

Happiness, then, comprises four elements: individual moral purpose, individual capacity, collective moral purpose, and collective capacity. If we lack one of these elements, the pursuit of happiness becomes impossible; if that pursuit is foreclosed, society crumbles.

Our society was built on recognition of these four elements. The fusion of Athens and Jerusalem, tempered by the wit and wisdom of our Founding Fathers, led to the creation of a civilization of unparalleled freedom and replete with virtuous men and women striving to better themselves and the society around them.

But we are losing that civilization. We are losing that civilization because we have spent generations undermining the two deepest sources of our own happiness—the sources that lie behind individual moral purpose, communal moral purpose, individual capacity, and communal capacity. Those two sources: Divine meaning and reason. There can be no individual or communal moral purpose without a foundation of Divine meaning; there can be no individual capacity or communal capacity without a constant, abiding belief in the nature of our reason.

The history of the West is built on the interplay between these two pillars: Divine meaning and reason. We receive our notions of Divine meaning from a three-millennia-old lineage stretching back to the ancient Jews; we receive our notions of reason from a twenty-five-hundred-year-old lineage stretching back to the ancient Greeks. In rejecting those lineages—in seeking to graft ourselves to rootless philosophical movements of the moment, cutting ourselves off from our own roots—we have damned ourselves to an existential wandering.

We must make our way back toward our roots.

Those roots took hold at Sinai.

CHAPTER 2

FROM THE MOUNTAINTOP

Imagine a world in which you are a plaything of nature, or the gods. You have a fate, but you have no true agency over it. You may seek to appease the gods through sacrifices, but they're as volatile and uncaring as other human beings. Those gods have invested kings and potentates with power; you are a commoner, trying to scratch your life from the dirt. You comfort yourself with the things around you, with simple pleasures; perhaps you even find communal meaning in service to the regime. But you are essentially a cork, bobbing on the eddies of an ocean you do not control—an ocean no one truly controls.

Now imagine everything changes.

Imagine someone tells you that you are worthwhile. You, a mere commoner scrabbling in the dirt. You're not a slave; you're a free and powerful human being with inherent value. You're no longer a cork on the waves of life—you're captain of your own ship. And you and your family and your community have but one job: to direct that ship toward the God that made you, the God that cares about you.

This is the Jewish and Christian God. This is the Judeo-Christian civilization. This is the foundation for the greatest culture and civilization in world history—the West, the greatest force for material prosperity and freedom in the history of the planet. The Light that allegedly shone at Sinai incontestably illuminated the world.

The revelation at Sinai, in approximately 1313 BCE according to traditional Biblical belief, changed the world by infusing it with meaning for those who knew the story. In particular, Judaism (and later, as we'll see, Christianity) granted individual purpose and communal purpose. It did so through four faith-based claims that were utterly different from the pagan religions before it.

First, Judaism claimed that God was unified, that a master plan stood behind everything.

Second, Judaism stated that human beings were held to particular behavioral standards for *moral*, not utilitarian reasons—we were ordered to be moral at the behest of a higher power, even if God's rules could benefit us in this life.

Third, Judaism claimed that history progressed: that revelation was the beginning, but it was not the end, that man had a responsibility to pursue God and bring about a redemption of mankind, and that God could use a particular example—a chosen people—to act as a light unto the nations.

Finally, Judaism claimed that God had endowed man with

choice, that men were responsible for their choices, and that our choices mattered.

Christianity took the messages of Judaism and broadened them: it focused more heavily on grace, and successfully spread the fundamental principles of Judaism, as emended by Christianity, to billions of human beings across the planet.

In today's West, such a contention is deeply controversial. Western leaders routinely use phrases like "Western values" to remind citizens that we have a moral purpose, that there is something special about the West. And there is.

But those same leaders all too often attack the roots of those values. They portray religious believers as fools or bigots, mock them as antirational and backward, suggest that true enlightenment rests on the destruction of the Judeo-Christian heritage. They place the religious beliefs that undergird Western civilization in direct opposition to Western values, as though Western civilization can only be preserved through destruction of its own roots.

Those same leaders suggest that we live in a world of destructive chaos—that there is no plan, no progress, no personal accountability. They've argued that we are nothing more than victims of the systems into which we are born—we are inescapably earthbound. There's political benefit to this kind of demagoguery: it allows politicians to proclaim themselves materialist messiahs, prepared to save us from uncaring fate.

The last time this kind of thinking was widespread, there was no Western civilization. And it's easier to return to the *status quo ante* than any of us will admit.

GOD'S ORDERED UNIVERSE

Before there was God, there were gods.

It is difficult for most Westerners to conceive of the notion of multiple gods nowadays, because the Judeo-Christian God has loomed so large for millennia. But the vast majority of religions prior to Judaism were polytheistic. That's not because polytheists were fools. It's actually because polytheism is sophisticated and natural in many ways.

Polytheism is sophisticated in its willingness to absorb new, strange gods. The ancient Egyptians, Greeks, and Romans were polytheists, and would routinely incorporate the gods of other religions into their own religion. As the famed British Orientalist Henry William Frederick Saggs points out, "Accepting a polytheistic view of life, the ancients were under no pressure to deny the existence of the gods of other peoples. . . . Difficulties only surfaced when one group assertively denied the very existence of other gods. This was the case with the Jews, who in consequence became the least tolerant of all ancient peoples."[1]

Paganism also recognizes that the universe is a chaotic place, one we can't fully understand. A prime mover—a singular God instead of myriad gods—would require that logic govern the universe, a predictable set of rules discernible by the human mind. There are no such obvious rules; therefore, the universe must be an interplay of various minds battling with one another for supremacy.

Pagan religious creation stories demonstrate colorfully how such beliefs manifest. The Mesopotamian creation story—which is similar to both Polynesian and Native American creation stories in a wide variety of ways—states that Apsu, god of the fresh water, was murdered, and that his wife, Tiamat, goddess of saltwater, threatened to destroy the other gods; Marduk murdered her and split her in half. One half of her became heaven; the other half became the earth.[2] The plethora of gods were created to explain a world without rules. In that way, polytheism is more pessimistic and more cynical than Judeo-Christian monotheism.

Finally, polytheism is rooted in a hardheaded belief in that which we can see. As former British chief rabbi Jonathan Sacks points out, "The pagan perceives the divine in nature through the medium of the eye."[3] The simplest explanation for a multitude of objects is a multitude of creators. Or, more simply, God *is* nature, and nature God—a pantheistic notion that continues to resonate down until today in "spiritual but not religious" circles, as well as in many Eastern religions. The Mesopotamians worshipped literally thousands of gods, and built massive ziggurats that were supposed to provide an earthly abode for the gods. Idols were built for the gods to inhabit, and the gods were worshipped through service, including feeding them on a regular basis.[4] The Egyptians had a different creation myth based in each major city, and a plethora of gods as well.

Judaism denied all these central tenets of polytheism.

Judaism claimed that God was now singular. The first of the Ten Commandments was simple and direct: "I am the Lord your God, who brought you out of Egypt, out of the land of slavery. You shall have no other gods before me."[5] God was the first and the last, the creator.

Furthermore, Judaism claimed that God had rules—and that He abided by those rules. The universe wasn't random;

the rules were generally discoverable and largely understand-
able. The Bible isn't a set of just-so stories designed to explain
why the rain falls and the sun shines. Instead, the Bible lays
forth, for the first time, an argument for the internal logic of
the universe. God, according to the Bible, worked through a
singular, unified system; nature operated according to a set of
predictable rules from which God could stray if He so chose.
In Genesis, for example, the patriarch Abraham asks God to
abide by His own rules for right and wrong: when God says
he wants to destroy Sodom and Gomorrah, Abraham *argues*
with God over right and wrong, and asks God whether collective punishment is appropriate if there are good people still
living in the city. God answers him; God doesn't merely ignore
Abraham or silence him. Rather He engages with him. In a chaotic world with no master moral values, the story of Abraham
would make no sense.

Now, Judaism does not claim that we are capable of understanding all of God's motives or actions. In Exodus, Moses specifically asks God to show him His face; God refuses, answering,
"I will cause all my goodness to pass in front of you, and I will
proclaim my name, the Lord, in your presence. I will have
mercy on whom I will have mercy, and I will have compassion
on whom I will have compassion. But . . . you cannot see my
face, for no one may see me and live."[6] This metaphor is God's
way of saying that we humans cannot completely understand
God. In fact, as Genesis makes clear, the human notion of good
and evil doesn't mirror the Divine notions of good and evil. But
God does have a standard, even if we can't fully comprehend
it. God does not randomly change His standard—"He is the

Rock, his ways are perfect, and all his ways are just. A faithful God who does no wrong, upright and just is he."[7] The notion of a moral universe is a Judaic creation. It's woven into the name of Israel itself: *Yisrael*, in Hebrew, means "struggle with God." And God *wants* human beings to struggle with Him—so much so that He will refuse to intervene to correct human beings even if they are wrong. The Talmud famously retells this shocking incident:

[During a debate about a matter of Jewish law] Rabbi Eliezer brought all possible proofs to support his opinion, but the rabbis did not accept his answer. . . . Finally, Rabbi Eliezer said, "If the law is in my favor, Heaven will prove it." A Divine Voice then stated, "Why are you arguing with Rabbi Eliezer, as the law is in accordance with his opinion everywhere?" Rabbi Joshua stood and stated [quoting Deuteronomy 30:12], "It is not in heaven." Rabbi Jeremiah said, "Since the Torah was already given at Mount Sinai, we do not listen to a Divine Voice, as You already wrote at Mount Sinai, in the Torah, to follow the majority." [Exodus 23:2] Years later, Rabbi Nathan encountered Elijah the prophet and asked him, "What did the Holy One, Blessed be He, do at the time of that debate?" Elijah answered, "He smiled and said, 'My children have triumphed over Me; My children have triumphed over Me.'"[8]

Finally, Judaism rebuked the notion of a corporeal god in ringing fashion. Judaism is antimaterialism; it specifically rejects the idea that what we can see is all there is, or that the spiritual must be made physically manifest. The Second Commandment bars Jews from making graven images. Jews are specifically enjoined to destroy idols.[9] This isn't nearly as tolerant as paganism, but it is also less human-bound, less sensory. It requires us to reach beyond that which our senses perceive. We must think beyond our physical limits—and we must recognize our own limited thinking, since any description of God is bound to be physical, and thus homonymic rather than literal. The notion of a Divine Being who reaches out to humanity with words, who runs the universe according to certain rules, and who stands beside us even if we can't see Him—that places God within human reach, even if God will always lie just beyond us.

GOD'S EXPECTATIONS FOR MAN

Before the Bible, man was merely cosmic chattel, a speck being bruited about by the forces of the divine. The gods expected little of man beyond simple bribery; there was no linkage between what we would deem "moral" behavior and divine expectation. As Saggs states, "There were no doctrines in the sense of definitions of required belief, and accepted standards of conduct were not explicitly linked to religion."[10] The gods were arbitrary. They were unchained to rules. This meant that human behavior wasn't tied to divine behavior.

The Bible offered a different perspective. A singular God meant a singular standard for behavior. Consequences couldn't merely be attributed to the interplay between the various self-interested gods; instead, consequences were life lessons, meant to teach us to be moral. Sin had consequences in the real world. Now, that didn't mean that every sin would be punished with a prompt and proportional consequence—God doesn't play whack-a-mole with human sin. But it did mean that following God's commandments would usually lead to better life results than doing the opposite. Polytheism argued that the gods were holy, and thus human beings ought to serve them; Judaism argued that we ought to be holy in imitation of God.[11]

Why, then, does the Bible focus so much on seemingly pagan sacrifices? Because Biblical sacrifices aren't designed merely to appease a higher power. They're designed to change *us*, to teach us something. Maimonides argues that sacrifices were originally designed to woo polytheists toward monotheism by repurposing an ingrained cultural ritual and directing it away from sheer appeasement and toward self-betterment. According to Maimonides, sacrifices are intended to remind us that we ought to pay for our sins ourselves, and that only the mercy of God allows us to escape that accountability.

The Talmud openly acknowledges that we could use reason to learn certain character traits;[12] Judaism suggests that we can in fact determine certain moral injunctions—even ignoramuses, Judaism believes, can determine that there is a God and that murder is wrong, for example.

But such learning is incomplete, Judaism holds. Reason can teach us how not to be bad—how not to harm others, for example. The seven Noahide Laws that governed humanity before revelation are all designed to minimize human cruelty: bans on murder, theft, idolatry, sexual immorality, animal cruelty, cursing

God, and the positive commandment to set up courts of law in order to punish crimes. And those Noahide Laws are incumbent on everyone, regardless of whether they even know about the Bible, specifically because they're so perfectly obvious.

But revelation teaches how to be *good*: it teaches us which values we ought to hold dear, which characteristics we ought to cultivate. Revelation is necessary to raise us beyond the realm of the mediocre.

GOD: THE FORCE BEHIND PROGRESS

History in many cultures has no beginning and no end. Greek thought saw the universe as permanent and moving in circular fashion—history would recur, grow, and decay. There could be no vision of a progression in history, an inexorable movement toward a better time or Messianic era.[13] Progress itself was, for many of the ancients, an illusion, or not even that: it was an idea that had no place in the rational universe.

That view of history isn't unique to the Greeks. Ancient Babylonians believed that "past, present, and future were all part of one continuous stream of events in heaven and earth. . . . Gods and men continued ad infinitum."[14] In Native American cultures, reality itself was circular: "Sacred hoops and medicine wheels, in their seamless curvature, represent the cyclical, no-beginning, no-end, turn-and-turn-again, 'mythic' view of reality of Native American peoples."[15] Hinduism sees history as circular; Buddhism sees time as "without beginning and without end . . . the uniqueness of each moment essential to the notion of history is not clearly expressed in Buddhism."[16]

In this view, the gods are not interested in history; they may intervene, but only for their own purposes, and often in conflict with one another. In *The Iliad*, the gods routinely intervene to save their favorites, and even take sides in the war based on their own interests. But those interests are variable and unpredictable. The Trojan War takes on little historic importance—it generates no progress, nor do the gods ever evidence any intent to do so.

The Bible takes a different view. The Bible immediately sets God in the context of a time-bound history: God exists outside of time, but He is intimately involved in creating progress. The Jewish creation story notes that God intervenes day by day to create new levels of complexity in the material world, and then He rests.

When God intervenes in the world, it is to better the lot of mankind, or to teach lessons. God inserts Himself in history by preserving Noah and his family; He restrains himself from stopping history ever again by destroying His creatures, no matter their choices.[17] God manifests Himself to Abraham to send the first monotheist on a journey to a place Abraham doesn't know—and God then makes a covenant with Abraham to build him up into a great and mighty nation, connected with a particular parcel of land: Israel. God chooses Abraham. He chooses Isaac. He chooses Jacob. And then He chooses the people of Israel to act as exemplars of morality across history—to spread His word, with Moses as His prophet. "You are to be holy to me because I, the Lord, am holy, and I have set you apart from the nations to be my own," God states in Leviticus 20:26.

The story of history is the story of God's romance with His chosen nation: His decision to take that nation out of slavery and bring it forth into freedom, and to use that nation as a vehicle for the transmission of His message. "Has any god ever tried to take for himself one nation out of another nation, by testings, by signs and wonders, by war, by a mighty hand and an outstretched arm, or by great and awesome deeds, like all the things the Lord your God did for you in Egypt before your very eyes?"[18]

But the plot has twists and turns. The story of humanity is a story of the romance between an honorable God and a straying nation—a nation that knows better, but must learn and relearn to love God once more, and a God who occasionally turns away His face but waits patiently for His people to return to Him.

With each relearning comes progress, a movement toward that historical finish line. We are all part of the great drama of history. History gives us a place. It gives us a rationale. We may live as individuals, but we are part of the tapestry of time, and even if our thread comes to an inglorious end, God weaves with us.

History, in short, *can* progress. It can progress because God cares about us as individuals, and because He is invested in our history. And the eventual culmination of history will come with the universal recognition of God and His handiwork, with the Jews as the treasured jewel shining forth light from Jerusalem. As historian Paul Johnson writes:

No people has ever insisted more firmly than the Jews that history has a purpose and humanity a destiny. At a very early

stage in their collective existence they believed they had de-
tected a divine scheme for the human race, of which their
own society was to be a pilot. They worked out their role in
immense detail. They clung to it with heroic persistence in
the face of savage suffering. . . . The Jewish vision became
the prototype for many similar grand designs for humanity,
both divine and man-made. The Jews, therefore, stand right
at the centre of the perennial attempt to give human life the
dignity of a purpose.[19]

THE MOST IMPORTANT VERSE IN HUMAN HISTORY

Polytheism left little room for the individual to make his way in
the world.

This wasn't true for rulers, who were ranked among the gods
themselves. They had freedom of action, being made in the image of the gods. In ancient Egypt, beginning with the Fourth
Dynasty (2613 BCE), Egyptian rulers were honored with the
title "Son of Ra"—Ra being the foremost Egyptian god.[20] In
Mesopotamia, the tradition of kings declaring themselves divine
began with Naram-Sin of Akkad in the twenty-third century
BCE. Self-deification continued intermittently for centuries, all
the way down to Augustus, who was declared a god upon his
death in Rome in 14 CE.[21] The spark of the divine invested in
great leaders allowed them freedom of action. Hammurabi, for
example, describes himself this way at the outset of his code:
"When Marduk sent me to rule over men, to give the protection
of right to the land, I did right and righteousness in . . . , and

brought about the well-being of the oppressed."[22] Epic heroes of the ancient myths are identified with the gods; commoners never even appear in these narratives.

Judaism fought the notion of human inequality before God tooth and nail. We are all created equal in our endowment with a certain level of free will. Perhaps the most important sentence ever penned was this, from Genesis 1:27: "God created man in His image, in the image of God He created him; male and female He created them." No longer was divine choice restricted to great leaders: in fact, God mocks such pretensions in Genesis 6:2, when He decides to flood the earth after the "sons of the gods"—the rulers—begin running roughshod over the rights of commoners, prompting God to scoff at the arrogant humans who "are mortal."[23]

Instead of a ruling caste with the power of free will, now *all* human beings—each and every one of us—was granted the value of choice. God had stamped us all, breathed life into us, formed us out of the clay of the ground. The creation story itself is designed to demonstrate how the first man, Adam, used his innate power of choice wrongly—and we are all Adam's descendants. One of the most moving segments of the Bible takes place just before Cain slays his brother Abel: God sees that Cain is jealous that Abel's offering has been accepted, and passionately informs Cain, "Why are you annoyed, and why has your countenance fallen? Is it not so that if you improve, it will be forgiven you? If you do not improve, however, at the entrance, sin is lying, and to you is its longing, but *you can rule over it*."[24]

This is a constant recurring theme. God lays out the importance of choice—of proper exercise of free will—in Deuteronomy:

See, I set before you today life and prosperity, death and destruction. For I command you today to love the Lord, your God, to walk in obedience to him, and to keep his commands, decrees and laws. . . . Now choose life, so that you and your children may live.[25]

Because we choose, we are God's partners in creation. We are signatories to a covenant with God, in which we must play our role and choose to abide by our commitments. Free choice is the central element here. When God brought the Jews out of Egypt and stood them before Sinai, He required them to sign on to the program; they made an affirmative decision to contract with God, and did so without even waiting to hear the terms: "We will do, and we will hear."[26] Freely willed action preceded justification.

WHAT JERUSALEM TELLS US . . .
AND WHAT IT DOESN'T

Let's return to our original standard for happiness: individual purpose, individual capacity, communal purpose, and communal capacity. What does Judaism alone have to say about these necessary elements?

When it comes to individual purpose, Judaism has quite a lot to say. Judaism says that God expects things of us—that He has standards for our behavior, that He demands our holiness, that He cares about our commitment. A human being on a desert island can find purpose in living the life God wants for Him, and it is laid out for Him through a series of rules to be found in His holy book. As King Solomon concludes in Ecclesiastes, the purpose of human existence is simple: "Fear God and keep his commandments, for this is the whole duty of man."[27] In doing so, Ecclesiastes says, we will find joy: "I know that there is nothing better for people than to rejoice and do good while they live . . . there is nothing better for a person than to rejoice in his work, because that is his lot."[28]

With regard to individual capacity, the Bible speaks clearly as well. The Bible states openly that we are free agents with the capacity to choose sin or holiness, and that we have the obligation to do so. We are holy; we are made in God's image. And we are equal in the capacity to act as Godly creatures, although we may have different capabilities. The Bible also makes clear that our job is to use our minds to discover God—to seek Him out, to ask questions, to struggle with Him. We believe that God abides by certain rules morally, and that he has set out certain rules for the world He created—that life is not an arbitrary scheme of chaotic last-minute decisions made by a variety of gods fighting for supremacy. In terms of science, this notion—the notion of a predictable, discoverable God—is vital. The assumption of regularity in the universe's rules is vital for the development of Western civilization—and for the development of science in particular. The entirety of science is based on the notion of looking for universal rules that govern the world around us. If the universe were a random agglomeration of unrelated events, governed by no higher logic, the scientific search would be rather frustrating.

The Bible does *not*, however, set out the notion that our own search for universal truths will bring us closer to happiness. God is, in the Jewish view, the only universal truth. Jews seek out God and hold Him to *His* word, not ours—His standards of truth matter, not our own.[29] The notion of a search for truth outside of God is foreign to Biblical thought.

How about communal purpose? Certainly, Judaism provides the notion of a communal purpose. God tells Abraham in Genesis, "I will bless those who bless you, and I will curse those who curse you, and all the peoples on earth will be blessed through you."[30] Never has a prophecy been truer—from one man in search of God in the wilderness came three monotheistic faiths that dominate humankind and shape human culture on the broadest possible scale.

Judaism taught that communal purpose was both particular and universal—that we must live within our communities and model our behavior to others. Judaism said that the nation of Israel would serve as proof of God's provenance, as demonstration of God's place in history.[31]

The attitude of historical progress, coined by the Jews and adopted by Christianity, drives Western civilization as a whole. Barack Obama was fond of quoting Martin Luther King Jr.: "The arc of the moral universe is long, but it bends toward justice." He even had that quotation inscribed on a rug in the Oval Office. But King himself only thought the moral arc existed in the context of a religious narrative of history. Here's the original context in which King spoke those words: "Evil may so shape events that Caesar will occupy a palace and Christ a cross, but that same Christ will rise up and split history into A.D. and B.C., so that even the life of Caesar must be dated by his name. Yes, 'the arc of the moral universe is long, but it bends toward justice.'" If history has a direction, it does so only if we have faith in a God who stands at the end of it, urging us forward.[32]

Finally, communal capacity: What does the Bible have to say about the best system for fulfilling individual and communal purpose? Surprisingly little. Judaism believes that power ought to exist in the first instance in the family; secondly, in the community of faith; and finally, in the government.

Judaism is ambivalent at best about the notion of state power. The Bible separates powers between the Levites and a judicial system. In fact, the Bible expresses fear of divine monarchy repeatedly. Moses says that the people will choose to appoint a king—he doesn't say that God will mandate a monarch. He then spells out a series of restrictions to be placed on the king, ranging from limitations on wealth to restrictions on the number of wives, and concluding with an order that the king must write his own copy of the Torah, so as to be reminded of his legal duties each and every day. The king must "not consider himself better than his fellow Jews and turn from the law to the right or to the left."[33] Once the Jews enter the land, they are ruled by judges for generations; the prophet Gideon explicitly declines to rule over the Jews, stating, "I will not rule over you, nor shall my son rule over you, the Lord shall rule over you."[34] When the Jews finally decide to throw over the prophet Samuel for a king, Samuel warns that a monarch will impoverish the people and act as a tyrant, concluding, "in that day you will cry out because of your king, whom you have chosen for yourselves, but the Lord will not answer you in that day."[35]

Judaism has a healthy suspicion of centralized power. Criminal penalties require two witnesses who warn the perpetrator *before the crime*, and then witness the crime. While religion has been used as cover for theological tyranny, there is ample basis in the Bible for the notion that various forms of state organization for purposes of enshrining both individual and collective purpose can work. That truth would become obvious during the pre-Enlightenment period, when widespread reading of the Bible would overturn centuries of theocratic power.

In short, the Bible presents a fulsome view of human happiness—but one that requires further elucidation. The Bible tells us what God expects of us and tells us that we have the duty to fulfill those expectations; it tells us that we are special, and that we are loved by an infinitely good, caring, and powerful Being. It tells us that we have a duty to reach out to Him. The Bible makes God accessible; it brings God down to earth. In doing so, it offers man the opportunity to raise himself. But the Biblical tradition does not stress the ability of people to reason a priori; revelation stands above reason.

And revelation alone is not enough. The soul with which God endowed man seeks the Divine through reason—the uniquely human quality that lifts human beings above animals, and places us at the foot of God's throne.

To seek a higher moral purpose, human beings would have to cultivate their reason.

For that, they turned to Athens.

CHAPTER 3

FROM THE DUST

There is a battle currently raging on college campuses regarding the role of the university. Is it to create a safe space for students to "find themselves"? Is it a place to experience the wonder of a wide variety of thought? Or is it a place to inculcate the basic thought underpinning Western civilization?

In the past, the answer was clearly the last option: people went to college to be steeped in the classics. The Founding Fathers were well versed in Latin and Greek; their writing is replete with references to ancient literature. In 1900, half of all American public *high school students* were obligated to take Latin classes.[1] But many current scholars and students find the classics trite and boring, old and hackneyed—ethnocentric and culturally stagnating. Jesse Jackson famously marched at Stanford in the 1980s, arm in arm with students, chanting, "Hey, hey, ho, ho, Western Civ has got to go." As of 2010, not a single top university required students to take a course in Western civilization; only sixteen even offered such a course.[2]

What happened? A generalized scorn for Western civilization itself led to a sharp critique of learning about the classics. Western civilization, in the view of many on the radical Left, was a bastion of imperialism and racism; students should be devoted to learning about those shortcomings, rather than about the glories of ancient philosophy. In fact, study of ancient philosophy and civilization dramatically limits our understanding of the West's innate evils. Edward Said made this case most explicitly in *Orientalism*, in which he suggested that the legacy of Greece and Rome was one of "othering" the East—and that classicists were most concerned with the denigration of non-Western traditions. Furthermore, Westerners were forbidden from writing about "Orientalist" cultures—as outsiders, they were destined to pervert the teachings of these cultures.[3] Education, in this view, is merely a different form of perpetuating power relationships—and focusing in on Western civilization thus contributes to ongoing tyranny. Better to ignore the classics in favor of a more well-rounded education focusing on various cultures.

Now, there's nothing wrong with reveling in that which we can learn from a multitude of cultures—the Supreme Court's hearing room contains Moses, Hammurabi, Solon, and Confucius in its tableau of lawgivers.[4] But to ignore the legacy of the Greco-Roman philosophical tradition is to perpetuate the lie that Western civilization brought us more exploitation than liberty. The promulgators of multiculturalism in education all too often aren't promoting breadth of learning, but lack of learning. This attitude reaches its apotheosis in the anti-classics movements we see on college campuses like Reed, where one student group lobbies against basic humanities courses because they allegedly "perpetuate[] white supremacy. . . . The texts that make up the [Humanities 110] syllabus . . . are 'Eurocentric,' 'Caucasoid,' and thus 'oppressive.'"[5]

This is a dramatic, deliberate misreading of the history of Western civilization—the greatest force for good in world history. That statement is not meant to ignore the myriad evils in which Western civilization has participated. But Western civilization has freed more people than any other, by a long shot; it has reduced poverty, conquered disease, and minimized war. Western civilization is responsible for the economic betterment of the global population, and for the rise in human rights and democracy.

And that civilization has deep roots. Why should Americans bother to learn about ancient Greeks? Because the classical roots of Western civilization in Athens still have much to teach us. Athens teaches us what we are capable of doing as human beings. Athens teaches us that we have the ability to use our reason to reach beyond ourselves. Athens teaches us not only how liberty can flourish, but why it *should*. I've argued that without Jerusalem, there could be no West; without Athens, the same holds true.

Religious faith is empowering because it tells human beings that they are loved, and that they have the capacity to choose between good and evil. But religious faith also requires us to acknowledge the inherent limits on human capacity—it requires us to say that there are things we will never understand, that we are earthly creatures bounded by dust. But if the project of Sinai was about elevating man above the animals by associating him with a Godly mission and granting him a Godly soul, the project of Athens was about elevating man using man's own faculties. Religion doesn't discount the capacity of mankind, of course, but that capacity is always secondary to God's will; Athens elevates man's capacity and makes it primary.

Greek thought, of course, didn't suggest that man could overcome all. The notion of Greek tragedy revolves around man reaching for the stars, but being prevented from his aspirations because of his own inherent limitations. But the heroes of Greek legend are those who challenge the fates, seeking to glorify their own independence: Prometheus, Antigone, Achilles . . . even Socrates himself. As famed drama critic Walter Kerr puts it, "Tragedy speaks always of freedom."[6]

This tragic quest for knowledge is endemic to Greek thought. It is a tragedy shot through with hope. Plato's allegory of the cave is the most famous example of striving to reach the light. In that allegory, Plato paints a picture of men chained to a wall in a cave, prevented from seeing the source of light outside the cave; their ignorance restricts them to the belief that "the truth is nothing other than the shadows of artificial things." But a few noble people can be released from those bonds, acclimated to truth, and brought out into the light; those happy few can then return to the cave and help build a truer society for their fellows—but they will risk the wrath of their fellow prisoners, and may pay the ultimate price for having debunked popular notions of truth.[7]

Utilizing human reason to escape the cave, and bringing knowledge of the light, that was the task of ancient Athens—a task uniting Plato (428–348 BCE) and Aristotle (384–322 BCE). The ancient Greeks gave us three foundational principles: first, that we could discover our purpose in life from looking at the nature of the world; second, that in order to learn about the nature of the world, we had to study the world around us by utilizing our reason; and finally, that reason could help us construct the best collective systems for cultivating that reason. In short, the Greeks gave us natural law, science, the basis of secularly constructed government. Jerusalem brought the heavens down to earth; Athens's elevation of reason would launch mankind toward the stars.

FINDING PURPOSE IN NATURE

The first contribution of the ancient Greeks was the philosophy of natural law.

We live in the physical world. The physical world has nothing to say to us about purpose or meaning. It's a bunch of stuff. Why should a bunch of stuff have any information to give us about how we direct our lives? We live in a world filled with things and facts. Facts do not determine values. A tree is not good or bad—it's just a tree. The world is filled with brute facts; we ourselves are brute facts, with no capacity to rise above the basic realities of nature.

That's the conclusion of many modern philosophers. It was also the conclusion of certain ancient Greeks like Democritus (460–370 BCE), a philosopher who lived contemporaneously with Plato and Aristotle and believed that all of human life could be boiled down to fundamental particles of matter he called "atoms."[8] Nature was merely nature; ethics takes a backseat.

Plato, Aristotle, and the Stoics thought differently. Plato and Aristotle rejected Democritus's atomic theory. In their view, the human mind was freely capable of deciphering nature's rules—and they believed that those rules did, in fact, exist. We could determine rules and values from nature itself. Nature had a purpose—or the God behind it did.

How could they reach such a conclusion? Their reasoning was simple and profound. They posited that virtually every object in creation is directed toward an end—a telos, in Greek. The value of an object lies in its capacity to achieve the purpose for which it was designed. Facts and values aren't separate things—values are embedded within facts. For example, a watch is virtuous if it tells time properly; a horse is virtuous if it properly pulls a cart.

What does this mean for human beings? What makes a man virtuous is his capacity to engage in the activities that make him a man, not an animal—man has a telos, too. What is our telos? Our end, according to both Plato and Aristotle, is to reason, judge, and deliberate. Plato put it this way in *The Republic*:

> Is there some work of a soul that you couldn't ever accomplish with any other living thing that is? For example, managing, ruling, and deliberating, and all such things—could we justly attribute them to anything other than a soul and assert that they are peculiar to it? . . . Further, what about living? Shall we not say that it is the work of a soul?[9]

Aristotle agreed: he believed that using our reason, we could determine the purpose of everything around us. Aristotle believed that everything in being relied on a rationale for its existence (in philosophy-speak, a "final cause").[10] So, for example, the roots of a plant only exist to fulfill their final cause—providing nutrients to that plant. And our final cause is the use of reason: "the work of a human being is an activity of soul in accord with reason."[11]

So, according to both Plato and Aristotle, what makes us "virtuous" is doing our job: look at the world with our reason, discerning the final causes for which things exist. This is our purpose. Just as Adam is tasked with naming the animals in the Bible, so we are tasked with recognizing the telos of the world around us in Greek thought.

The modern mind rebels at this notion—the notion of something's virtue tied to its inherent purpose. Nature, we believe, is blind and valueless—we don't blame a snake for biting or a baby for crying. But that's not what the ancients meant by virtue. They didn't mean our modern moral sense of "virtue"—being a nice person, or something similarly vague. They meant fulfilling the telos for which you were created.

Part of fulfilling that telos was the cultivation of those aspects of character that made you most human. Ancient systems of thought carried one significant difference from modern thought with regard to virtue: they focused on virtue in terms of character development. As Jonathan Haidt writes, "Where the ancients saw virtue and character at work in everything a person does, our modern conception confines morality to a set of situations that arise for each person only a few times in any given week: trade-offs between self-interest and the interests of others."[12] Whereas modern systems of morality focus far more on whether given actions are good or evil, ancient ethical systems worried less about rules for action, and more about making men and women virtuous people—people capable of fulfilling their telos as human beings, and utilizing reason and character to carry out complex moral equations.

Now, this still leaves us with a problem: in order for us to share a community, we have to agree on our telos. As philosopher Leo Strauss suggests, no society can be built on a multiplicity of end goals.[13] In order to avoid arguing incessantly over end goals, therefore, the Greeks had to posit an objective, underlying logic to the universe: a Grand Designer, an Unmoved Mover. Were the universe a chaotic, arbitrary, and random place operating according to no design, it would have no telos. But if a grand plan stands behind all of creation, our job is merely to investigate that plan—to uncover the natural law that governs the universe.

The ancients realized that any theory of telos had to rely on the presence of a designer. As such, they were philosophical monotheists, even if they were religious polytheists. Anaxagoras (510–428 BCE) found a system of universal logic undergirding the world; he called it *nous*. Heraclitus (535–475 BCE) was the first known philosopher to use the term *Logos* to describe the system of unified reason behind the world we see and experience. Man could understand the universe because a force had created the universe; man's mind mirrored that force to the extent that man could uncover its purposes. As historian Richard Tarnas writes, "As the means by which human intelligence could attain universal understanding, the Logos was a divine revelatory principle, simultaneously operative within the human mind and the natural world." And philosophers were tasked with uncovering this Logos; by doing so, they would be fulfilling both their own telos and discovering the telos of mankind more broadly.[14]

THE BIRTH OF SCIENCE

This investigation led to the birth of science. The science and technology that has bettered our world—the iPhones college freshmen use to denigrate Western civilization—was built on Greek origins.

The ancient belief that virtue was to be located in use of our reason necessitated the investigation of nature. The ancients believed that by studying the nature of things, we could discover the nature of being. While the Biblical worldview said that God had created nature, it didn't have much to say about nature itself, or whether investigating nature would lead to God. The Bible didn't even have a word for "nature"; the Hebrew word *yetzer* is the closest term, and that generally means "will." But Greek philosophy was different: it suggested that the best way to investigate the nature of human purpose was to look at reality itself, and attempt to discover the systems behind it. This made it imperative to investigate our universe in order to find a higher meaning.

Pythagoras (570–495 BCE) led this quest—he believed that human beings could achieve consonance with the universe by seeking to understand that universe. Pythagoras's philosophy led him to mathematics, an attempt to uncover the supposedly perfect harmony of the cosmos. And that led him to the Pythagorean theorem, among other discoveries.[15]

Plato and Aristotle both believed in the notion of objective truth as well. But Plato and Aristotle disagreed with regard to what constituted objective truth: the Forms, or knowledge of the physical world. In the end, this disagreement would wind up creating the basis for the scientific method: deduction would present human beings with a scientific hypothesis; facts presented by empirical evidence would become the basis for judging that theory; the hypothesis would then be accepted or rejected or changed. Aristotle's establishment of logical rigor with regard to empirical observation would provide the basis for all further scientific thought.

THE CREATION OF REASON-BASED GOVERNMENT

Finally, the Greeks gave us the roots of democracy.

Based on the notion of virtue—use of reason to act in accordance with nature—Plato, Aristotle, and the Stoics developed ethical systems. Those ethical systems didn't merely recommend personal cultivation. They also encompassed the creation of new forms of government. Some of their ideas regarding government were good; others were bad. But they began the process of applying reason to governmental structures—a process that has continued down to our day.

The ancients believed that in order to cultivate virtue, the polis—the city-state—must be at the center of human life. As philosopher Alasdair MacIntyre points out, the Athenians universally believed that good citizenship was a prerequisite to being a good man.[16] Plato's ethical system tied together happiness and virtue: the truly virtuous man will be happy. Plato defined various virtues, too: justice, moderation, and the like. But these virtues aren't *individual* virtues, in Plato's view— they only exist in the context of a community. The virtue of justice, for example, exists when each person fulfills his or her function in relation to the polis. Our virtues exist in relations with others.[17]

Because the polis is the context in which virtue is cultivated— and because cultivating virtue is the ultimate goal of man—the polis must be governed rigorously so that human beings are inculcated with virtue, according to Plato. That means that those who govern must be the best and wisest among us—that we must rigorously condition a class of philosophers to rule. Otherwise, chaos will ensue. "Unless," wrote Plato in the voice of Socrates, "the philosophers rule as kings or those now called kings and chiefs genuinely and adequately philosophize, and political power and philosophy coincide in the same place . . . there is no rest from the ills for the cities, my dear Glaucon, nor I think for human kind . . . in no other city would there be private or public happiness."[18]

In Plato's view, conflict within the state lies in failure of people to recognize their own station. To solve such conflicts, Plato set up a rigorous hierarchy in his utopian vision, between workers, warriors, and philosopher kings. He also recommended a communistic vision of his ideal state in which the philosopher kings are raised. This led philosopher Karl Popper to protest that Plato's ideal state was "purely totalitarian and anti-humanitarian," and accuse Plato of re-enshrining "class rule and class privilege . . . the principle that every class should attend to its own business means, briefly and bluntly, that *the state is just if the ruler rules, if the worker works, and if the slave slaves*."[19] In defense, Plato scholars Leo Strauss and Allan Bloom rejected Popper's critique by suggesting that Plato's entire scheme was at least partially facetious, an attempt to prove the unworkability of full communitarian control.[20]

Aristotle's system of virtue also involved one's status as a citizen. But unlike Plato, who believed that the Forms could be understood by a select few who could then rule benevolently over the rest of a well-organized society, Aristotle rejected such utopianism. He tore into Plato's suggested regime, calling it unrealistic and stating that it would rend apart the society itself. "Let us remember," Aristotle says, "that we should not disregard the experience of ages."[21] Aristotle instead said that a regime combining aspects of democracy with aspects of aristocracy would be best—a clear philosophical iteration of a system of checks and balances.

The logic of both Plato and Aristotle tied together the existence of the state to its ability to forward and abide by natural law. Their philosophical heirs, like Cicero, would express that view more fulsomely. Thus, Cicero writes in *The Republic*:

> True law is right reason in agreement with nature; it is of universal application, unchanging and everlasting; it summons to duty by its commands, and averts from wrongdoing by its prohibitions. . . . There will not be different laws at Rome and at Athens, or different laws now and in the future, but one

eternal and unchangeable law will be valid for all nations and all times, and there will be one master and ruler, that is, God, over us all, for he is the author of this law, its promulgator, and its enforcing judge.[22]

Cicero's elegant defense of what he termed a mixed system—a system of shared governmental responsibility, in which citizens have a share in control of their government, checked by a monarch, checked in turn by an aristocracy—was treasured by the American Founding Fathers.[23] This system, Cicero thought, would ensure the prevention of tyranny and the violation of virtue.

WHAT ATHENS TELLS US . . .
AND WHAT IT DOESN'T

Yes, classical studies are still necessary. The college students who fulminate against them are undercutting the very foundations upon which they stand—they're ignoring reason, science, and democracy. We'll see later in this book just how that abandonment undercuts the strength of the West. But there is no question that without Athens, the West simply would not exist as it is—and that the world would suffer greatly for that fact.

With that said, Athens alone is insufficient to explain the greatness of the West.

The world of Athens has shaped us in profound ways—and it shapes us particularly strongly as products of a secular age. It's easier to spot our debts to Athens than our debts to Jerusalem:

they seem to require less faith, less of a belief in the miraculous and the divine. But Athens wasn't enough—the West still required Jerusalem.

To understand why, we must once again return to our fourfold framework for meaning: individual purpose, individual capacity, communal purpose, and communal capacity.

In the Athenian framework, it's nearly impossible to disassociate individual purpose from communal purpose. Plato, Aristotle, and the Stoics would have all rejected such a division as counterproductive and fruitless: individual purpose lay in acting virtuously—fulfilling our telos by pursuing right reason in accordance with nature. Virtue, in turn, could only be defined with reference to the community. The individual, in this view, tends to disappear into the community.

Where the Athenians were tepid with regard to individual purpose in the absence of community, they were religious in their belief in individual capacity. They passionately advocated the notion of an order to the universe, and insisted repeatedly that mankind had not just the capacity but the obligation to uncover that order. Uncovering natural law meant seeking to know nature, and Plato, Aristotle, and the Stoics were united in their belief that human beings could turn their minds to nature in pursuit of answers. Humans were graced with a divine power, reason; the human mind reflected objective truths discoverable in the universe. Perhaps the most inspiring legacy of Athens is the unwavering faith in the power of the human mind.

As already noted, communal purpose was wrapped up with individual purpose: if the goal of the individual was to find happiness through virtuous citizenry, the goal of the community had to be promotion of that virtue. In this communitarian vision, individual freedom in the modern sense completely disappears. Athens rejected the concept of individual freedom beyond the freedom to pursue the virtuous in pursuit of telos; freedom merely meant self-control, the very opposite of what we often mean by freedom today. Freedom in the modern notion is explicitly rejected by Plato, who felt it would lead to anarchy; according to Aristotle, freedom only exists in the individual context when you are involved in philosophical pursuits.[24]

What, then, of communal capacity? The community was tasked with two separate functions: instilling virtue in the citizenry, and protecting the citizens from the violation of natural law. Plato thought that fulfillment of the first function could prevent the necessity for the second: if the government could train perfect philosopher-kings to govern, there would be no need to worry about violations of natural law. Aristotle and the Stoics both worried at such utopianism, and believed that the state had to be designed to prevent the violation of natural law through a mixed system of checks and balances.

The Athenian system of thought establishes certain fundamental notions crucial to happiness: the notion of telos, discoverable by us; the importance of reason-led investigation, leading to the birth of science; the recognition that social ties bind us to one another. But Athenian thought still leaves several serious questions to be answered. The Greeks found happiness in philosophizing, not in action. If you aren't a philosopher, how do you achieve happiness? Are we really expected to be happy as workers or warriors, in Plato's tripartite society? How do we avoid the tyranny of the polis, given the link between virtue and good citizenship?

Most of all, how does philosophy translate over into action? Where the law of Moses is written in stone, the natural law often seems vague or even illusory. How can the world of thought be united with the world of practice? Could the thundering voice of God, demanding action from the mountaintop, somehow be linked with the quiet, questioning voice of the philosophers, demanding reason from nature?

CHAPTER 4

COMING TOGETHER

The worlds of Jerusalem and Athens seemed largely irreconcilable. Judaism was a small but important religion—estimates suggest that perhaps 10 percent of the Roman Empire was Jewish by the end of the first century CE[1]—and Greek thought had largely been subsumed within the rubric of Roman thought. But the two building blocks of Western civilization, Judaic revelation and Greek reasoning, were at war.

It was, at best, highly unclear whether consonance could be successfully attempted.

There were three serious conflicts between Jewish thought and Greek thought. The first conflict surrounded the nature of God: the God of Moses and the God of Aristotle were not identical. Where Judaism posited an active God in the universe, Greek thought posited an Unmoved Mover largely unconcerned with human affairs. "The changeless, Unmoved Mover was the God of Plato and Aristotle," Rabbi Jonathan Sacks says. "The God of history was the God of Abraham. They simply did not belong together." Judaism believed, as Greek thought did, in a God who stood behind creation; but unlike Greek reason, Judaism also saw God's presence in human events, not merely nature. God was intimately involved, in this view, with man's action. The Greeks believed far more in fate than in a divine presence with a moral sense.[2]

Second, Greek reason sought universality in all things; revelation found universality through the specific communication between God and man at Sinai. Greek natural law thinking centered on the notion that human beings could, through pure contemplation of the world around them, arrive at certain universal truths. Those universals were true for everyone, and represented the ultimate level of knowledge.

Jewish revelation, by contrast, suggested that human beings were not fully capable of discovering all universals—that revelation would be necessary, a voice speaking from on high to human beings, dictating morality. Thus, the Torah suggested that God wanted human beings to use reason to find general truths, but that His "chosen" people had also been given additional responsibilities. That people was designated His "light unto the nations," to enact His commandments and, by doing so, spread those universal truths. Universalism suggests that human logic leads to the light outside the cave; particularism suggests that God's hand can be found in His guidance of one particular nation.

Third, Greek commitment to the polis contradicted Jewish commitment to the divine. The Greek vision of citizenship focused centrally on the place of the individual within the polis, the city-state; Hellenic thought focused heavily on how to shape individuals to best serve as citizens, and how to cultivate virtues that would be useful in such citizens. Judaism, however, had another commitment: the commitment to individual and collective service to Divine law. These two notions came into direct conflict in 167 BCE, when the Greek king Antiochus IV attempted to defile the Jewish Temple on behalf of the Greek religion and banned many Jewish practices. He used as his proxy Hellenized Jews, who saw traditional Judaism as an obstacle to assimilation. The Maccabees rose up in revolt, and reestablished the Hasmonean dynasty in Judea; that uprising is commemorated by Jews to this day in the form of Hanukkah.

Could these two traditions be brought together? Could reason alone provide purpose? Could religion alone provide capacity? Or would the two find consonance?

These questions would drive philosophy and religion for the next thirteen centuries, transform the philosophy and history of the European continent, and provide the next layer of foundational ideas in the building of modernity.

THE BIRTH OF CHRISTIANITY

The birth of Christianity represented the first serious attempt to merge Jewish thought with Greek thought. The Christian admixture was far more Jewish than Greek in its vision of God and of man's quest in the world, but it was also far more Greek than Jewish in its universality.

Christianity universalized the message of Judaism. The Gospels were deliberately written in Greek, not the Aramaic used by the Jews of the period. Jesus's story was meant to extend to the entire world. Because Jesus was no longer a Jewish figure in the Christian view, but the material incarnation of the divine, that meant that Jewish law could be abandoned in favor of universalism. As historian Richard Tarnas writes, "That supreme Light, the true source of reality shining forth outside Plato's cave of shadows, was now recognized as the light of Christ. As Clement of Alexandria announced, 'By the Logos, the whole world is now become Athens and Greece.'"[3] The Judaic notion of God, so focused on law and the Jewish people as God's torch burning in the darkness through fulfillment of that law, was turned aside. Instead, Jesus became all:

> Christ is the culmination of the law so that there may be righteousness for everyone who believes. . . . If you declare with your mouth, "Jesus is Lord," and believe in your heart that God raised him from the dead, you will be saved. . . . For there is no difference between Jew and Gentile—the same Lord is Lord of all and richly blesses all who call on him.[4]

Access to God became universal, and far more easily attainable: the answer lay in belief. This key Christian concept—the notion of faith in one personal redeemer, the representative of God's logic in the universe—broadened the appeal of Judaism to billions of people over history in a way Judaism never would have: Christianity's focus on grace rather than works makes it a far more accessible religion than Judaism in a practical sense. The commandments of Judaism are intricate and difficult. Christianity dispensed with the need for them. Faith is paramount.

In making faith paramount, however, Christianity demoted the role of Greek reason in the life of human beings; despite Christianity's vision of God as the Logos, the logic lying behind all of the universe, Christianity conflated that Logos with the person of Jesus. The great early Christian thinker Tertullian (155–240) summed up the idea well: "What has Jerusalem to do with Athens, the Church with the Academy, the Christian with the heretic? . . . After Jesus we have no need of speculation, after the Gospel no need of research."[5] Likewise, Saint Augustine (354–430) suggested that investigating the universe was a waste of time for those who accepted the truth of revelation: "Many scholars engage in lengthy discussions on these matters, but the sacred writers with their deeper wisdom have omitted them. Such subjects are of no profit for those who seek beatitude, and, what is worse, they take up very precious time that ought to be given to what is spiritually beneficial. . . . The truth is rather in what God reveals than in what groping men surmise."[6] Augustine was not a full opponent of reason; if not for original sin, Augustine said, reason alone could have connected man with God. But grace had to fill the gap between man and God after the Fall; reason couldn't be the primary fuel for crossing that boundary.

Christianity solved the dilemma of the polis vs. the individual by suggesting that Jesus's transformation of the world was essentially spiritual, not material. Judaism had posited that the messiah would be a political figure, not primarily a spiritual one—and that very idea put Judaism inherently in conflict with any powerful material empire. Christianity redefined the concept of the messiah entirely: Paul morphed the Jewish belief in a political messiah who would usher in an age of worldly peace to the Christian belief in a spiritual messiah who had to die to atone for human sins.

This division was made clearest by Augustine, who, in the aftermath of the fall of the Roman Empire, was deeply concerned with rejecting the idea that Christianity's rise had led to the collapse of the Empire. Augustine dealt in dichotomies, chief among them the division between what he called the City of God and the City of Man. The City of God revolves around virtue; it is the community of Christians who have been initiated by grace into Jesus's love. The City of Man is the material city, the polis so treasured by the Greeks—grasping, materialistic, incapable of bringing happiness, in Augustine's description.[7]

This dichotomy suggested that the existing governments need not feel threatened by Christianity, which, after all, just sought the hearts of men in worship. Christianity was beyond politics; citizenship was to be governed by the City of Man. Augustine wrote:

> Christ's servants—whether kings or princes or judges, whether soldiers or provincials, rich or poor, free or slave, men and women alike—are told to endure, if need be, the worst and most depraved republic and, by their endurance, to win for themselves a place of glory in the most holy and majestic senate of the angels, so to speak, in the heavenly republic whose law is the will of God.[8]

The realm of man was man's; the realm of God was God's. In reality, of course, the Church would quickly centralize temporal as well as spiritual power. Augustine's dichotomy be-tween the City of God and the City of Man actually *supported* that power seizure, since the best City of Man would presumably be one that utilized the values of the City of God. Augustine con-troversially followed the path of power on occasion, too: when a schismatic sect called the Donatists threatened him and the regime under which he lived, Augustine used the Roman au-thorities to quash them, arguing, "You are of opinion that no one should be compelled to follow righteousness; and yet you read that the householder said to his servants, 'Whomsoever ye shall find, compel them to come in.' . . . sometimes the shep-herd brings wandering sheep back to the flock with his rod."[9] Defenders of Augustine said that this was less doctrinal than an emergency defense; either way, the Catholic Church would not shy away from the arrogation of power over the course of coming centuries.

THE VICTORY OF CHRISTIANITY

The spread of Christianity was immediate and far-reaching. Historian Rodney Stark estimates that there were about one thousand Christians in the year 40 CE; by the year 300, there were some six million Christians, a growth rate of some 40 percent per decade.[10] What drove Christianity's spread? There have been several theories, aside from the obvious spiritual ones. First, concurrent historians suggested that Christianity's rise had been driven by admiration for its system of care for the poor: the emperor Julian, a committed opponent of the Church, spoke of pagan shortcomings when compared with the "moral character, even if pretended," of the Christians, including their "benevolence toward strangers and care of the graves of the dead." Julian saw Christians' attention to the impoverished as a chief outreach method.[11]

Then there was the fact that Christianity was the only religion actively seeking converts: after the destruction of the Jewish Temple in 70 CE, Judaism had stopped religious outreach (there is controversy as to whether Judaism sought religious conversion even before that event). Because Christianity proposed both universal salvation *and* exclusive salvation, furthermore, it drew adherents from Roman society—it's easier to evangelize those of foreign religion if they are barred from eternity by failure to join.

Early Christians were persecuted brutally by the Romans, who saw them as a rebellious and millennialist offshoot of the Jewish tree. But Christianity's division between the spiritual and material worlds allowed various emperors to treat the religion as either a scapegoat or as a potential source of support. Emperor Diocletian launched the most vicious round of persecution against the Christians in 303 CE, but in 311 CE, Emperor Galerius issued an edict of toleration granting Christianity the status of legal religion within the Eastern Empire; two years later, the Edict of Milan extended that toleration to the Roman Empire as well. Finally, in 325, Emperor Constantine took part in the First Council of Nicaea, an ecumenical council designed to settle the main points of Christian canon. The result of that meeting, the Nicene Creed, set the theological framework for Christianity. On his deathbed, Constantine finally converted to the religion he loved. In 380, Emperor Theodosius made Christianity the official state religion of the Roman Empire. The astonishing rise of a tiny Jewish sect to the religious leadership of the most powerful empire on earth was complete.

But the Roman Empire was already tottering on its last legs. In 476, the last emperor of Rome, Romulus Augustus, abdicated at point of sword. (The Eastern Empire, based in Constantinople, remained, transforming into the Byzantine Empire and lasting all the way until the fifteenth century.) The collapse of the Roman Empire in the West fragmented the continent in terms of political control. The Catholic Church moved quickly to fill the gap, centralizing both temporal and spiritual power.

From the fall of Rome through the twelfth century, Christianity would spread from its base in the Italian peninsula to the British Isles, France, Germany, and eventually the Nordic countries as well. While Augustine had posited a great divide between the City of God and the City of Man, the Catholic Church was quite active in the City of Man—the Church received tithes from Christians the continent over and had its own ecclesiastical courts. By the tenth century, the Church was the single largest landowner in Western Europe.[12] Kings found their legitimacy through the conduit of the Church, and battled with the Church to expand their own power: Holy Roman Emperor Henry IV walked barefoot in the snow to earn back the approval of Pope Gregory VII; Henry II of England (1133–1189) had himself flogged in order to win back the approval of his Christian population after accidentally ordering the death of Archbishop Thomas Becket.

Popular history maintains that this period represented the

"Dark Ages." But that's simply inaccurate. Progress continued as Christianity spread. The monastic system centralized learning in monasteries, where priests and nuns devoted themselves to ascetic pursuit of Divine understanding. In educational terms, this devotion revolved around scripture. The Benedictine monks, for example, lived under the rules created by Saint Benedict (480–547), a set of orders regarding the hierarchy of monasteries, the behavior by which to abide, and the requirements of work. The arts thrived in the monastic system; manuscripts were preserved by monks devoted to writing new copies and beautifying them. In the monastic system, the liberal arts taught by the Greeks and the Romans—as championed by Cicero and Seneca, among others—survived, albeit in spiritualized form: Augustine himself, despite his distaste for paganism, suggested that the liberal arts education could be hijacked for service to God. Augustine likened such cultural appropriation to the Jews taking Egyptian gold during the Biblical Exodus: "This is their gold and silver, which they have not created themselves but have extracted from certain ores, as it were, of precious metal, wherever they found them scattered by the hand of divine providence. . . . These we need for our life here below, and should appropriate and turn them to a better use."[13] These liberal arts were categorized by the philosopher Boethius (481–525) into the famous *quadrivarium* (music, arithmetic, geometry, and astronomy) and *trivium* (grammar, rhetoric, logic).

Meanwhile, the Middle Ages saw technological revolution in agriculture, the rise of commerce, and the institution of new forms of art ranging from polyphonic music to Gothic architecture; it also saw new developments in the art of war, with technological advances that would allow the West to defeat its enemies in the course of coming centuries.[14] While many historians tout the power of Islamic civilization during this time period—and Islamic civilization did thrive on the Arabian Peninsula particularly—when Islamic civilization came up against Western civilization at the Battle of Tours, Islamic forces were soundly defeated.

By the eighth century, Christian leaders were crusading against enslavement (except, notably, for the enslavement of Muslim war captives); monasteries were engaging in proto-capitalism as well.[15] Furthermore, the Catholic Church was responsible for learning and teaching. Virtually all literacy sprang from monasteries.

Still, the modern world could not have been created under these circumstances alone. Faith provided individual moral purpose; faith provided collective moral purpose. But while individual capacity was bolstered by the doctrinal belief in free will and the value of work, reason had been made secondary to faith; while collective capacity was bolstered by the presence of a strong social fabric, the all-encompassing power of the Catholic Church and the rule of monarchs meant that individual choice was heavily circumscribed. Even education had been radically reoriented toward the Church; all true knowledge lay in the Bible, and the liberal arts were only useful so far as they bolstered the Biblical story. For science and democracy to take hold in the West, reason would have to be elevated once more.

That process began with the reintroduction of Greek reason

to the West in the eleventh century. Christianity, comfortable now in its dominance, could afford more exploratory thinking when it came to secular learning. This bred a new movement, called scholasticism—and that movement encouraged Christians to extend the provenance of God's dominance over all of the areas of human knowledge. Scholasticism would open the door for a renewed investigation into the unity between God and His created universe, and between faith and reason. Leading scholastic Hugh of Saint-Victor (1096–1141) famously stated, "Learn everything, later you will see that nothing is superfluous"; he followed through on his own injunction by attempting to write a book that covered the gamut of human knowledge, known as a summa.[16]

Scholasticism became the dominant philosophy of the Church. The Church launched a program of support for universities: the University of Paris, also known as the Sorbonne; the University of Bologna; and the University of Oxford. As Thomas E. Woods Jr. writes, "The Church provided special protection to university students by offering them what was known as benefit of clergy. . . . The popes intervened on behalf of the university on numerous occasions."[17]

But the grandest attempts to reunify Athens and Jerusalem came in the twelfth and thirteenth centuries. During the twelfth century, Aristotle's works, long buried, were rediscovered in the West. They had been maintained in the Arabic-speaking world for generations, but they were only retransmitted in Europe over the course of that century, breaking anew and with massive impact in the thirteenth century.[18]

Athens was back.

There were several leaders in the newfound attempt to unify Athens and Jerusalem: Maimonides (1135–1204), whom we will discuss later, was the most profound thinker among Jews. Among Christians, the leader in this respect was Thomas Aquinas (1225–1274). Aquinas became father of a philosophy named after him: Thomism. The basic idea was a merger of Aristotelianism and Christianity—a commitment to reason and logic, as well as to revelation. Aquinas stated, "They hold a plainly false opinion who say that in regard to the truth of religion it does not matter what a person thinks about creation so long as he has the correct opinion concerning God. An error concerning the creation ends as false thinking about God."[19] As God was the master of heaven and earth, His creation was evidence of Him, and knowledge of that creation would bring us closer to Him. But to know God meant first to believe in Him. God made man to know God.

Aquinas, like Maimonides and Muslim philosophers like Al-Farabi (872–950), concerned himself, therefore, with proofs of God's existence. This was, in and of itself, somewhat revolutionary in the Christian world. Judaism offered no proof of God beyond revelation; God was simply the Creator. End of story. And Christianity offered no logical proofs for God's existence; Jesus walked the earth and rose from the dead. End of story.

But Aquinas sought to use reason to bolster faith. He offered several proofs of God's existence, the most convincing of which was a form of the cosmological argument promoted by Aristotle. Essentially, Aquinas argued that all things in life are a combination of actual and potential—that a candle, for example, is a candle right now, and has the potential to become a pool of wax when operated on by fire. The reason the candle is currently in its state is because of *something* acting upon it. That something, in turn, is dependent on something else. But, Aquinas argues, that chain cannot continue forever; in the end, there must be a final cause, an Unmoved Mover standing behind things as they are. That Unmoved Mover will not be a combination of actual and potential at all—it will be pure actuality, since if it had potential, that potential could only be actualized by another force, which would continue the regress. This final Unmoved Mover, says Aquinas, is what we call God. And that Unmoved Mover must exist immaterially, exist outside of time and space, and be perfect—otherwise, the Unmoved Mover would not be pure actuality.[20]

Aquinas went further still. If reason supports the notion of an intelligent God who crafts nature and stands behind its ever-present glory, Aquinas posited, then human beings can examine the natural world as a pathway to understanding Him. God made nature; to discover nature is to investigate the works of God. In fact, God wanted man to do this—God wanted man to seek Him everywhere. And God granted human beings the power of free will and reason to do so—as Aquinas celebrates, "man acts from judgment, because by his apprehensive power he judges that something should be avoided or sought . . . forasmuch as man is rational it is necessary that man have a free-will."[21]

In Aquinas's thought, Jerusalem and Athens are reunified. God orders us to use our reason, and reason impels us to discover the natural law—laws designed by God.

Aquinas is completely comfortable with the notion of scientific discovery and progress; he openly states that if the astronomers of his day were proved to be wrong, that would not refute any of his metaphysics, since "perhaps the phenomena of the stars are explicable on some other plan not yet discovered by man."[22]

If reason suffices to bring us all this way, according to Aquinas, then why is revelation even necessary? Aquinas here borrows from Augustine: were we perfect, reasoning beings, revelation might be unnecessary. But we are not. Revelation thus bridges the gap. As theology professor Ernest Fortin suggests, Aquinas believes that "between the truths of Revelation and the knowledge acquired by the sole use of reason and experience there is a distinction but there can be no fundamental disagreement."[23]

Aquinas's faith in human reason—and his faith that human reason would not be able to tear down the revelation of God—led to a consonance that would blossom into the scientific revolution. The development of Western science was rooted in the notion that man's task was to celebrate God through knowledge of His creation. Contrary to the propaganda of a postmodern atheist movement, nearly every great scientist up until the age of Darwinism was religious. The Scholastic movement produced the earliest roots of the scientific method, all the way up through the discovery by Nicolaus Copernicus (1473–1543) of a heliocentric solar system.[24]

Perhaps the greatest exponent of the Scholastic method was Roger Bacon (1219–1292), a Franciscan friar who devoted himself to understanding the natural world. Like Aquinas, Bacon was a devoted Aristotelian who suggested gathering facts before coming to conclusions. He wrote fulsomely on optics, alchemy, and astronomy; he suggested revising the Julian calendar, which he found obtuse; he even set down the first European formula for gunpowder. The age of scientific progress didn't begin with the Enlightenment. It began in the monasteries of Europe.

FLAWS IN THE CONSONANCE

This consonance could not last, and it didn't.

To see why, we must examine where the legacy of Augustine and Aquinas fell short, and where those shortcomings were brought to fruition in the rise of the Enlightenment. Let us, then, return to our basic framework for happiness, and examine it in light of the dominance of Catholic European thought: individual purpose, individual capacity, communal purpose, and communal capacity.

The rise of Scholasticism provided a serious answer to the question of purpose: human beings are placed here by a loving God, who seeks from us to do good and avoid evil. This is the same answer provided by Judaism, modified only by simplification of Judaic legalism into Athenian-seeming universal natural laws, discoverable through reason. According to Aquinas, human beings have natural inclinations, placed there by God; when we rule those natural inclinations through reason, we discover the good.[25] Augustine would have preached that belief in Jesus provided that sole window to knowing God; Aquinas, while not rejecting that New Testament ordinance, found another window through the use of reason.

Aquinas also provided a strong belief in human capacity. Both Augustine and Aquinas believed in free will, but Aquinas's faith in reason stretched beyond Augustine's. That faith in reason would allow Aquinas to make room for exploration of the material world, without fear that such exploration would detract from the religious mission to know God. Aristotelian focus on the immanent replaced Platonic speculation about the transcendent.

What of communal purpose? Christianity provided a sense of communal purpose in fighting for the good. But Christianity, like all religions, focuses on the spiritual to the exclusion of the physical. And that failure to take into account the drive for betterment in the physical world would be used as a club wielded against Christianity itself before long.

When it comes to communal capacity, however, the dominance of the Catholic Church provided a stumbling block. Neither Augustine nor Aquinas would have contemplated a separation between church and state in any real sense. Augustine sought to defend religion against the predations of a secular state but would have preferred a Christian monarch to a secular one; Aquinas, like Aristotle, believed that the promotion of the common good through the state was worthwhile, even if he demoted that promotion to secondary status behind the promotion of spiritual salvation.

While the end of the Middle Ages provided yet another major stone in the foundation of Western civilization, then, those foundations were not yet complete. They would not be complete without learning two more critical lessons: the dangers of communal power and the human capacity for material betterment.

CHAPTER 5

ENDOWED BY THEIR CREATORS

If one attitude characterizes modern politics, it's an attitude of complete and utter moral certainty. Those on the political Left are certain that those who oppose them are Nazi-esque monsters hell-bent on domination of individual lives; those on the political Right are certain that the opposite is true. Most important, both sides of the political aisle seem determined, at times, to use the power available in culture and government to cram down their vision of the world on their opponents—to establish a heavenly kingdom of hegemonic, one-party rule.

That demand for certainty cuts against the foundations of our very civilization.

The history of the West teaches us that while we must share a common vision for our civilization, the means by which we pursue that vision need not be shared. That lesson was learned over the course of centuries, at the cost of tremendous quantities of blood and tears. The bricks of the West were mixed from Athens and Jerusalem, yes—but the catalyzing factor was a large dose of humility.

By the end of the thirteenth century, Western civilization was completely dominated by Catholicism. That dominion stretched across Europe, giving new freedom to thinkers like Aquinas—but it also masked serious religious tensions among various orders, as well as even deeper tensions with secular rulers who felt threatened by the arrogation of power to the Church. Furthermore, the reign of Catholicism masked serious conflicts within the Church itself. All of these conflicts frequently broke out into open conflict; in 1303, for example, Pope Boniface VIII found himself arrested by forces in the pay of France's King Philip IV, which resulted in the temporary exile of the papacy from Rome itself.

From this era of challenges, two strong new ideas emerged: first, human beings are capable of exploring the world and bettering their material condition in it; second, each human being is free and endowed with natural rights. Skepticism of centralized political power grew from centuries of political and religious conflict; optimism in the power of science grew from new discoveries made in light of the liberated individual mind. The Renaissance and the Enlightenment completed the foundations of the West that built our world.

THE POWER OF SCIENCE

The explosion of science in the West is perhaps the West's best-known, most-celebrated legacy. The story of technological development has never changed—human beings want to live more comfortably in the world. But the story of science changed radically beginning with Thomas Aquinas and Franciscan friar William of Ockham and their successors: human beings sought the cosmos through science, and used that newfound knowledge to develop technologies that would later be thought to obviate the need for God Himself. The secularist myth holds that religion held back science for millennia. The reverse is true. Without Judeo-Christian foundations, science simply would not exist as it does in the West.

Contrary to popular opinion, new discoveries weren't invariably seen as heretical or dangerous to the dominion of the Church; in fact, the Church often supported scientific investigation. Nicole Oresme (1320–1382), the discoverer of the Earth's rotation about its axis, was a bishop of Lisieux and a graduate of the University of Paris. Nicholas of Cusa (1401–1464), cardinal of Brixen, theorized that the Earth was not stationary, but moved through space.[1] Nicolaus Copernicus studied in parochial school and served the church of Warmia as medical adviser; his publication of *De revolutionibus*, his theory that the Earth moved around the sun and not the other way around, in March 1543, included a letter to Pope Paul III.[2]

Eventually, the backlash to the inclusion of secular knowledge in the Christian worldview—a backlash led by thinkers like Martin Luther (1483–1546) and John Calvin (1509–1564)—led to the Church's famous persecution of Galileo. Galileo Galilei (1564–1642) famously posited that the Earth moves around the sun, and was forced to recant by the Church for his failure to state that his theory was not fact. Copernicus had been treated with decency by the Church of his own time—but in 1616, in response to the new fundamentalist religious wave, Copernican ideas were banned. The ban would last until the early nineteenth century, and Galileo's official pardon from the Vatican would only be issued at the end of the twentieth century.[3]

Still, the Thomistic allegiance to both reason and faith could not be quashed. Despite his differences with the Church, Galileo never abandoned his own faith that science could be a pathway to God. He wrote, "I say that as to the truth of the knowledge which is given by mathematical proofs, this is the same that Divine wisdom recognizes, [although] our understanding . . . is infinitely surpassed by the Divine. [Yet] when I consider what marvelous things and how many of them men have understood, inquired into, and contrived, I recognize and understand only too clearly that the human mind is a work of God's, and one of the most excellent."[4]

Galileo was no exception. He was a representative of the rule: religious men saw a duty to examine the universe, and to do so with the best possible methodology. This philosophy permeated the wisdom of the Enlightenment's greatest scientists. Johannes Kepler (1571–1630), the discoverer of the laws of planetary motion, explained: "The chief aim of all investigations of the external world should be to discover the rational order and harmony which has been imposed on it by God and which He revealed to us in the language of mathematics."[5] Kepler routinely described his own physics as part and parcel of Aristotelian metaphysics, and explained that the laws of nature "are within the grasp of the human mind. God wanted us to recognize them by creating us after his own image so that we could share in his own thoughts."[6] Kepler's philosophy was also that of Isaac Newton (1642–1726): "Opposite to [God] is Atheism in profession & Idolatry in practice. Atheism is so senseless & odious to mankind that it never had many professors."[7]

SCIENTIFIC PROGRESS, CONTINUED

The progress of science was motivated by a determination to know God's universe, but it became increasingly clear that one significant by-product of that quest for knowledge was the betterment of man's material status. Like Ockham, Francis Bacon (1561–1626) dispensed with the Aristotelian notion of final causes in science—he saw that human beings could all too easily substitute their own conclusory reasons for hard data. "To go beyond Aristotle by the light of Aristotle is to think that a borrowed light can increase the original light from which it is taken," Bacon wrote.[8]

Bacon's rejection of Aristotelian science also led him to reject Aristotelian teleology more broadly. Man's purpose was not, in Bacon's view, to act in accordance with his nature as a reasoning being. Bacon instead sought purpose in "extend[ing] more widely the limits of the power and greatness of man." Bacon wanted to turn the pursuit of knowledge toward "the benefit and use of men . . . for the glory of the Creator and the relief of man's estate."[9] In tones that remind us of those of today's modern social scientists, Bacon also suggested the use of science to determine the best mode of governance and ethics.[10]

Unlike modern social scientists, however, Bacon took his cue for governance and ethics from the Judeo-Christian tradition. While Bacon upheld the importance of the scientific method and a belief in the pure value of innovation to better the material lives of human beings, Bacon was no atheist. He derided the notion of a Godless universe in harsh terms, suggesting that while "a little philosophy inclineth man's mind to atheism, depth in philosophy bringeth men's minds about to religion."[11] Bacon wrote this prayer in *Novum Organum*: "let none be alarmed at the objection of the arts and sciences becoming depraved to malevolent or luxurious purposes and the like, for the same can be said of every worldly good: talent, courage, strength, beauty, riches, light itself, and the rest. Only let mankind regain their rights over nature, assigned to them by the gift of God, and obtain that power, whose exercise will be governed by right reason and true religion."[12] This last statement is an attempt to read ancient thought and Christianity back into science, over his own objections.

Bacon's confidence in man's mind to better the world—in accordance, of course, with "right reason and true religion"— saw further development from René Descartes (1596–1650), who also discarded "speculations" on behalf of "useful knowledge." He saw meaning not in theology, but in science—full knowledge of which would surely carry mankind forward toward "the perfect moral science." As with Bacon, the good of man lay not in the search for God or the pursuit of a virtuous telos, but in the quest to better the material state of man. Morality would surely follow in the wake of man's technological progress and increased scientific knowledge.[13]

Such knowledge, Descartes believed, could not be pursued without radical skepticism of received wisdom: "I ought to reject as absolutely false all opinions in regard to which I could suppose the least ground for doubt, in order to ascertain whether after that there remained aught in my belief that was wholly indubitable." This led Descartes to doubt all of his senses—except his knowledge of his own thinking. Thus, Descartes stated, "*Cogito, ergo sum*"—I think, therefore I am. From this basis, he reintroduced a good God who would not create senses that lie to us.[14]

Both Bacon and Descartes, while discarding the teleology of the ancients, maintained faith in the Bible and in God. But they also laid the groundwork for the rise of Deism—and in time, for the fall of religion itself. By cutting final causes from science, by separating God from the natural world, the modern scientific project would eventually remove religion and purpose from the domain of reason—a project that both Bacon and Descartes would have abhorred.

THE RISE OF CLASSICAL LIBERALISM

The rise of science was coincident with the simultaneous rise of human freedom. The dominance of the Catholic Church over the course of the Middle Ages and Renaissance led some to rebel against the notion of centralized authority altogether. One of the first to do so was Marsilius of Padua (1275–1342), who fought against the notion of papal plenitude of power—the notion that the Church ought to rule in the City of Man as well as the City of God. Marsilius saw that the Catholic Church's power could threaten secular authorities—and that those secular authorities could then turn on the Church. Instead of theocracy, Marsilius proposed sovereignty of citizens. His philosophy actually bordered on calls for democracy—he suggested that freedom to worship God itself prohibited theocracy. No wonder Pope Clement VI stated that he had almost never read a worse heretic than Marsilius.[15]

Marsilius's skepticism regarding the Church would be taken to the next level by Niccolò Machiavelli (1469–1527). Like Marsilius, Machiavelli saw oppression in the guise of the Catholic Church: in *The Prince*, Machiavelli openly mocked the Church.[16] Machiavelli believed that those who proclaimed that the state could be governed in accordance with virtue were merely lying for the sake of convenience. His cynical suggestion: that states be governed in accordance with *virtù*, a mix of cruelty and kindness generating both fear and love. The goal of such governance: to prevent utopian schemes designed to instill virtue in the citizenry through the power of the sword.

In *The Prince*, Machiavelli proposed that human beings are not driven by reason—thereby tacitly rejecting the ancient notion of Aristotelian virtue—but that they were instead driven by passion. In his *Discourses on Livy*, Machiavelli suggested that we presuppose that "all men are bad and that they will use their malignity of mind every time they have the opportunity." The best way to ensure the freedom of human beings, then, would be to check passion with passion: "The desires of free peoples are rarely harmful to liberty, because they arise either from oppression or from the suspicion that they will be oppressed . . . the people, although ignorant, can grasp the truth, and they readily yield when they are told the truth by a trustworthy man."[17] Machiavelli thus discarded the ancient search for a utopian republic and disdained the notion that a state can exist to make men virtuous. Naturally, as with Marsilius, the Catholic Church banned Machiavelli's *Prince* in 1559.

But the Catholic Church's woes were just beginning. The rise of Lutheranism challenged both the spiritual and temporal power of the Church. Luther, in his ardent attempt to reclaim the Bible from what he deemed the thoroughgoing corruption of the papacy, worked to decimate the hierarchy of believers, leaving merely individuals before God, capable of comprehending God's direct word: "A shoemaker, a smith, a farmer, each has his manual occupation and work; and, yet, at the same time, all are eligible to act as priests and bishops." In pursuit of that egalitarian vision, Luther discarded the notion of sanctuary from the secular law: "It is intolerable that in canon law, the freedom, person, and goods of the clergy should be given this exemption, as if the layman were not exactly as spiritual, and as good Christians, as they, or did not equally belong to the church." Luther's translation of the Bible into German also made practical his notion of individuals communing directly with God. As history professor Joseph Loconte of King's College writes, "Luther offered more than a theory of individual empowerment. He delivered a spiritual bill of rights."[18]

In the realm of government, Luther was no democrat. He believed that the state's authority did not derive from the authority of the people, but from God Himself: "We must firmly establish secular law and the sword, that no one may doubt that it is in the world by God's will and ordinance." In consigning reason to secondary status behind faith, Luther demeaned popular sovereignty, though he saw the value of placing restrictions on absolute monarchs—Christians were not to obey anti-Christian commands, for example. Similarly, Calvin believed in an aristocracy governed by checks and balances, but, like Luther, he saw the presence of a particular government as a sign of God's will in action.[19]

Nonetheless, it would be Luther and Calvin's religious fragmentation and their devolution of authority down to the individual that would lead to a true transnational movement away from authoritarian government. The horrors of religious conflict from the mid-sixteenth century culminated in the Thirty Years' War (1618–1648)—a war that resulted in some eight million deaths—and forced the choice of religious toleration or mass carnage. It was in making this choice that the notion of human rights was born.

The earliest author of that concept was Hugo Grotius (1583–1645). Grotius, unlike Machiavelli, Luther, and Calvin, saw human reason as paramount and society as a way for man to develop his capacity in concert with others; his thought reflects far more the thought of the ancients. Grotius, like Plato and Aristotle, saw natural right as an extension of natural law: you had a right to do that which was in accordance with your telos. As Grotius put it, natural law is the "dictate of right reason which points out that an act, according as it is or is not in conformity with rational nature, has in it a quality of moral baseness or moral necessity; and that in consequence, such an act is either forbidden or enjoined by the author of nature,

God."[20] Such right reason could be discovered by looking to the law of nations—including the Noahide Laws of the Bible.[21]

Grotius extended the concept of human rights further than that: he stated that human beings also had rights to *do things*— the right to act in pursuit of justice by capturing criminals, for example. Once Grotius combined the notion of a right to act with the idea that sovereigns were subject to the dictates of natural law, it was a relatively short step to Thomas Hobbes (1588–1679).

THE RISE OF THE INDIVIDUAL

Hobbes is often considered the first rationalist political philosopher. He attempted to map out human behavior with the regularity of mathematics. In doing so, he rejected the philosophy of Aristotle as insufficiently realistic, and, following Machiavelli, suggested instead that human passions were the chief motivator for human conduct. And the chief passion, Hobbes believed, was the passion for saving your own skin. Forget the polis; forget the community. No longer was the goal of human life to fulfill the ends of reason—it was to prevent your own death, as shown by the so-called state of nature, in which men harmed one another so far as their self-interest dictated they should do so. "I put for a general inclination of all mankind, a perpetual and restless desire of power after power, that ceaseth only in death," Hobbes stated.[22]

Men's first right, then, was the right to self-preservation. Hierarchies disappear in this regime of natural rights—large, small, smart, stupid, we are all equal in our right to survive. But in a state of nature, with no one to guarantee our safety, how do we survive? We don't rely on the cultivation of virtue. Instead, we grant power to the state. We require a leviathan—a sovereign heading a powerful state—to free human beings from the war of all against all. And that sovereign ought to be seen as representing the collective will of the people. His power is absolute and unchallengeable, granted by social contract from individuals in the state of nature.[23]

Hobbes, however, had opened a door that he could not close again: If human beings had *individual rights*, did those rights end merely with survival? Or, in a state of nature, did human beings enjoy inalienable rights beyond merely breathing and eating and not being murdered?

The philosopher who asked that question was John Locke (1632–1704). Following in Hobbes's footsteps, Locke believed that sovereignty resided in the individual. Locke—a deeply religious Christian—believed in both natural law discoverable by reason and Hobbesian natural right inherent in human existence. Natural law, like the ancients supposed, could be discovered in nature: a law dictating through right reason both correct behavior and the purpose for life. Locke based his beliefs in human reason, sovereignty, and equality not merely in ancient philosophy but in the book of Genesis, in God's suggestion that man is made in His image.[24] Natural rights, according to Locke, were those rights that sprang from exercise of natural law: a right to property, since we had a corresponding duty not to steal; a right to life, since we had a duty not to kill; a right to liberty, since we had a duty not to oppress. Those rights carried with them duties, as well: the right to property carried with it the duty to cultivate that property, for example, since God had granted the earth to all people in common, but that our self-ownership to the exclusion of others allowed us to mix our labor with the land, thereby transforming it.

Locke radically disagreed with Hobbes about the state of nature. For Hobbes, the state of nature made life nasty, brutish, and short; for Locke, the state of nature was a place of "men living according to reason, without a common superior on earth, to judge between them." Notice that Locke, a believer in individual natural rights, did not discount community as Hobbes did. The state of nature was not supposed to describe a sort of Eden-on-earth, but man's status in a pre-political society—in a family or a community of voluntary association. Over time, such communities would grow, and sovereignty would have to be surrendered to a broader government to guarantee the exercise of fundamental rights.

According to Locke, then, the formation of a government requires the exercise of *consent*—or, alternatively, the behavior of the government in accordance with natural law, for example a government's willingness to protect natural rights. The goal of law is to *preserve* freedom, not to trade freedom away for security as Hobbes would have suggested: "the end of law is not to abolish or restrain, but to preserve and enlarge freedom: for in all the states of created beings capable of laws, where there is no law, there is no freedom."[25]

Locke suggested a republic of checks and balances as the key to creating such a government. Government, he stated, required two separate powers: the legislative and the executive. Montesquieu (1689–1755) would later set down the more well-known balance of powers enshrined in the American Constitution: legislative, executive, and judicial.

Most important for American history, Locke openly recognized a right to rebel against a government that violated the rights of its citizens. Any government doing so would allow citizens to revert to a state of nature, in which the citizens could set up a new government: "whenever the legislators endeavor to take away, and destroy the property of the people, or to reduce them to slavery under arbitrary power, they put themselves into a state of war with the people, who are thereupon absolved from any farther obedience, and are left to the common refuge, which God hath provided for all men, against force and violence . . . [power] devolves to the people, who have a right to resume their original liberty."[26]

Locke's philosophy would not merely influence the Founding Fathers of the United States, as we will see—it would shape the foundations of free market enterprise. The vision of Adam Smith (1723–1790) of natural liberty almost precisely mirrors Locke's vision of natural right:

> The obvious and simple system of natural liberty establishes itself of its own accord. Every man, as long as he does not violate the laws of justice, is left perfectly free to pursue his own interest his own way, and to bring both his industry and capital into competition with those of any other man, or order of men.

Smith posited that the government had but three fundamental duties: preservation of life; preservation of liberty through administration of justice; and funding for public goods. His viewpoint would be deeply influential in the formation of the greatest economy in the history of mankind.[27]

THE AMERICAN TRIUMPH

This long philosophical journey would come to fruition in the first country in history to be crafted based on philosophy: the United States of America. The Founding Fathers were devotees of Cicero and Locke, of the Bible and Aristotle. They'd done their reading. And they based their new national philosophy on the lessons garnered from that reading: natural law, rooted in reason and enshrined by religion; individual natural rights, balanced by corresponding duties; a limited government of checks and balances designed to protect those rights in accordance with natural law; and inculcation of virtue, to be pursued by individuals and communities, again in accordance with the dictates of natural law. The founders weren't heedless narcissists, unconcerned with the dangers of radical individualism—they feared a society of religion-less individuals. Nor were they tyrannical collectivists—they feared mob rule and the heavy hand of government cramming subjective definitions of "virtue" down the throats of individuals.

All of this is clearly visible in the Declaration of Independence. Thomas Jefferson attempted to enshrine the brilliance of his philosophical forebears in our founding document; in 1825, he explained, "it was intended to be an expression of the American mind. . . . All its authority rests then on the harmonizing sentiments of the day, whether expressed in conversation, in letters, printed essays, or in the elementary books of public right, as Aristotle, Cicero, Locke, Sidney, etc."[28] John Adams, the chief congressional sponsor of the Declaration, mirrored Jefferson's language exactly: "the principles of Aristotle and Plato, of Livy and Cicero, and Sidney, Harrington, and Locke; the principles of nature and eternal reason; the principles on which the whole government over us now stands."[29]

The Declaration begins with a ringing statement of authority: that of "the Laws of Nature and of Nature's God." This isn't the passivity of Hobbes or Augustine or Luther with regard to the value of the current regime. This is the unification of ancient natural law with the force of Biblical drive. It is an active statement that men can take power into their own hands so long as that power is utilized in pursuit of the natural law, and in accordance with the human right to liberty.

Jefferson quickly makes that clear. "We hold these truths to be self-evident," he writes. But clearly such truths are *not* self-evident—they have not been self-evident for most of human history. Jefferson here references the "right reason" of the ancients: those who think properly, who look to the meanings behind nature, can discover fundamental truths that should undergird human life and human action.

What, precisely, are those truths?

First, that "all men are created equal." Obviously, Jefferson did not mean that all human beings are created with equal capacity. He would have disagreed radically with that notion, since he wasn't a fool. Jefferson originally worked from a draft of George Mason's Virginia Declaration of Rights, which was far more specific: "all men are born equally free and independent."[30] Jefferson merely compressed these ideas into the pithier "all men are created equal."

The notion of all men having equal freedom and independence sprang originally from the Biblical notion of man being made in God's image, admixed with the Greek tradition of individual reason, and passed down generation after generation, transmuted over time into the understanding that not only are human beings made in God's image with will and reason, but with the liberty to exercise that will and reason in accordance with the pursuit of virtue.

Jefferson continues by stating that men are "endowed by their Creator with certain unalienable Rights, that among these are Life, Liberty and the pursuit of Happiness." In Locke, that phrase had been "life, liberty, and property." Why didn't Jefferson simply use the word *property* rather than *pursuit of happiness*? He certainly didn't ignore the right to property because he rejected it—Jefferson routinely talked of the right to the fruits of your labors.[31]

Jefferson used the *right to happiness* because in Jefferson's view, property and its ownership was not a full enough description of our rights. Jefferson, like Locke, believed that the pursuit of happiness encompassed ownership of our own labor, our own minds. Locke himself wrote at length about the pursuit of happiness—and he did not mean the modern misreading of his phrase, which suggests that we all define happiness in our own way. In his "Essay Concerning Human Understanding," Locke wrote, "the care of ourselves, that we mistake not imaginary for real happiness, is the necessary foundation of our liberty." This is Locke touting *virtue*, suggesting that we forgo our own subjectivism in pursuit of a higher happiness, discernible through right reason.[32] As Harry Jaffa of the Claremont Institute wrote, "It is difficult to imagine a more forthright Aristotelianism in Hooker or Aquinas."[33]

And the founders, despite common misperception of their religious practice, were well aware of the necessity for a community of virtue-seeking religious believers in their new republic.[34] The vitality of religion was a precondition for a healthy society. No wonder the founders placed such heavy emphasis on freedom of worship.

Rights and duties, according to the founders, were simply two sides of the same coin. While some critics of the founders have claimed that they ignored duties on behalf of rights, thereby setting the course for societal disintegration, that's a misreading of the founding philosophy: as George Washington stated in his first inaugural address:

> The foundation of our national policy will be laid in the pure and immutable principles of private morality . . . there exists in the economy and course of nature an indissoluble union between virtue and happiness.[35]

THE CULMINATION

The founding ideology was the basis for the greatest experiment in human progress and liberty ever devised by the mind of man. But then again, it was an idea developed through

Judeo-Christian principles and Greek rationality, molded and shaped over time by circumstance, purified in the flame of conflict. It was the best that men have done, and the best that men will do in setting a philosophic framework for human happiness.

Let us examine why—again, through our framework of the requirements of human happiness.

The founding philosophy acknowledges the possibility of individual purpose. That purpose isn't to be supplied by a government, or by molding individual citizens to the service of the polis. That purpose is supplied by a Judeo-Christian tradition of meaning and value, and a Greek tradition of reason. The founders thought that reason was paramount, and virtue worth pursuing. That virtue took the form of courage—willingness to sacrifice life, fortune, and sacred honor in pursuit of defending the rights necessary to pursue virtue itself. That virtue took the form of temperance—no better founding document has ever been penned than the Constitution of the United States, the product of compromise. That virtue took the form of prudence—the practical wisdom of *The Federalist Papers* has not yet been surpassed in political thought. And that virtue took the form of justice—the rule of law, not of men, and the creation of a system where each receives his due.

The founding philosophy also glorified the power of individual capacity. The founders were fully cognizant that human beings had the capacity for evil as well as good, for passion as well as reason. But they had immense faith in the power of reason to impel human beings toward proper thinking. Jefferson stated in the Bill for Establishing Religious Freedom in Virginia in 1779, "the opinions and belief of men depend not on their own will, but follow involuntarily the evidence proposed to their minds; that Almighty God hath created the mind free, and manifested his supreme will that free it shall remain by making it altogether insusceptible of restraint."[36] John Adams identified liberty itself with the power of reason: "It implies thought and choice and power; it can elect between objects, indifferent in point of morality, neither morally good nor morally evil." The only thing, according to Adams, that would turn reason toward good, was a societal inculcation of good, and a general pursuit of knowledge itself: "My humble opinion is, that knowledge, upon the whole, promotes virtue and happiness."[37]

What of communal purpose? Communal purpose could be sought, according to the founders, in common values: in Judeo-Christian traditions and the heritage of Western rights. Culture and philosophy came together in the young United States to form a united country. And that country's job would be to spread liberty, both domestically and abroad. "We should have such an empire for liberty as she has never surveyed since the creation," Jefferson wrote to Madison in 1809, "and I am persuaded no constitution was ever before so well calculated as ours for extensive empire and self-government."[38]

The founders were well aware of the need for collective capacity as well. On the one hand, the founders believed in the individual capacity of Americans to pursue virtue. On the other hand, they distrusted human beings to do so absent social institutions that could encourage such virtuous behavior. And Americans built, cherished, and maintained those social institutions: in *Democracy in America*, penned in the 1830s, Frenchman Alexis de Tocqueville wondered at the fact that "Americans of all ages, all conditions, all minds constantly united . . . Thus the most democratic country on earth is found to be, above all, the one where men in our day have most perfected the art of pursuing the object of their common desires in common and have applied this new science to the most objects." De Tocqueville wisely warned that the replacement of these voluntary associations by government would risk the "morality and intelligence of a democratic people."[39]

The founders agreed, which is why they sought to limit the power of government so dramatically. In order to protect the rights of individual human beings—and in order to ensure their collective capacity for social action—the founders refused to grant strong central powers to the government. James Madison summed up the sentiment well in *Federalist #51*:

> If men were angels, no government would be necessary. If angels were to govern men, neither external nor internal controls on government would be necessary. In framing a government which is to be administered by men over men, the great difficulty lies in this: you must first enable the government to control the governed; and in the next place oblige it to control itself.[40]

Never were stronger foundations set for human happiness than in the founding philosophy. Of course, that philosophy was not sufficiently universalized even by the founders: it had to be extended in practice to black Americans and women, for example. The evils of their time did not leave our founders unaffected. The founding was rife with self-contradiction: that great exponent of liberty, Jefferson, a man who called slavery "a cruel war against human nature," was a slaveholder and the father of six children by a slave, Sally Hemings; Madison, another slaveholder, said that slavery based on "mere distinction of colour" was "the most oppressive dominion ever exercised by man over man."[41]

But the principles of the founding were indeed universal—just as universal as Nature and Nature's God. Frederick Douglass, a former slave turned abolitionist, said it best in a speech decrying the thoroughly wrong, thoroughly evil *Dred Scott* decision, which suggested that black people were not men under the Constitution:

> The Constitution, as well as the Declaration of Independence, and the sentiments of the founders of the Republic, give us a platform broad enough, and strong enough, to support the most comprehensive plans for the freedom and elevation of all the people of this country, without regard to color, class, or clime.[42]

The philosophy of the founders, made material in the creation of the United States and in the continuing quest to fulfill their ideals, has been the greatest blessing for mankind in human history. The United States has freed billions of people; it has enriched billions of people; it has opened minds and hearts.

But that founding philosophy—the crown jewel of the West—

has not prevailed. It has, instead, been gradually decaying. With that decay, the foundations for human happiness have been eroding. We, in our day, may be watching them collapse completely.

How could such a collapse occur?

Gradually, slowly . . . and then all at once.

CHAPTER 6

KILLING PURPOSE, KILLING CAPACITY

Seemingly every year in the United States, a great debate breaks out regarding the separation of church and state. The headlines change, but the underlying conflict does not. It may be a court case about removing a Ten Commandments monument from a public space, or about prayer in the public schools, or about forcing a religious baker to create a custom cake for a same-sex wedding. The root conflict is always the same: Was America built on secular grounds, or religious grounds, or both? More important, will America be made better by curbing religion in the name of secularism, or vice versa?

Now, I have argued that the founding philosophy was based on both secular reason and religious morality, that modernity was built on these twin poles, cultivated and perfected through the fires of religious warfare and secular argument. We built a civilization that was practical and purposeful, religious and rational, virtuous and ambitious. Individual capacity and communal capacity had been brought into harmony: citizens had committed to Judeo-Christian values and individual rights, working to bolster one another. Individual purpose and communal purpose had been aligned: individuals were set free to cultivate virtue, and communities were built to set the framework for that pursuit of happiness.

But advocates for the so-called Enlightenment offer a different theory. They suggest that the philosophy of the modern West—the philosophy of individual rights, particularly—sprang from rejection of religion and embrace of reason. The proponents of the self-proclaimed age of reason flatter themselves that we live today in accordance with the thought of great Enlightenment thinkers, bold new minds who sprang forth from the ground, wholly formed, ready to do battle with, and triumph over, the ancients. In fact, the very term *Enlightenment* suggests a pre-Enlightenment era in which religion inhibited human development rather than fostering it—and by extension, suggests that belief in Judeo-Christian values and God Himself was at best an obstruction to modern Western civilization. Furthermore, the most ardent believers in the Enlightenment deride the Greek search for telos as misguided, resting as it does on the assumption of a reality lying behind material reality; they believe that Enlightenment thought could only progress by jettisoning teleology itself, and substituting materialism. They argue that the Enlightenment only became the Enlightenment by killing God and discarding the idea of an objectively discoverable purpose. The Enlightenment, they say, shed the vestigial organs of religion and Greek teleology, and took civilization to new, uncharted heights.

Unfortunately, these claims are manifestly false.

As we've seen, history is necessary. If it weren't, Enlightenment could have sprung up anywhere, at any time; perhaps it should have arisen *earlier* in societies without the barriers of Greek telos and Judeo-Christian religion. It didn't.

It didn't, because the philosophy of individual rights, springing from the Biblical beliefs that individual human beings are created in God's image and that individual virtue matters, were key to the Enlightenment. So was the search for knowledge—a search rooted in the belief that God had a master plan for the universe, that human beings were blessed with the free will and the reason to investigate that plan, and that we had a moral duty to seek God and to better our own stations materially and spiritually through that search. A devotion to progress in history began with Judeo-Christian religion as well. Most important, Judeo-Christian thought and Greek thought both held in common the belief in purpose.

But, advocates of the revisionist Enlightenment history say, what if the Judeo-Christian belief system and the Greek devotion to reason were necessary to *build* Western civilization, but later prevented Western civilization from fully realizing its potential? What if the ideas of Judeo-Christianity and Greece weren't foundational? What if they were more like a scaffolding, to be removed from the structure as Western thought solidified? What if we could pick and choose our favorite ideas from the Enlightenment canon, and junk all the rest?

As we'll see, we tried it. It failed.

In reality, just as with every other philosophical development in history, the Enlightenment had its upside—the glories of American founding philosophy and Western classical liberalism, both of which were direct outgrowths of Athens and Jerusalem—and it had its downside. What was that downside? That downside began with the purposeful destruction of Judeo-Christian values and Greek teleology. It turns out that those thinkers who maintained the wisdom of those twin foundations built the power and glory of the modern West. Those who sought to chip away at those foundations would eventually emerge victorious—and their victory would plant the seeds for an existential crisis of meaning from which the West suffers more deeply every day. And even their supposed devotion to reason itself would be consumed by their reflexive instinct to tear down the old, no matter how objectively good it was.

FROM VIRTUE TO MORAL RELATIVISM

The original drive to discard God in Western thought grew from three intertwined forces. First, the drive against religion sprang from the dissolution of Catholic dominance; that dissolution created religious schisms and vacuums that all too often invited brutal violence. Critics of Judeo-Christian faith saw in the internecine religious warfare proof that religious fundamentalism inhibited human freedom rather than deepening it. Second, atheism and agnosticism saw a dramatic upswing among intellectuals thanks to the rise in religious fundamentalism: both Lutheranism and Calvinism were, at least in part, responses to the perceived secularization of the Catholic Church. And the Catholic Church moved to mitigate such religious insurgencies by cracking down on its own tendencies toward secular learning. Religion *did* become more of an obstacle to secular learning as Catholic homogeneity receded. Finally, the fragmentation of control by the Catholic Church led to more room to breathe for dissenters. The Peace of Westphalia was explicitly designed to promote more religious freedom for minority religions—and that also allowed new, agnostic philosophies to flourish.

The earliest signs of a philosophical movement breaking with Judeo-Christian morality and Aristotelian virtue came from Machiavelli. An active and rigorous debate rages on about whether Machiavelli was a religious man or a covert atheist—but suffice it to say that his reverence for the Bible was questionable. In *The Prince*, he cites Moses as an example of a war leader (while jokingly calling him a "mere executor of the will of God") and brazenly explaining, "It was necessary, therefore, to Moses that he should find the people of Israel in Egypt enslaved and oppressed by the Egyptians, in order that they should be disposed to follow him so as to be delivered out of bondage."[1]

As to Greek allegiance to virtue, Machiavelli, in typical mocking fashion, hijacks the term itself. No longer should men be governed by virtue, he states—now, they should be governed by *virtù*, a combination of evil and good designed to achieve a certain end and overcome the chaos of fortune (*fortuna*). As Harvey Mansfield writes, "Machiavelli wants to give Renaissance humanism a hard face: to deflate its esteem for classical rhetoric, to attack its adherence to philosophical tradition, to unsettle its accommodation with Christianity, to refute its belief in the virtues of the classical gentleman, and to remind it of the value and glory of the military."[2]

Machiavelli's early iteration of a break from traditional purpose found its first open embrace in Hobbes. Hobbes applied the standards of rigorous logic to religious revelation itself—and found revelation wanting. "To say [God] hath spoken to him in a dream is no more than to say that he dreamed God spake to him, which is not of force to win belief from any man that knows dreams are for the most part natural and may proceed from former thoughts," Hobbes wrote. "If one Prophet deceive another, what certainty is there of knowing the will of God, by other way than that of Reason?"[3]

Hobbes doesn't merely dismiss the Judeo-Christian moral system as divine. He also discards the Aristotelian telos: "For there is no such *Finis ultimus*, (utmost aim,) nor *Summum Bonum*, (greatest Good,) as is spoken of in the Books of the old Moral Philosophers. . . . Felicity is a continual progress of the desire, from one object to another; the attaining of the former, being still but the way to the latter."[4] In other words, the search for meaning cannot be found in seeking final causes; nature contains no such information. Instead, morality must be boiled down to mere competition of interests, and the desire of human beings to avoid suffering and untimely death. In a state of nature, "nothing can be Unjust. The notions of Right and Wrong, Justice and Injustice have there no place. Where there is no common Power, there is no Law; where no Law, no Injustice."[5] If moral relativism began anywhere, it began in Hobbes.

Hobbes's skepticism of Judeo-Christian morality and Aristotelian teleology found alliance in a most unlikely philosopher: a brilliant lapsed Jew named Baruch Spinoza (1632–1677). Spinoza grew up an Orthodox Jew in the Netherlands but was excommunicated for heresy in 1656. His crime involved his declarations that the Bible did not mention immortality, that God might take physical form in the universe, and that the immortal soul might not actually be immortal, but mere life-force.[6] He proceeded to write some of the most well-read philosophical treatises in history—and his anti-religious thought took center stage.

Where Hobbes was playfully vague as to his views of the Bible, Spinoza took no prisoners: he blasted religious authorities for being close-minded. He encouraged the faithful to seek the message of the Bible only in their own hearts, and ripped the textualism of Biblical fundamentalists: "instead of God's Word, they are beginning to worship likeness and images, that is, paper and ink."[7] He declared that Moses did not write the Torah; he stated that the Torah had been written centuries later by another figure. He dismissed miracles, the text of the Bible, and its commandments. As proof of the Bible's non-divinity, Spinoza wrote in terms that would make Richard Dawkins proud: "religion is manifested not in charity, but in spreading contention among men and in fostering the bitterest hatred, under the false guise of zeal in God's cause and a burning enthusiasm."[8] Spinoza believed that the Bible had been written for the foolish and carried forward by them—but he was also politically astute enough not to disparage the New Testament as he did the Old Testament.

Spinoza was similarly dismissive of the notion of a natural law. He turned his intense intellect to the very notion of final causes and dismissed them with relish. Humans, Spinoza argued, designed a God who had made the universe especially for mankind, and reasoned in circular fashion that God had crafted a human purpose. Like Hobbes, this leads Spinoza to disparage the very notion of "good" or "bad."[9] And like Hobbes, this led Spinoza to a sort of rational egotism as the nature of man: human beings want to avoid pain and seek pleasure. The best way to do this, according to Spinoza, is through a Stoic passivity—seeking knowledge of the universe and acknowledging that we are not at the center of it.

While Hobbes's new morality led him to the foot of an all-encompassing state, Spinoza recommended the opposite: a minimal state designed merely to prevent insurrection from those whose rights are violated. Freedom of religion and speech, in this view, aren't rights so much as spheres of privacy the state ought to avoid if it knows what's good for it. This is a libertarianism based on practicality, not on principle per se: we don't know what is right or good or virtuous, and therefore the decent man will not foist his opinion on others. But in order for that sort of freedom to prevail, the state must agree not to become the tool of the powerful to quash disagreement.[10]

The final step away from Judeo-Christian ethical monotheism and Greek teleology and toward outright atheism came courtesy of the jolly British empiricist David Hume (1711–1776). Like Hobbes and Spinoza before him, Hume discounted the possibility of miracles—he said that the laws of nature speak to us more frequently than any human testimony, and therefore the evidence for miracles was annihilated. He even argued that polytheism was as rational as monotheism. He also attempted to demolish classical proofs of God's existence. He took on the cosmological argument by stating that it is quite possible for something to come from nothing, so the notion of an Unmoved Mover was unnecessary; he also attacked the idea that order requires design (he says that an acorn can grow an oak tree without design, for example). Most of all, Hume rejected the idea of a just God because of the presence of evil in the universe.

Like Hobbes and Spinoza, Hume totally dismissed the notion that human beings could discern purpose or virtue from the bare facts of the material world. Hume famously summed up this problem in his "is-ought" distinction: just because the natural world *is* a certain way doesn't mean we *ought* to do a certain thing. Discoverable purpose disappeared in Hume's philosophy.

BUILDING ON REASON ALONE

Hume's atheism remained a minority position in his time; most philosophers still believed in at least a deist conception of the universe, though they increasingly rejected the tenets of Judaism and Christianity. Most philosophers were also unwilling to concede to Hobbesian positivism—the idea that good and bad are human constructions dependent on power relationships. Instead, philosophers increasingly focused on rebuilding universal morality in the absence of the Bible. Having dethroned God as an active moral arbiter for human behavior and instead redefined God as the Aristotelian Unmoved Mover alone, man was free to search for a moral system using reason alone. But these same philosophers could no longer rely on Aristotelian teleology—they could not look at the nature of the universe and determine moral ends.

New moral systems, therefore, had to be constructed from scratch. Human beings, these Enlightenment thinkers proposed, could construct systems to maximize human happiness. Now, in reality, most Enlightenment thinkers still operated off the moral assumptions of Judeo-Christian values as well as Aristotelian teleology—their intellectual engines were running on the fumes from a gas tank they had already purposefully emptied. It was only a matter of time until those fumes ran out. But the remnant vapors were responsible for some of humanity's most fascinating and complex attempts at creating a God-free objective morality.

Leading the way was Voltaire (1694–1778). Voltaire was a deist—he famously stated, "It is perfectly evident to my mind that there exists a necessary, eternal, supreme and intelligent being. This is no matter of faith, but of reason."[11] Voltaire believed in the search for morality in reason; in his philosophical dictionary, he stated, "We cannot repeat too frequently that dogmas differ, but that morality is the same among all men who make use of their reason. Morality proceeds from God, like light; our superstitions are only darkness."[12] But Voltaire plainly considered Judeo-Christian tradition superstitious; his writings are filled with nasty asides against Jews in particular. Like an eighteenth-century Bill Maher, Voltaire delighted in ridiculing the most facially ridiculous statements of the Bible and declaring the Bible's morality abhorrent on its face.[13]

How, then, could morality be constructed through reason? It couldn't be done through Aristotelian teleology. Voltaire famously scoffed at the idea of a discoverable telos in nature, mocking the brilliant philosopher Gottfried Wilhelm Leibniz (1646–1716) on those grounds. Leibniz argued that since God was good, and since God had created but one world, the world He had created was by necessity the best possible world. Voltaire mercilessly skewered that perspective in *Candide*:

> Pangloss taught metaphysico-theologico-cosmo-nigology. He could prove to wonderful effect that there was no effect without cause. . . . "It is demonstrable," he would say, "that things cannot be other than as they are: for, since everything is made to serve an end, everything is necessarily for the best of ends. Observe how noses were formed to support spectacles, therefore we have spectacles. Legs are clearly devised for the wearing of breeches, therefore we wear breeches . . . those who have argued that all is well have been talking nonsense; they should have said that all is for the best."[14]

Pangloss ends up contracting syphilis, loses an eye and an ear, and is hanged. So much for the best of all possible worlds, according to Voltaire. And so much for the notion that we can look at the nature of things and discover morality there. Voltaire scoffs at the idea of the Aristotelian "good"; noses obviously weren't made for glasses.

So where did Voltaire find purpose and morality? Like Francis Bacon, one of his intellectual heroes, he found it in the betterment of the human condition materially. And this led him toward a hedonistic, materialist morality as well. For those capable of exercising reason properly, the maximization of pleasure and minimization of pain were the paramount goals of life. His poetry is filled with unambiguous condemnation of religious prudery, and embrace of the pleasures of the world: "Enjoying pleasure in each state and hour, / Mortals acknowledge God's eternal power . . . The modern Stoic would each wish control, / And of its very essence rob my soul."[15]

Voltaire's morality tends toward the fully libertarian, then—freedom from control, liberty in behavior. But such a system, absent the virtue of a citizenry, quickly collapses. Voltaire knew that, which is why he wished that those of lesser rational capacity worship an omnipotent, omniscient God—God was necessary for others, but not for Voltaire. Unfortunately, he would be proven right in his estimation of human nature in short order. By removing the supposed shackles of virtue, Voltaire also removed the constraints preventing chaos and tyranny. When Voltaire's version of freedom was mixed with the passion of Jean-Jacques Rousseau (1712–1778), the result was the guillotine.

Juxtaposed to the vainglorious, acidic Voltaire, Immanuel Kant (1724–1804) appears a secular saint. Kant never left Königsberg, Prussia; he was certainly no hedonist. But like Voltaire and Locke, Kant was a devotee of reason above all, even if he explored its limits to the utmost. In his essay, "What Is Enlightenment?," Kant spelled out the central philosophy of the era: "*Dare to know! (Sapere aude.)* 'Have the courage to use your own understanding,' is therefore the motto of the Enlightenment."[16]

And what of morality? Kant thought that the search for virtue could be found not through reason applied to the universe, but through investigation of the moral instinct. We all have an instinct for morality, Kant believed. Reason was limited, as human perception was limited; Kant remained skeptical of the human capacity to know the world. By looking at our moral instinct, Kant believed we could derive a universal morality:

Two things fill the mind with ever new and increasing admiration and awe, the more often and steadily we reflect upon them: *the starry heavens above me and the moral law within me.*[17]

Kant sought to locate the new meaning and purpose in a priori knowledge—things we can know without experiment or experience. Kant believed that certain truths were not dependent on the human experience—2+2 would always equal four, whether or not human beings experienced it. Kant thus embarked on an almost Platonic quest for knowledge beyond the material—but where Plato looked to the realm of Forms, Kant looked instead to the human heart. The human heart, he said, had embedded within it a moral logic. And that moral logic relied on categorical imperatives: absolute truths. Those categorical imperatives included injunctions never to use other human beings as means, but rather to treat them as ends. Actions are good in and of themselves, not because they have good effects. And acting in pursuit of the good makes us free. The measure of religion itself is its adherence to this moral law of the heart.[18] In short, "Act only according to that maxim whereby you can at the same time will that it should become a universal law."[19]

To our secular minds, this is beautiful stuff—and the closest thing philosophy has ever crafted to a serious sense of meaning and purpose. But Kant's idealism could not sustain itself—

his philosophy of morality soon fell apart. Kant's categorical imperative—the idea that every law must be generalizable—provides a nice guidepost for human activity, and one that seems to mirror the Golden Rule. But Kant's categorical imperative does not answer more complex moral calculations. Is it really correct that we do a wrong whenever we lie, even to hide a Jew when the Nazi is at the door, for example, as Kant seems to suggest?

Furthermore, Kant's categorical imperative isn't objectively *mandatory*. Why not simply assume that everyone else should abide by Kant's rule, and break all the rules yourself? And even if you don't wish your own self-serving priorities to rule, there are other moralities just as logical as Kant's. Indeed, Kant's categorical imperative was but one system for organizing human morality along the lines of a priori reason. Jeremy Bentham (1748–1832) similarly sought to construct a moral system by using reason—and his system, unlike Kant's, wasn't based on universal moral principles but on utility. Bentham believed that human action should be constructed to "promote or oppose" happiness, which could be measured in terms of pleasure and pain. Bentham believed, along the lines of Hobbes, that no rights preexisted the state, and called natural rights "nonsense upon stilts."[20]

Voltaire, Kant, Bentham—all assumed that reason could construct morality from scratch. But their moralities did not coincide. Practically speaking, their morality lifted elements, even if unconsciously, from the Judeo-Christian tradition and Greek telos they suggested they had exploded.

All of this left an unanswered question: If reason could not construct objective systems of morality, what could? What if faith in reason was misplaced—and something darker actually motivated human beings?

THE DEATH OF CAPACITY

The death of Judeo-Christian values and Greek telos didn't mean the liberation of reason from superstition. For some key philosophers, it meant the destruction of reason itself. That may seem counterintuitive—after all, philosophers had tossed out the Bible and Aristotle in the name of reason. But the Enlightenment did not merely involve utilizing reason to question Judeo-Christian values and telos. It involved turning reason in on itself, examining the human mind. It meant obliterating mankind as the jewel of the cosmos, bringing him low, returning him to the animals rather than allowing him to aspire to join the divine. By throwing God out of the kingdom of man, the Enlightenment also reduced man to a creature of flesh and blood, with no transcendent reason to guide the way.

Machiavelli and Bacon had both recognized the power of passion—but they had also upheld the rule of reason above passion. Machiavelli believed that passion could be manipulated to useful effect by reason-driven leaders, and that passion could be used to check passion; Bacon believed that reason could be successfully applied to the universe to unlock its secrets for the betterment of mankind. Neither Machiavelli nor Bacon significantly undermined the belief in the free will of humans. Machiavelli's devotion to *virtù* sprang from his desire to oppose *fortuna*—the vagaries of fortune, which could thwart even the best-laid plans. Machiavelli sought to overcome fortune with will, with the concerted use of means to achieve goals.

Not so with Hobbes.

Hobbes, who was deeply devoted to tearing down Greek teleology, attacked not only the idea that the universe had discoverable purpose, but that human beings were capable of exercising reason more broadly. "The Passions of men," Hobbes writes, "are commonly more potent than their Reason." Reason cannot bring happiness, nor can it be used as the goal of a philosophical life. There is no happiness. There is only striving and security and passion. Reason cannot save us from the war of all against all; only the Leviathan, the power of the state, can.[21]

Hobbes's skepticism of reason was mirrored by Descartes, who suggested that human beings were driven by passion rather than reason.[22] But Spinoza made the most radical break with the past when he discarded the notion of free will altogether. He likened human beings to stones cast through space, but believing that they move themselves: "Such a stone, being conscious merely of its own endeavor and not at all indifferent, would believe itself to be completely free, and would think that it continued in motion solely because of its own wish. That is that human freedom, which all boast that they possess, and which consists solely in the fact that men are conscious of their own desire, but are ignorant of the causes whereby that desire has been determined."[23] Through reason, human beings are capable of better understanding their plight, and this grants them some limited measure of freedom—but their freedom of action is heavily circumscribed.

It was left to Hume, once again, to completely circumscribe reason. "Reason is, and ought only to be, the slave of the passions," Hume famously wrote, taking to its logical extreme the thought of his predecessors. "[Reason] cannot be the source of moral good or evil, which are found to have that influence."[24]

Hume's contemporary and friend Jean-Jacques Rousseau accepted Hume's essential argument about human nature— but then elevated the passions in a way Hume never did. No, said Rousseau, passions were *good*. Man was perfectible. And morality was based on empathy. In the beginning, Rousseau argued, man lived in harmony with nature, comfortable and "indolent," until he formed societal bonds. Those societal bonds were formed in an attempt to *perfect* human nature—to develop human nature itself. Human beings gathered together and lived as communities in "the happiest and most stable of epochs" before greed came to the fore, pushing men to create surplus rather than surviving at subsistence levels. Property was the death of the natural man. "The first man who, having enclosed a piece of ground, bethought himself of saying *This is mine*, and found people simple enough to believe him, was the real founder of civil society," Rousseau wrote. But now that society had been created, human beings could only find happiness through an administration of the "general will"—as Mary Ann Glendon writes, "an agreement by which everyone would give himself and all his goods to the community, forming a state whose legislation would be produced by the will of each person thinking in terms of all." And that state would be led by a transformative leader dedicated to "changing human nature."[25]

This move away from reason and toward passion—the rejection of Judeo-Christian values and Greek teleology—may have been popular among philosophers, but it remained a rather fringy perspective. All that changed, however, with the rise of Darwinism. Charles Darwin's *On the Origin of Species* (1859) provided the first scientific grounding to the notion of a world without God, and a world beyond the mind of man.

With Darwin's evolutionary biology, a unifying field theory of life could suddenly be proposed: accident. God did not create man in His image; man was merely the next step in a chain of evolution propelled forward by natural selection. There was no telos to the universe—there was merely nature, and man was part of it. Man was an animal. God was unnecessary. Reason itself disappeared into higher brain function designed for better environmental adaption. Objective truth itself became an article of faith, since the human mind was designed not for its discovery, but for finding the nuts and berries necessary to ward off death and pain. Morality, too, was an outgrowth of simple convention and adaptive innovation: animals could engage in rudimentary "moral" behavior, without any semblance of human reason.

Darwinism was seen by the intelligentsia of the time as a final permission to break with the ways of the ancients. Finally, at long last, the superstitions of religion could be put aside; finally, at long last, the legacy of the ancient Greeks could be escaped. Mankind, in joining the animals, had finally liberated himself from the chains of the divine. In fact, the excitement of Darwinism can still be felt today in the literature of atheists like Daniel Dennett, who writes, "Darwin's idea is a universal solvent, capable of cutting right to the heart of everything in sight. The question is: what does it leave behind?" Dennett claims that "we are left with stronger, sounder versions of our most important ideas."[26]

But were we?

As the scientific world celebrated its newfound elevation over Judeo-Christian values and Greek telos, two figures emerged to warn the West of what was to come. One was a Russian novelist; the other, a German philosopher.

THE WARNING

Fyodor Dostoyevsky (1821–1881) worried deeply about mankind unbound from moral obligation. He saw in the rise of an atheistic world the face of the Marquis de Sade (1740–1814), the famed French sadist, rapist, and pedophile who embraced passion, discounted human responsibility, and saw in his own pleasure the highest good. De Sade infamously dismissed God and added, "We rail against the passions, but never think that it is from their flame that philosophy lights its torch."[27] Dostoyevsky saw the Sade-ian perspective as the logical endpoint of a system without God, theorizing that without immortality, all constraints on human behavior would disappear. He foresaw that materialist man was far more of a threat than religious man—that human beings who think themselves mere agglomerations of matter, without the responsibility of choice, will throw decency aside. He saw that man would find in his search for purpose something far darker than the Judeo-Christian tradition and Greek teleology that built the modern world.

Dostoyevsky feared the materialism that had come to dominate European thought. In the famous "Grand Inquisitor" chapter of *The Brothers Karamazov*, in which Ivan Karamazov tells his tale of a Spanish inquisitor grilling Jesus, Dostoyevsky suggested that the day had come when human beings would give up on meaning in favor of worldly goods: "Dost Thou know that the ages will pass, and humanity will proclaim by the lips of their sages that there is no crime, and therefore no sin; there is only hunger?" Dostoyevsky suggested the cure for hunger would be the dictator—the man who satiates hunger will be worshipped as a deity. Human beings, Dostoyevsky suspected, were too frightened to use God-given freedom of will to seek God Himself; instead, they would retreat into infantilism, happy to follow leaders who will relieve them of their need for bread and provide them the comfort of conformity, promising them that their sins mean nothing: "We shall show them that they are weak, that they are only pitiful children, but that childlike happiness is the sweetest of all."[28]

The dark side of the Enlightenment was no secret to Dostoyevsky, who saw the rumblings of a coming cataclysm looming through the mists of the future. He knew that reason alone, unmoored from God, could not hold back the tide; in fact, reason itself would provide the impetus for evil, he argued.

In *Notes from the Underground*, Dostoyevsky decried the scientific optimism of the materialists, scoffing at their suggestion that human weakness would be eradicated by "common sense and science . . . completely re-educat[ing] human nature." He laughed at the notion that men could be told that they lack the ability to choose, but could simply be guided toward morality by the application of scientific rules. No, Dostoyevsky stated, man would rebel against such logic. Human beings were not made for it: "What man wants is simply independent choice, whatever that independence may cost and wherever it may lead. And choice, of course, the devil only knows what choice."[29]

Human beings are creatures who seek more than that which reason and science purport to give them—and they are more than the self-interested animals reason and science seek to make them. The search for meaning, untrammeled by Judeo-Christian values and Greek telos, freed from moral responsibility by scientific determinism, would burst forth in a conflagration that will set the whole world on fire, Dostoyevsky predicted. The result would be blood and suffering, a maelstrom of horror, followed by an epoch of emptiness. God's death, Dostoyevsky thought, was man's death as well.

THE TRIUMPH OF THE WILL

The death of God, Friedrich Nietzsche (1844–1900) saw, left no room for purpose through reason. Like Hume, Nietzsche believed that morality through reason alone was a lie, a cover for instinct wearing the costume of reason: "Your decision, 'this is right,' has a previous history in your impulses, your likes and dislikes."[30] Nietzsche, in other words, had consolidated the lessons of the eighteenth and nineteenth centuries, and ripped the mask of nicety from the face of the Enlightenment.

Reason and passion are both aspects of something deeper, something primordial, Nietzsche stated: the will to power. Nietzsche suggested that we stop brooding over the "moral worth of our actions." Instead, he said, let us "seek to become what we are,—the new, the unique, the incomparable, making laws for ourselves and creating ourselves!"[31] Nietzsche knew that the only answer to scientific materialism was radical subjectivity, and with it would come the death of morals. He celebrated that fact, and reveled in the power of the will.

What, exactly, is the will to power? It is the will to self-perfection. In *Thus Spake Zarathustra*, Nietzsche poeticizes:

> Before God!—Now however this God hath died!—Ye higher men, this God was your greatest danger. . . . Now only travaileth the mountain of the human future. God hath died: now do we desire—the Superman to live. The most careful ask to-day: "How is man to be maintained?" Zarathustra however asketh, as the first and only one: "How is man to be surpassed?" The Superman, I have at heart; that is the first and only thing to me—and not man: not the neighbor, not the poorest, not the sorriest, not the best . . .[32]

Nietzsche advocated the destruction of Judeo-Christian values. He properly understood that all other systems of morality, from utilitarianism to Kantian categorical imperatives, are based at root on the moral discoveries of the Judeo-Christian tradition—and he said that man can only be freed by destroying that moral vestigial structure. That structure, he believed, had held man back; it was "slave-morality," which sacrificed strength for weakness, which celebrated poverty and powerlessness.

What was required is a new morality. Man could create his own morality, but only on the basis of strength and will. That morality will no longer be based on human happiness—it would not be based on how to "maintain himself best, longest, most pleasantly." These were petty virtues, Nietzsche claimed. Instead, Nietzsche valued honesty and struggle, strength and courage. He valued man unbound.

What Nietzsche observed, and what he lauded, had been under way for generations. Philosophy spent two centuries killing Judeo-Christian values and Greek teleology—or at least discarding them in favor of brave new utopias filled with perfectible human beings, or crystal palaces ruled by men of reason, or worlds of determinism filled with avoidance of pain and maximization of pleasure.

Either man would rule supreme, or he would destroy all in his path. Which would it be? The world would soon find out the answer to that question.

CHAPTER 7

THE REMAKING OF THE WORLD

W hy can't we all just be reasonable?

This is the characteristic call of our age. Forget values; forget judgment. Let's just be reasonable with one another. Tolerance can supplant Judeo-Christian ideas. We all know what's right, deep down. If we follow our star, civilization won't just survive—it will thrive and flourish.

This idea is a vestige of the Enlightenment mentality. But it ignores the dark side of the Enlightenment hope. It ignores the history of the nineteenth and twentieth centuries. It ignores the fact that the Enlightenment had two strains—one based on Athens and Jerusalem, the other bereft of them. History performed a comparative study in which form of Enlightenment worked best—and the results were clear and convincing.

The Enlightenment straddled two sides of a thin line. On the one side was the American Enlightenment, based on the consummation of a long history of thought stretching back to

Athens and Jerusalem, down through Great Britain and the Glorious Revolution, and to the New World; on the other was the European Enlightenment, which rejected Athens and Jerusalem in order to build new worlds beyond discoverable purpose and divine revelation.

The juxtaposition between the American Revolution and the French Revolution demonstrates the contrast between the strains of Enlightenment thinking. The American Revolution, based on Lockean principles regarding the God-given rights of individuals, the value of social virtue, and a state system created to preserve inalienable individual rights, broke sharply with the French Revolution, based on Rousseau's "general will," Voltaire's generalized scorn for traditional virtue, and an optimistic sense of the perfectibility of mankind through the application of virtue-free reason.

The French Revolution was born with a utopian sense of purpose: man would finally be freed of old constraints. Those constraints were not merely political. They were constraints of the soul, chains on human freedom itself. The most obvious chains were those imposed by religion itself, which the French philosophes saw not as the bulwark for Western morality and rationality, but as the chief obstacle to them. It was Denis Diderot, the editor of the famed *Encyclopédie*, who said that he wished to strangle the last king with the guts of the last priest.[1] Once the last priest was dead, then presumably mankind could reach back toward the nature within, and find within himself the capacity for godlike power and wisdom. Nicolas de Condorcet, the French philosopher and early revolutionary, stated that science would rescue man from his flaws, "foresee the progress of humankind, direct it, and accelerate it."[2]

Reason without boundaries, combined with natural passion, would soon make for a toxic admixture.

While the United States moved toward the embrace of an Enlightenment based on Locke, Blackstone, Montesquieu and the Bible—the first meeting of the United States Senate occurred on March 4, 1789—the French Revolution moved toward utopian rebuilding. On July 14, 1789, French citizens stormed the Bastille. And they quickly dethroned the kings and the priests. The Cult of Reason became the first official religion of the new France: it worshipped "one God only, *Le Peuple*," according to revolutionary Anacharsis Cloots.[3] God himself was stripped of His holiness, and reason accorded His place.

Frenchmen were to celebrate the Festival of Reason. That festival saw churches across France transformed into Temples of Reason, with the chief temple being the cathedral at Notre Dame. There, the musicians of the National Guard and Opera performed hymns to Liberty, serving Liberty as a deity; the opening anthem was "Descend, O Liberty, Daughter of Nature." An inscription "to Philosophy" was placed at the entrance, and the flame of the goddess of Reason was lit on the Greek altar.[4] Maximilien Robespierre, who disdained the excesses of festivals of the Cult of Reason, founded a more sober-minded Cult of the Supreme Being, but it was similarly atheistic, and worshipped similar principles; festivals were so well-staged that Jacques-Louis David, the revolutionary artist, scripted "the moment when mothers must smile at their children, the old men at the youths and their grandsons."[5]

In March 1794, Robespierre had the leaders of the Cult of Reason executed. In July 1794, Robespierre himself was executed. When Napoleon took power, he reacted to the cults by banning them outright. The end of the rejection of Judeo-Christian churches in favor of secular churches was the guillotine.

The French Revolution also replaced the virtue of the ancients—seeking an objective code for living by investigating the universe using our right reason—with the virtue of the collective, or with radical subjectivism, or both. Robespierre defined virtue in a speech extolling the new French republic: it is "nothing else than love of the *patrie* and its laws." To defend that virtue required everything up to and including political violence: "If the driving force of popular government in peacetime is virtue, that of popular government during a revolution is both *virtue and terror*: virtue, without which terror is destructive; terror, without which virtue is impotent."[6] Diderot, a materialist who disdained even Deism, defined virtue in pure terms of moral relativism: "There is only one virtue, justice; one duty, to be happy; one corollary, not to overrate life, and not to fear death."[7] French historian Robert Mauzi writes that Diderot believed that "to be happy is to be oneself; that is, to preserve the truth which is peculiar to our being, and which may choose to express itself through a passion incompatible with virtue."[8]

The rejection of Judeo-Christian values and ancient virtue on behalf of the general will was expressed in glowing terms in the French Declaration of the Rights of Man, approved by the National Assembly on August 26, 1789. Unlike the Declaration of Independence—a document expressing a collective desire for individual rights—the Declaration of the Rights of Man expresses the belief that man's place in the universe revolves around his role as part of a larger collective. Every individual right expressed in the French Declaration is curbed by the collective's right to overrule that individual. So, for example, the French Declaration states, "Men are born and remain free and equal in rights. Social distinctions may be founded only upon the general good." But the second clause renders the first absolutely meaningless—if men are equal in right, how can their rights be subject to the opinions of a majority?

The answer is obvious. In the French Declaration, rights do not spring from God or preexist government: "The principle of all sovereignty resides essentially in the nation. No body nor individual may exercise any authority which does not proceed directly from the nation." All rights come from the state. All rights therefore belong to the state. This is the Hobbesian Leviathan come to life. While the French Declaration pays homage to the nonaggression principle—it explicitly states that "Liberty consists in the freedom to do everything which injures no one else. . . . These limits can only be determined by law"—such niceties disappear as soon as the document states that "Law is the expression of the general will." Religious rights are secondary to "the public order established by law." Freedom of expression is guaranteed . . . except as "shall be defined by law."[9] The collective rules the individual, and the general will trumps the individual will.

The leading philosophical twin lights of the Revolution were Voltaire and Rousseau—although both writers (particularly Voltaire) might well have disdained their legacy. Fully thirteen years after Voltaire's death, the famed artist Jacques-Louis David organized a procession one hundred thousand strong to usher Voltaire's disinterred body to the Panthéon—the rechristened church of Sainte-Geneviève, secularized by the revolution. As historian Raymond Jonas writes, "Voltaire's procession neatly aped the Catholic rituals associated with Corpus Christi—the stops at the Bastille and the Louvre resemble the processional pauses at *reposoirs*—and even recalled Genevieve's triumphant procession resulting in the cure of the *maladie des ardents.*"[10]

Rousseau was a key influence on Robespierre particularly—Robespierre wrote of him, "Divine man, you have taught me to know myself."[11]

It wasn't until after Robespierre's execution that Rousseau received the same treatment as Voltaire—but it was glorious indeed. His body was exhumed and then moved from Ermenonville to Paris, his coffin put in public view in the Tuileries and then placed in the Panthéon near Voltaire. A statue of Rousseau came along for the ride, and a copy of *The Social Contract* was gently cradled on a velvet cushion. All across Paris, his plays were revived, and all across France, similar processions took place.[12]

The French Revolution was bloody, vicious, and awful. Tens of thousands of people were murdered by the regime between 1793 and 1794, with another quarter million dead in a civil war over a draft designed to fight foreign invasion. And what followed the French Revolution—the rise of Napoleon Bonaparte—would cast the continent into a new era of upheaval.

Where, exactly, did the French Revolution—born with dreams of liberty, equality, and fraternity—go so wrong? It went wrong because the Enlightenment of the French Revolution rejected the lessons of the past; it saw in the history of the West mere repression and brutality, and longed for a tomorrow full of visions and dreams based on vague notions of human goodness.

The man who best critiqued the French Revolution lived just across the English Channel. His name was Edmund Burke (1729–1797), and he was a member of Parliament sympathetic to the American colonists but utterly opposed to the French Revolution. Burke argued that the French Revolution had failed because it had ignored the lessons of human nature, the morality of Christianity, and the traditions of the past. Written at the outset of the revolution in 1789, *Reflections on the Revolution in France* became a seminal text for modern-day conservatives, who saw in it a call away from radicalism and toward sensible governance. "The effect of liberty to individuals is, that they may do what they please: We ought to see what it will please them to do, before we risque congratulations, which may be soon turned into complaints,"[13] Burke wrote. He feared that the revolution had done away with the two foundations of Western civilization: "the spirit of a gentleman, and the spirit of religion." He warned that the triumph of supposed rationality over tradition and Judeo-Christian values would turn reason into a mere byword to be vulgarized by political forces: "Their liberty is not liberal. Their science is presumptuous ignorance. Their humanity is savage and brutal."[14] And he warned as well that such brutality would extend to seizure of property and life itself.

How did Burke foresee the tragedy? Because he held true to the ancient precepts of Western civilization—Greek telos and Judeo-Christian morality. Philosopher Russell Kirk writes of Burke's worldview:

> Revelation, reason, and an assurance beyond the senses tell us that the Author of our being exists, and that He is omniscient; and man and the state are creations of God's beneficence. . . . How are we to know God's mind and will? Through the prejudices and traditions which millennia of human experience with divine means and judgments have implanted in the mind of the species. And what is our purpose in this world? Not to indulge our appetites, but to render obedience to divine ordinance.[15]

Burke was correct—but the French Revolution had already initiated a cycle of reaction that would continue for the next 156 years. Its slogan, "Liberty, Equality, Fraternity," had already proved chimerical a mere five years after Burke's opus. Yet that creed would provide the impetus for a century and a half of political utopianism and its disastrous aftermath. Liberty would collapse into moral relativism and then tyranny; fraternity would collapse into nationalistic tribalism; equality would collapse into a new caste system, with all-wise rulers in control of the commanding heights.

THE UTOPIA OF NATIONALISM

Revolutionary France, which forcibly conscripted its own citizenry and turned itself into the first modern militarized state, celebrated the nation-state as the apotheosis of the general will. In doing so, the French were merely carrying forward the legacy of Rousseau.

It was the French Revolution that made romantic nationalism a driving force in history. The very definition of citizenship changed in Revolutionary France, from subjects at the beck and call of more powerful actors to citizens with an equal stake in the formation of the general will. But that definition of citizenship quickly devolved into a new form of subject status: in France, citizens owed their rights *to* the state. As Professor William Rogers Brubaker of Harvard University writes, "The Revolution, in short, invented not only the nation-state but the modern institution and ideology of national citizenship." Karl Marx (1818–1883) suggested, "The gigantic broom of the French Revolution . . . swept away all these relics . . . thus clearly simultaneously the social soil of its last hindrances to the superstructure of the modern state edifice." By centralizing power, the Revolution discarded all boundaries between man and the state, and made individuals feel part of a greater whole.[16]

The new state of France revolutionized war-making. In 1793,

as a result of both civil unrest and the decision to make war on Austria, the National Convention instituted the first mass draft in the history of the world. Where joining the military had been a preserve of a certain few, and high-ranking officers had been culled from aristocratic families, the French now substituted mass war-making and a certain level of meritocracy. The *levée en masse* of August 23, 1793, stated:

> From this moment until such time as its enemies shall have been driven from the soil of the Republic, all Frenchmen are in permanent requisition for the services of the armies. The young men shall fight; the married men shall forge arms and transport provisions; the women shall make tents and clothes and shall serve in the hospitals; the children shall turn old lint into linen; the old men shall betake themselves to the public squares in order to arouse the courage of the warriors and preach hatred of kings and the unity of the Republic.[17]

This radically changed the nature of war—and the perception of both the state as a historical tool and the role of the citizen within the state. Prussian general Carl von Clausewitz, the most famous military historian of all time, said that this decree accessed the "passions of the people," and in doing so showed the world that a united citizenry could stand up in the face of overwhelming military odds. "People at first expected to have to deal only with a seriously weakened French army," Clausewitz wrote, "but in 1793 a force appeared that beggared all imagination. Suddenly war again became the business of the people . . . the full weight of the nation was thrown into the balance. . . . War, untrammeled by any conventional restraints, had broken loose in all its elemental fury."[18] The French Revolution, then, led not only to the rise of the nation-state and nationalism more broadly, it also opened the door to total war—the end of the distinction between civilian and military, and the willingness to weaponize an entire population toward the ends of governments.

Despite the internal collapse of the French Revolution, the power of the French military never wavered. Napoleon's coup merely made clear what had already become obvious: military nationalism was the wave of the future, and other states would have to struggle to respond in kind. The nation-state was the tool of progress and of history. And other states would not be long in reacting to the rise of France with similar enthusiasm for nationalism—and more dangerously, enthusiasm for ethnically based, expansionist nationalism.

Now, nationalism on its own can be a powerful force for good. Philosopher Yoram Hazony defends nation-states built on two principles: first, what he terms the "moral minimum required for legitimate government," which would include "minimum requirements for a life of personal freedom and dignity for all"; second, the "right of national self-determination," rights accruing to nations "cohesive and strong enough to secure their political independence." A multiplicity of nation-states can be a guarantee against universal tyranny, and a guarantor of philosophical, legal, and political diversity. It was respect for such diversity that brought about the Peace of Westphalia. American exceptionalism fulfills Hazony's criteria: the Declaration of Independence and Constitution operate as creedal unifiers, and a shared history and culture operate as the glue holding together the nation.[19]

But nationalism can also be a force for evil. Nationalism turns toxic when it fails to reach that moral minimum—when it tyrannizes its own citizens, or locks people out based on immutable characteristics. Nationalism turns poisonous when it becomes imperialism—when it suggests that it represents a universalism that can override the legitimate rights of other states, or when it uses national interest as an excuse for conquest on behalf of a "volk." Revolutionary France quickly bled over into imperialism. That was no coincidence.

But the rise of Revolutionary France led other nations to embrace its romantic nationalism. In Prussia, Johann Fichte (1762–1814) famously suggested, "Of all modern peoples it is you in whom the seed of human perfection most decidedly lies and to whom the lead in its development is assigned."[20] Perhaps the key philosopher espousing the power of nationalism in history—and one of the most influential philosophers of the century overall—was Georg Hegel (1770–1831). According to Hegel, individuals were defined by "the life of the state"; the state may be created by individuals, but eventually it supersedes them. The state shapes men and civilizations, and those who impose its will are the civil servants, guided by reason—the class of men both made by the state and who work for it. And states, as the embodiment of the rational state of a nation, settle matters between themselves through conflict.[21] The individual's mind is suffused into a zeitgeist—a spirit of the age.

That zeitgeist carries with it the seeds of history—and is brought into being by history itself.

History is the great arbiter of right and wrong, in Hegel's view. Hegel saw God not in morality or reason but in the progress of history; history moved forward, using and discarding men at will, ushering in the betterment of the world through the clash between thesis and antithesis, which would be eventually brought together in synthesis. War could be a key tool in this process. "Through consciousness (rational) spirit intervenes in the order of the world," Hegel wrote. "This is spirit's infinite tool, also bayonets, cannons, and bodies."[22]

The nineteenth century's embrace of the new concept of romantic nationalism offered a purpose without Judeo-Christian values or Greek telos: the nation, spurring forward the progress of history, unified by ethnicity and background, proselytizing with its power. Nationalism also unified the question of individual and collective capacity by suggesting that they were one and the same: your individual identity lay in your identity as a member of the collective. And the collective existed to give you spirit and strength and purpose.

It's an obvious truism that nations find collective identity in language and culture. But the question is whether that culture forwards fundamental God-given rights, or whether that culture becomes an excuse to take away rights in the name of collective self-preservation. Romantic nationalism is not patriotism. But the appeal of romantic imperialistic nationalism has never died. And that fiery appeal, unmoored from any transcendent values, has burned millions in its heat.

THE UTOPIA OF LEVELING

The French Revolution's murder of the Judeo-Christian God meant substituting a supposedly more realistic materialism for transcendental values. The Bible contended that man could not live by bread alone; the French Revolution contended that without bread, nothing else mattered. Thomas Paine, author of the most important political pamphlet in modern history, *Common Sense*, saw the French Revolution as a powerful, necessary move in favor of social leveling. An ardent atheist, Paine rejected the value of Judeo-Christian morality, and instead promoted redistributionist materialism. In particular, Paine targeted the class distinctions that so characterized Europe. "The Aristocracy," he wrote, "are not the farmers who work the land . . . but are the mere consumers of the rent." And those aristocrats were living off the backs of a "great portion of mankind . . . [who suffer] in a state of poverty and wretchedness." Paine wrote, "One extreme produces the other: to make one rich many must be made poor; neither can the system be supported by other means." Paine would also argue that "the working hand perishes in old age, and the employer abounds in affluence." No wonder Revolutionary France made Paine an honorary citizen.

Paine quickly became a devotee of proto-socialist Gracchus Babeuf. "Property," Babeuf's followers argued, "is, therefore, the greatest scourge on society; it is a veritable public crime." Paine quickly began to believe the same, and advocated for a system of "ground-rent" for property ownership, the proceeds from which would be distributed among the citizenry. Paine argued that private property was a mere convention, and that all private property was actually the work of society at large: "Personal property is the effect of society; and it is as impossible for an individual to acquire personal property without the aid of society, as it is for him to make land originally." Thus the state is master over all private property. And a revolution would be necessary to effectuate that reality.[23]

The French Revolution didn't end in a communist utopia. But according to Karl Marx, it was the first step in the gradual evolution of markets toward communism. In *The Eighteenth Brumaire of Louis Napoleon*, a pamphlet written in 1852 regarding the French coup of 1851, Marx wrote that the French Revolution had set for itself "the task of unchaining and setting up modern *bourgeois* society," but that its own commitment to classical republican ideals had prevented the class uprising that could liberate its citizens from the shackles of class;[24] that revolution, Marx thought, had nearly been achieved in the communist movements that spread across the continent of Europe like wildfire. And soon, that communist utopia would be achieved. As Marx and Friedrich Engels wrote in *The Communist Manifesto* in 1848, "A spectre is haunting Europe—the spectre of communism."

So, what was this specter?

Today, Marx's more aphoristic credos have become legendary—"From each according to his ability, to each according to his need," and "Workers of the world, unite!" and the like. But his philosophy represented a radical new attempt to find meaning in a world without God. Like Paine before him, Marx saw free markets as a system of exploitation. According to Marx, the value of a product could be measured by its "socially necessary labor time"—the average number of work hours needed to create a product. Manufacturers could only gain profit by artificially driving down the socially necessary labor time, or by forcing laborers to work longer hours. The capitalist can only become rich by exploiting workers; workers never see the fruits of their labor thanks to capitalists taking the "excess" labor off the top for themselves.[25]

This system, Marx believed, demeaned human beings. Human beings are built to produce "in accordance with the law of beauty," not merely for survival; labor makes men free, Marx stated. But "in tearing away the object of his production from man, estranged labor therefore tears him away from his species-life, his true species-objectivity . . . his inorganic body, nature, is taken from him."[26] What sort of human beings would be produced by a truer system of labor? The man freed to be an individual by the collective. Marx posited that "only in community" does an individual have "the means of cultivating his gifts in all directions; only in the community, therefore, is personal freedom possible. . . . In a real community the individuals obtain their freedom in and through their association."[27]

Eventually, human nature would be restored by the collapse of capitalism—and this collapse would, in turn, drive the creation of a new man, a better human being. Marx's promise was a transcendental promise, not merely a material one. Like Rousseau, Marx believed in the power of the collective.

And like Rousseau, Marx saw a return to human nature as a good to be bought at the cost of civilization. Communion with the collective, in Marx's view, can only be brought about by changing history. Like Hegel, Marx attempted to uncover the plot of history, which he thought inevitably led to a brighter future. But unlike Hegel, Marx believed that human beings had to take an active part in their history-making in order to change themselves. Human beings, Marx posited, were animals, and thus part of their environment—but they could also change the environment in which they lived, and, by doing so, change themselves. All that would be required was the will to overthrow old systems. Mankind could be perfected through a program of rigorous and continuous revolution. Abolishing private property would end alienation; abolishing the family would end the exploitation of children by parents and wives by husbands. "Does it require deep intuition to comprehend that man's ideas, views, and conceptions, in one word, man's consciousness, changes with every change in the conditions of his material existence, in his social relations and in his life?" Marx and Engels wrote in *The Communist Manifesto*. Yes, of course the old morality would be abolished—but more important, it would be made utterly obsolete by the creation of new human beings, since all prior morality was reliant on "the exploitation of one part of society by the other."[28]

The Judeo-Christian God would have to be buried. "The abolition of religion as the illusory happiness of the people is a demand for their true happiness," Marx stated.[29] Greek search for purpose would have to be directed at revising society itself. A new age would be born. And a new human being would rise to occupy it.

Fortunately, Marx had a program that could achieve this

world-changing transformation. First, the proletariat would "use its political supremacy to wrest, by degree, all capital from the bourgeoisie, to centralize all instruments of production in the hands of the State"—and naturally, this would entail "despotic inroads on the rights of property" that could appear economically untenable, but would soon work themselves out. This would involve abolition of property in land, a heavy progressive tax, confiscation of all property of emigrants and rebels, centralization of credit in the state, centralization of all means of communications and transportation by the state, extension of those means of production by the state, forced labor ("equal liability of all to work"), forcible resettlement of populations, and free education. Then, magically, the ills of modern society would disappear—the conditions for the existence of class antagonisms will disappear, and the glory of the collective will be established for all time: "In place of the old bourgeois society, with its classes and class antagonisms, we shall have an association in which the free development of each is the condition for the free development of all." The individual will define himself by association with the collective, and the collective will work as a unified individual.[30]

Marx offered a transformative vision of humanity, a system of meaning and purpose. He acknowledged that suffering would follow from his recommended policies but suggested that such suffering would in the end result in a Messianic age of man, in which collective reason would unify with individual meaning. Marx's specter would indeed come to dominate the world, looming astride civilization like a vengeful anti-deity. His philosophy would damn millions to slavery—and haunt the openness and freedom of the post-Enlightenment world with the specter of glorious utopianism.

THE UTOPIA OF BUREAUCRACY

The rise of nationalism and the rise of collectivism were both driven, at their root, by the Rousseauian worship of the general will. But how could such a general will ever find its way to practical implementation? Individual action outside the rule of the general will would only undercut the general will; individual action outside the nationalistic state could only detract from the power of the state; individual excellence would only undermine the leveling process necessary for transforming man.

Unless, that is, individual excellence was yoked to the service of the state. That yoke would be termed *bureaucracy*. The term *bureaucracy* is a mashup of the French word *bureau*, meaning the material used to cover desks, and the Greek term *kratos*, meaning power. So the term itself literally meant "desk power" or "office rule." Bureaucracy was already prevalent in France before the French Revolution, but the Revolution created a bureaucracy of its own, despite its own insistence that such bureaucracy was an evil of the ancien régime.[31]

Proponents of state power quickly began to praise the rise of an expert bureaucracy that could do the people's will—without, of course, consulting with the people, who were, after all, a bunch of rubes. Whereas democrats like Alexis de Tocqueville considered the bureaucracy a new form of oppressive oligarchy, Hegel called bureaucrats the "universal class," since their goal was to fulfill the general will. Bureaucrats were to be trained in ethics and organization. And if properly governed, people would naturally resonate to patriotism: "the consciousness that my interest, both substantive and particular, is contained and preserved in another's (i.e., in the state's) interest and end."[32] Hegel's reverence for bureaucracy would later be deepened and broadened by German sociologist Max Weber (1864–1920), who declared that merit-based bureaucracy could bring about a better world, predicating "the exercise of control on the basis of knowledge."[33]

But didn't such an oligarchic worship of centralized control cut against the supposed foundations of the Enlightenment itself? Didn't individual rights come into direct conflict with a small clique of all-knowing experts, ruling from above?

The man who solved this conundrum was Auguste Comte (1798–1857). Comte is often disparaged today based on his belief in pseudoscientific silliness like phrenology—the study of the shapes of skulls to determine differences among human beings. But we are still living in Comte's framework.

Comte provided a philosophical basis for bureaucratic oligarchy: atheistic science. Widely considered the father of sociology, Comte believed that human development had begun with religious pseudo-authority—human beings paying attention to obscure moral codes they believed had come from God, thanks to their own superstition. But during the French Revolution, power moved from the priests and the kings toward science. Now, Comte recognized that the French Revolution had been a failure, but only because human beings weren't capable of moving directly toward governance by science—the Revolutionaries had made the mistake of seeking meaning in universal values like human rights. Those individual rights ran directly counter to the necessity and power of the state. But the Revolution's failure demonstrated the truth: the only truths could be found in hard scientific fact, in scientific positivism.[34]

In 1822, Comte wrote his *Plan for the Scientific Work Necessary to Reorganize Society*—his suggestion then, as it was throughout his career, is that human knowledge could lead to the imposition of rational laws that could reorganize all of humanity. Expertise was the basis of governance. And all inquiries into transcendental values were worthless, except insofar as they served man. Science was philosophy was religion. All were the same. It made perfect sense, therefore, when Comte founded the religion of humanity, designed to fill the gap left by churchgoing. Comte's church never met with success—it turns out that banning God and worshipping at the altar of pseudoscience will take a toll on membership—but it set the groundwork for the era of high-minded Western progressivism.

Continental progressivism—the philosophy of Hegel and Comte, among others—made its way across the Atlantic Ocean in the form of John Dewey (1859–1952), a man that Professor Robert Horwitz described as "the foremost American philosopher of democracy of the twentieth century." Dewey believed that social science could be used to engineer a new world and a new humanity. Dewey thought that the great ill plaguing the United States was its materialism—like Marx, Dewey said that production and consumption had locked human beings into a vicious cycle of meaninglessness. But there was good news: that cycle could be broken, and without Marx's brutal class warfare.

Instead, all that was needed was "intelligence." If we were simply smart enough, we could solve all of our problems. As Dewey wrote, "the most direct and effective way out of these evils is steady and systematic effort to develop that effective intelligence named scientific method in the case of human transactions."[35]

Dewey did recognize another problem, though. Science, he stated, is typically aimed at an agreed-upon end: we research how to stop cancer, for example, because we all agree that cancer is an evil that must be eradicated. So, what common end should unite us in politics? Is it freedom? Equality? Virtue? Certainly not—Dewey disowned such notions as universal truths, mocking the founders for their bizarre loyalty to "immutable truths good at all times and places."[36] Dewey's answer was simple: ask Darwin.

What, you may ask, does Darwin have to do with anything? Well, says Dewey, Darwin showed that everything changed and became more complex over time—and that was good. It was our job to facilitate human "growth": physical growth, emotional growth, intellectual growth. Our "purpose is to set free and to develop the capacities of human individuals without respect to race, sex, class or economic status."

But this raises yet *another* question: what about democracy? What about consent? What if I'm not interested in growing the way John Dewey thought I should be interested in growing? Well, then, I'm just not "intelligent" enough—the state should be able to scientifically investigate the various players in any democratic system and put its thumb on the scale on behalf of those associations that are most valuable for growth. Furthermore, the state ought to reeducate children toward the type of growth the intelligent bureaucrats have endorsed; children are, in effect, the property of the state.

Yet again, we ask, who will decide the direction of the state? Dewey's answer, in the end, is simple: we just don't know. Government must change and adapt toward the end of making its people better. *Pragmatism* is the watchword. Whatever works is moral. Government must use its means to promote empowering rights—things citizens need in order to "grow." The state would shape the citizen, and the citizen would shape the state until, as in Hegel's thought, the two merged: "The State is then the completed objective spirit, the externalized reason of man; it reconciles the principle of law and liberty, not by bringing some truce or external harmony between them, but by making the law the whole of the prevailing interest and controlling motive of the individual."[37]

The philosophy of scientifically based expertise proposed by Hegel and Comte and espoused by Dewey came to fruition in the administration of Woodrow Wilson. Woodrow Wilson studied Hegel; he was a devotee of Herbert Spencer, himself a fan of Comte and the philosopher who actually coined the term *survival of the fittest*.[38] And he thought that the American Founding Fathers had been wrong—that the social contract theory and inalienable rights of John Locke and Thomas Jefferson were a load of bunk. Liberty was malleable, changeable, just as Dewey said: "No doubt we are meant to have liberty; but each generation must form its own conception of what liberty is." And government was in the business of progress, not in the business of protecting eternal truths: "All that progressives ask or desire is permission—in an era when 'development,' 'evolution,' is the scientific word—to interpret the Constitution according to the Darwinian principle; all they ask is recognition of the fact that a nation is a living thing and not a machine."[39] In Wilson's vision, the community always took precedence over the individual; scientifically minded experts could best run the country; and the president—you know, someone like Woodrow Wilson—could act as the repository of the Rousseauian general will. "The President," Wilson stated, "is at liberty, both in law and conscience, to be as big a man as he can. His capacity will set the limit."[40]

From now on, American government would no longer base itself on the Declaration of Independence and the Constitution of the United States. It would base itself on the pragmatic progressivism of Dewey and Wilson—an ever-growing bureaucracy, self-assured and confident in its own scientific expertise, and aware of its own authority to help shape the formation of the American people from the top down.

THE CATACLYSM

In the absence of Judeo-Christian morality and Greek teleology, each of these visions offered a shining, exciting new purpose to humanity. The philosophy of the American founding represented the apex of a philosophy that could provide all four elements of meaning necessary for the building of a civilization: individual purpose and communal purpose, individual capacity and collective capacity.

But romantic nationalism, collectivist redistributionism, and scientific progressivism did away with the individual need for meaning. The four elements of meaning collapsed downward into two: communal purpose and communal capacity. The individual virtually disappeared in each of these domains. Individuals were only valuable as members of the collective: as sources of the general will, to be embodied in the unified culture of the state; as members of economic classes, who could unite to overthrow the nature of humankind itself; as citizens to be cultivated by the state, their expertise to be placed in service of the greater good.

And human beings *did* find meaning in the new systems.

But the new systems of thought, unchecked by the old morality, unconstrained by the willingness of single individuals to stand up to the collective, could only end one way: in blood. The worst sins of the nineteenth and twentieth centuries sprang from various combinations of romantic nationalism, collectivist redistributionism, and supposedly scientific governance.

The most obvious example, of course, came in Germany. The regime of Otto von Bismarck was characterized by its embrace of romantic nationalism, which culminated in the unification of Germany—and Bismarck's subsequent focus on Kulturkampf, the "cultural struggle" for German solidarity. That struggle led Bismarck to crack down in fascistic fashion on German Catholics, whom he saw as a threat to his autocratic rule. The National Liberal deputy Georg Jung summarized the principle of Kulturkampf well in the Prussian Landtag in May 1875:

> Gentlemen, anyone who believes in our day and age that he
> must carry his religion around with him, anyone who feels
> obliged to wear a particular dress, who swears grotesque

vows, who bands together in herds, and who, when all is said and done, swears unconditional loyalty to Rome, the bitterest enemy of our young German and Prussian glory—such people can have no place in our state. This is why I say: away with them as fast as possible.[41]

This was an early indicator of evil to come in Germany. And it was combined with collectivist redistributionism and the rise of an oligarchic regulatory regime. This combination, however, was seen as a model for a new sort of state: Woodrow Wilson praised Bismarck's system in 1887 as the "most studied and most nearly perfected," and noted approvingly, "Almost the whole of the admirable system has been developed by kingly initiative."[42]

Romantic nationalism continued to animate the German national experience. Its chief expositor, ironically enough, was the British-born Houston Stewart Chamberlain, who warmed to Germany after hearing the romantic nationalist music of Richard Wagner, the ardent anti-Semite and virulent critic of "Jewishness in music"—the title of Wagner's most famous anti-Semitic tract. In that tract, Wagner posed the supposed rectitude and depth of Germanness directly against the evil of the nefarious Jew, stating, "Emancipation from the yoke of Judaism appears to us the greatest of necessities." Jews, said Wagner, were "alien," their speech characterized by a "creaking, squeaking, buzzing snuffle," their music artificial and plastic; even conversion from Judaism could not relieve them of such characteristics (Felix Mendelssohn is Wagner's specific target of ire).[43]

Chamberlain not only bought fully into Wagner's *volkisch* view—a populist romantic nationalism—he became friendly with Richard's nasty widow Cosima, and expanded Wagner's dichotomy between Jewishness and Germanness into an entire worldview. That worldview took full effect in his bestseller, *The Foundations of the Nineteenth Century*. In it, Chamberlain characterized world history as a titanic struggle between the Aryan races and the Jewish race. The book made Chamberlain an intimate of Kaiser Wilhelm II, who adored it. Wilhelm was reportedly taken with Chamberlain's notion that "the Germanic race alone was the most vital and that the present and future belonged to the German Reich, which was its strongest political organism."[44]

This philosophy embedded itself in the German psyche. When Germany surrendered after World War I and the Kaiser was ousted in a coup, romantic nationalism did not dissipate: it was buried lightly under the soil, where it festered. In the aftermath of World War I, the German national myth of the "backstabbing" outsiders who had given away a battle victory spread far and wide. Germany had been betrayed, the logic went, and only a united Germany, beyond democracy and liberalism, could rise again to defeat its enemies.

It burst forth in full bloom with the Nazis.

The Nazi regime promulgated the most extreme romantic nationalism in world history—hundreds of thousands of Germans united in lockstep, cheering wildly at the sight of a dictator, greeting each other by hailing Hitler, hanging pictures of the Führer over their mantels. All of it was an obvious attempt to create a cult of personality, but it drew on deep-seated romantic nationalism embedded in the German mind since before the days of Wagner. Hitler himself had been entranced with that nationalism when as a teenager, he heard Wagner in Vienna. As Hitler biographer Ian Kershaw writes, "He wanted to become himself a new Wagner—the philosopher-king, the genius, the supreme artist." And he also imbibed deeply from Chamberlain, finding inspiration in the *volkisch* movement: "extreme nationalism, racial antisemitism, and mystical notions of a uniquely German social order, with roots in the Teutonic past, resting on order, harmony, and hierarchy."[45]

As the Weimar Republic collapsed, and with the threat of transnational communist agitation on the move in Germany, romantic nationalism became paramount in Germany. Philosopher Martin Heidegger embodied the feelings of millions when he urged his students in 1933, "May you ceaselessly grow in courage to sacrifice yourselves for the salvation of the nation's essential being and the increase of its innermost strength in its polity. . . . The Fuhrer himself and he alone is the German reality, present and future, and its law . . . Heil Hitler." Hitler merely channeled the widespread belief that German Sturm und Drang could only be recovered through an emphasis on the essence of "Germanness"; Heidegger wrote in 1929, "Either we restore genuine forces and educators emanating from the native soil to our German spiritual life, or we abandon it definitely to the growing *Jewification*." In pure pseudoscientific language, he added that Germans had to realize "the fundamental possibilities of the essence of the originally Germanic race."[46]

The appeal of such ideals may be confusing, but George Orwell brilliantly summed them up in a 1940 essay on Hitler's *Mein Kampf*: "Hitler, because in his own joyless mind he feels it with exceptional strength, knows that human beings don't only want comfort, safety, short working-hours, hygiene, birth-control and, in general, common sense; they also, at least intermittently, want struggle and self-sacrifice, not to mention drums, flags and loyalty-parades."[47]

The romance of tribe, as we will see, didn't end with the fall of the Nazis.

Meanwhile, concurrent with the rise of romantic nationalism in Germany, the ideals of collectivist redistributionism took precedence in the East. The end of World War I marked the final breath of the tsarist regime in Russia—and with it, the rise of Marxism.

Vladimir Lenin (1870–1924) had spent his entire life in pursuit of socialist revolution; he'd been arrested and exiled for it. He spent most of the First World War dreaming of the inevitable Marxist revolution that would unite class against nation and overthrow the existing order. But when the opportunity arose in his homeland, Lenin quickly shifted his activity toward the formation of a revolutionary vanguard in Russia, embracing and championing the passionate violence of Marx that Fabianism had subsumed.

Marx himself had not been averse to the possibility of violent revolution. In 1848, writing about revolutions taking place within the Austrian Empire, Marx stated, "there is only one way in which the murderous death agonies of the old society and the bloody birth throes of the new society can be shortened, simplified and concentrated, and that way is revolutionary terror."[48] And, of course, Marx had concluded his *Communist Manifesto* with a call to arms: "their ends can be attained only by the forcible overthrow of all existing social conditions. Let the ruling classes tremble at a Communistic revolution. The proletarians have nothing to lose but their chains. They have a world to win. WORKERS OF ALL COUNTRIES, UNITE!"[49]

Drawing on Marx's writings about armed revolution, Lenin suggested a revolutionary terror, to be followed by "true democracy"—a dictatorship of the proletariat. Sounding a lot like Bernie Sanders, Lenin wrote in 1917, "Democracy for an insignificant minority, democracy for the rich—that is the democracy of capitalist society." Instead, Lenin sought on the one hand "immense expansion of democracy, which *for the first time* becomes democracy for the poor, democracy for the people, and not democracy for the money-bags," and on the other hand, "a series of restrictions on the freedom of the oppressors, the exploiters, the capitalists. We must suppress them in order to free humanity from wage slavery, their resistance must be crushed by force; it is clear that there is no freedom and no democracy where there is suppression and where there is violence." Freedom required tyranny; tyranny was freedom.[50] The terror of Stalinism began with the terror of Leninism; historian Richard Pipes states, "It is difficult to convey the vehemence with which Communist leaders at this time called for the spilling of blood." Grigory Zinoviev, one of the original members of the Politburo and later to be executed by Stalin after a show trial, bragged about the launch of the so-called Red Terror: "We must carry along with us 90 million out of the 100 million of Soviet Russia's inhabitants. As for the rest, we have nothing to say to them. They must be annihilated." As Pipes points out, this constituted a "sentence of death on 10 million human beings."[51]

Stalin would carry Lenin's bloody legacy further, of course—by the end of his life, Stalin was responsible for the murder of tens of millions of people under his rule, including five million people during the forcible starvation of Ukraine for agricultural collectivization from 1931 to 1934 alone.[52] And in China, Mao Tse-tung would bring Stalinism to a new audience, in the process murdering some sixty-five million human beings, the vast majority during Mao's "Great Leap Forward"—an attempt to re-shape human beings by collectivizing their property and returning them to the soil. He did, but only as corpses—somewhere between thirty and forty million people died of starvation. Mao openly bragged about "bur[ying] alive 46,000 scholars." During the Cultural Revolution, Mao's forces committed atrocities upon intellectuals—and mirroring the USSR's gulags, Mao built a system of laogai that housed tens of millions of dissidents over the decades.[53] Today, the North Korean gulag state mirrors the glorious heritage of its communist predecessors.

While it is easy to revile the deeds of the Russian communists today, it is important to note the esteem in which they were held at the time. Walter Duranty of the *New York Times* won a Pulitzer Prize for covering up the crimes of the communists and repeating their propaganda, even though he knew that they were slaughtering their political opponents. Some seven decades later, the *Times* executive editor finally admitted that "the work Duranty did, at least as much of it as I've read, was credulous, uncritical parroting of propaganda."[54] It wasn't merely the press. As Jonah Goldberg notes in *Liberal Fascism*, "Nearly the entire liberal elite, including much of FDR's Brain Trust, had made the pilgrimage to Moscow to take admiring notes on the Soviet experiment." The experts were at the wheel in Moscow, these officials believed; as Stuart Chase, the father of the New Deal, stated, the communists didn't worry about grubby money. Instead, they were motivated by "the burning zeal to create a new heaven and a new earth which flames in the breast of every good Communist." John Dewey found the USSR wondrous, as did most of the top officials in the American labor movement. W. E. B. Du Bois gushed, "I may be partially deceived and half-informed. But if what I have seen with my eyes and heard with my ears in Russia is Bolshevism, I am a Bolshevik."[55] Until the USSR's fall, many on the mainstream Left believed it to represent a viable ideology.

Despite the fall of the USSR, the desire to find a new meaning in the collective remains, both in the United States and abroad. The romanticism about communism has never truly died on the American Left—in 2017, the *New York Times* ran op-eds about why "women had better sex under socialism," "when Communism inspired Americans," and why "socialism's future may be its past."[56]

Today, we hear about the wonders of Chinese central planning—the great strength to be found in organized economies, the rising power in the East. Thomas Friedman of the *New York Times* regaled readers in 2009 with tales of China's mastery: "There is only one thing worse than one-party autocracy, and that is one-party democracy, which is what we have in America today. One party-autocracy certainly has its drawbacks. But when it is led by a reasonably enlightened group of people, as China is today, it can also have great advantages."[57] None of it is true over any serious length of time, but the desire for collective purpose and collective capacity runs strong.

In fact, it runs so strong that Stalin remains an incredibly popular figure in Russia, decades after his death and half a century after his monstrous crimes against humanity were fully revealed.

In 2017, a poll by the Levada Center showed that a plurality of Russians named Stalin the most "outstanding" person of all time; modern Russian dictator Vladimir Putin, a former KGB officer, says that Stalin was a "complex figure," adding that "excessive demonization of Stalin is one of the ways Russia's enemies attack it."[58] Even victims of Stalin's crimes miss the power and glory that came with collectivization of purpose. In her Nobel Prize–winning oral history *Secondhand Time*, Svetlana Alexievich quotes a former communist factory worker imprisoned and beaten half to death by the regime. A year later, he was released. Then, during World War II, he met his interrogator, who told him, "We share a Motherland." As an old man, this cruelly wronged man said, "People always want to believe in something. In God or in technological progress. . . . Today it's the market. When I go into my grandchildren's room, everything in there is foreign: the shirts, the jeans, the books, the music—even their toothbrushes are imported. Their shelves are lined with empty cans of Coke and Pepsi. Savages! . . . I want to die a Communist. That's my final wish."[59]

The deep-seated need for collective purpose and capacity found its outlet in the United States in bureaucracy, the movement away from a government answerable to the population and toward a government run by so-called experts. But these experts weren't experts on human nature, it turns out: instead, they used science as a catchword for political priorities that maximized centralization. In the realm of economics, this meant the rise of a federal government dedicated to the proposition that unfairness in life could be rectified through central planning. During the FDR administration, economic policy was set from the top; ignoring the injunction by economically laissez-faire thinkers that no set of individuals can know more than the entire market at large, FDR and his cadre of geniuses lengthened the Great Depression by nearly a decade by manipulating the currency, setting wages and prices, and bullying those who objected into silence. As Harold L. Cole and Lee E. Ohanian of UCLA concluded, "The economy was poised for a beautiful recovery, but that recovery was stalled by these misguided policies."[60] Those misguided policies included FDR setting the price of gold based on his lucky number. Treasury Secretary Henry Morgenthau wrote in his diary, "If anybody ever knew how we really set the gold price through a combination of lucky numbers, etc., I think they would be frightened."[61]

Ironically, as Cole points out, "The fact that the Depression dragged on for years convinced generations of economists and lawmakers that capitalism could not be trusted to recover from depressions and that significant government intervention was required to achieve good outcomes."[62]

The enthusiasm for central planning led to particularly dark results in the areas of race and sex. Many of the most prominent proponents of the social science movement were devotees of so-called race science, the pseudoscience that suggested that all disparities were due to inborn traits—and that the future of a society lay in its willingness to find a "solution" to the problem of "undesirable" populations. This pseudoscience led many of those same "humanistic" thought leaders to propose eugenics as a solution to societal ills. As historian Thomas Leonard writes, "The roster of progressives who advocated exclusion of hereditary inferiors reads like a Who's Who of American economic reform. . . . They were joined by the founders of

American sociology."[63] Among these figures were Teddy Roosevelt, Woodrow Wilson, and Oliver Wendell Holmes.

Teddy Roosevelt wrote a letter in 1913 stating, "Society has no business to permit degenerates to reproduce their kind. . . . Some day we will realize that the prime duty the inescapable duty of the good citizen of the right type is to leave his or her blood behind him in the world; and that we have no business to permit the perpetuation of citizens of the wrong type."[64] Wilson pushed for compulsory sterilization of those with Down's syndrome in 1907, and signed a compulsory sterilization bill as governor of New Jersey in 1911.[65]

Holmes, a Supreme Court Justice, was a philosophical pragmatist and devotee of Dewey. His 1927 decision in *Buck v. Bell* resonates down the ages for its evil embrace of state sterilization of supposedly unfit populations: "We have seen more than once that the public welfare may call upon the best citizens for their lives. It would be strange if it could not call upon those who already sap the strength of the State for these lesser sacrifices, often not felt to be such by those concerned, in order to prevent our being swamped with incompetence."[66] Fully sixteen states embraced eugenic sterilization during the 1920s and 1930s; over the coming decades, the states would sterilize sixty thousand people.[67]

In 1922, author Harry Laughlin proposed compulsory sterilization of millions of Americans; in return for calling for generational death of the physically and mentally disabled, as well as alcoholics, he received an appointment as expert for the House Committee on Immigration and Naturalization for the Congress. He also testified on behalf of dramatically restricting immigration. In his book, he created a "Model Eugenical

Sterilization Law."[68] Two decades later, Karl Brandt, chief Nazi medical officer and Adolf Hitler's personal doctor, cited Laughlin and *Buck* in his defense at Nuremberg.[69]

And, of course, the creator of an organization that remains relevant down to our day favored eugenics as well: Margaret Sanger, founder of Planned Parenthood. Sanger wrote in 1921 that the question of sterilizing the disabled was "the most urgent problem today."[70] In one of her speeches, she suggested the sterilization or quarantining of some "fifteen or twenty millions of our population," who would—she put it rather gently—"be organized into soldiers of defense—defending the unborn against their own disabilities."[71] She declared birth control "nothing more or less than the facilitation of the process of weeding out the unfit [and] of preventing the birth of defectives."[72] For her work, Sanger was nominated for the Nobel Peace Prize a staggering thirty-one times—twice as many times as Gandhi.[73]

Making a better world, in this view, meant living for the collective—and, if necessary, compulsion on behalf of the collective. The exposure of the Nazi eugenics program stopped the American progressive eugenicists cold. But the drive for a centralized program of living, as proposed by bureaucrats, has never died.

A WORLD IN ASH

In World War II, all three of these prominent collectivist worldviews came into direct conflict—and somewhere between fifty and eighty million people died. Romantic nationalism engulfed

Nazi Germany, along with a worship of centralized bureaucracy and "scientific" governance—and six million Jews were mowed down by German bullets or gassed in death camps. The Soviet Union saw its own population as fodder for the preservation of the state, sending its citizens to die on the front lines of Stalingrad with no guns in their hands but guns at their backs. The United States interned 117,000 Japanese. By the end of the war, the great hope of the telos-free, Godless Enlightenment had faded from view—or, more precisely, it had been buried under the mountains of corpses from World Wars I and II.

The West was suddenly in crisis.

Despite massive technological improvements—and, in part, because of such improvements—the human race had nearly wiped itself off the planet. Science had not solved the search for purpose. In fact, with the discovery of atomic weaponry, it seemed that the West had come to the brink of its own annihilation. The great dream of redefining human beings, discovering transcendent values without reference to God or universal purpose, seemed to have died. While some still held out hope in the West for the eventual triumph of the Soviet experiment, with the revelation of Stalin's crimes, that hope too faded.

What would replace that hope now?

CHAPTER 8

AFTER THE FIRE

The world survived World War II, of course. Not only did the West survive—it got freer, richer, more prosperous than ever. Human wealth expanded exponentially. Life spans increased.

But there remained a hole at the center of Western civilization: a meaning-shaped hole. That hole has grown larger and larger in the decades since—a cancer, eating away at our heart. We tried to fill it with the will to action; we tried to fill it with science; we tried to fill it with world-changing political activism. None of it provides us the meaning we seek.

By the end of World War II, European optimism was dead and buried beneath six feet of human ash. The philosophies of the Europeans—Enlightenment ideals about the value of human beings and the need to move beyond God or Greek teleology—had ended in tragedy. Hitler claimed ideological forebears in Kant, Hegel, and Nietzsche;[1] Stalin took his cues from Marx; the eugenicists took their ideas from Darwin and Comte. The post-Locke Enlightenment project had been a Tower of Babel, with the common goal of supplanting reason for religion rather than seeking the congruence of the two. As the tower began to challenge God, its builders went to war with one another, speaking languages all their own.

And then the tower fell, and the land was left barren.

Europe had buried millions of its sons and daughters; the West had placed its bets on mankind, and reaped the whirlwind.

But God did not return. Magna Carta, the first great charter of Western liberties, was signed by King John in 1215, and set limits to monarchic powers based on "regard to God and for the salvation of our soul, and those of all our ancestors and heirs, and unto the honour of God and the advancement of his holy Church." Religious practice remained the norm in Europe until the advent of the middle of the twentieth century. Then, as the children born around World War II reached adolescence, religious observance plummeted.[2]

Faith in human reason, too, had waned. After the catastrophic insanity of not one but two Great Wars, the Biblical warning not to place faith in princes had been proved prescient. The Enlightenment hope in mankind's collective capacity to better itself had collapsed.

Without God, and without the collective, all that was left were individuals. Alone.

Thus, the philosophy of existentialism came to the fore.

Existentialism truly began in the nineteenth century with Søren Kierkegaard (1813–1855), a Danish philosopher bothered by the problem of Enlightenment reason, which he saw as arrogant—the notion that a universal ethical system could be discerned by human beings was a fool's errand, the idea that history was an unerring unfolding of Hegelian dialectics far too simplistic. The universe was cold and chaotic—man's search for meaning could not begin with an attempt to look outward for that meaning. Kantian universalism was too hopeful, Comtian scientism far too self-assured.

Instead, Kierkegaard posited that human beings had to find meaning by looking within. The system by which one chooses to live is a leap of faith—but in that leap, man finds his individual meaning. "Subjectivity is the truth," Kierkegaard wrote. "Objectively there is no infinite decision or commitment, and so it is objectively correct to annul the difference between good and evil as well as the law of noncontradiction and the difference between truth and untruth." Truth can be found in ourselves.[3] To Kierkegaard, this meant making the leap of faith to believe in a God beyond man-made ethics—his famous "teleological suspension of the ethical." Kierkegaard focused on passion as opposed to reason—he deemed passion the most important driving force in life, and concluded, "The conclusions of passion are the only reliable ones."[4] He hoped, of course, that the passionate leap would be toward the Christian God. But his belief system would lead not to God, in the end, but to worship of subjectivity.

If truth lay in the self, then all moral truth automatically became a matter of subjective interpretation. This was the view of Nietzsche, who stated that the greatest man would be he "who can be the most solitary, the most concealed, the most divergent, the man beyond good and evil, the master of his virtues, and of superabundance of will; precisely this shall be called *greatness*; as diversified as can be entire, as ample as can be full."[5]

But *all* truth was subjective, according to the existentialists, not merely moral truth. This was the view of Karl Jaspers (1883–1969), a German philosopher who wrote, "All knowledge is *interpretation*."[6] It was also the view of Martin Heidegger (1889–1976), who suggested that the essence of being human was *being*—not reason or passion, but existence. While Descartes had suggested that proof and meaning in human existence could be predicated on thinking—"I think, therefore I am"—Heidegger contended that our identity was wrapped up purely in existence itself. What did this mean practically? It meant mostly deconstructing ancient notions of eternal truths and human reason going all the way back to Plato and Aristotle. What would fill the gap? Authenticity—the true self, contemplating its own death and the meaninglessness of the universe, "taking hold of itself."[7] Heidegger prophesied a time "when the spiritual strength of the West fails and its joints crack, when this moribund semblance of a culture caves in and drags all forces into confusion and lets them suffocate in madness." He openly preached the power of will, and saw a choice between "the will to greatness and the acceptance of decline."[8] Heidegger's extension of this individual idea—taking hold of oneself and our place in the world—may have led to his original association with the Nazis.[9]

The truest expositor of existentialism, however, was Jean-Paul Sartre (1905–1980). Politically, Sartre was a committed Marxist; he spent his life bouncing between support for Soviet communism and Maoism. But his philosophical contributions lay more precisely in the realm of the individual. According to Sartre, unlike both the ancients and the Enlightenment philosophers, existence precedes essence: in other words, we are born, and then constantly remake ourselves in the face of the world, rather than being subject to the dictates of human nature. There is no sure good or evil; there is merely the world we are granted, and it is our job to make and remake ourselves, utilizing our freedom to do so. So Sartre writes:

> Nowhere is it written that the Good exists, that we must be honest, that we must not lie; because the fact is we are on a plane where there are only men. . . . If existence really does precede essence, there is no explaining things away by reference to a fixed and given human nature. In other words, there is no determinism, man is free, man is freedom. On the other hand, if God does not exist, we find no values or commands to turn to which legitimize our conduct. So, in the bright realm of values, we have no excuse behind us, nor justification before us. We are alone, with no excuses. That is the idea I shall try to convey when I say that man is condemned to be free. Condemned, because he did not create himself, yet, in other respects is free; because, once thrown into the world, he is responsible for everything he does.[10]

This is a beautifully expressed idea—an idea replete with the tragedy of existence, but hopeful about man's possibility of reaching within himself for something higher. But it also leaves human beings without a guidepost. It promises no communal purpose or communal capacity; it focuses almost entirely on the individual, but leaves individuals without any guide other than the guide within. Furthermore, Sartre's belief in an unfixed human nature opens the door to utopian schemes of all sorts—if we can merely change the system, as Marx argued, perhaps the New Man will arrive, cloaked in glory.

THE NEW "NATURAL LAW"

While Enlightenment worship of reason may have ended in tears during the first half of the twentieth century, its continued faith in science was amply rewarded. There is no question that the pace of scientific discovery rapidly increased in the period following the Enlightenment, with the average life expectancy in Europe in 1850 at 36.3 years old; by 1950, that number had nearly doubled, to 64.7.[11]

Science was the future.

The philosophy of scientific government had resulted in the horrors of two World Wars and the specter of centralized, tyrannical government. But that science could free mankind was still in the offing in the postwar period. And why not? As John F. Kennedy put it in one of his last speeches in 1963, "Science is the most powerful means we have for the unification of knowledge, and a main obligation of its future must be to deal with problems which cut across boundaries, whether boundaries between the sciences, boundaries between nations, or boundaries between man's scientific and his humane concerns."

The focus on science had radically shifted. Science had begun, in the Francis Bacon philosophy, as an aid toward the betterment of man's material conditions; it had morphed over time into an aid toward the betterment of man's moral condition, though not the source of morality itself. But now, with God out of the picture and the collective implicated in the worst crimes in human history, science was handed the task of creating a new morality, a new law. The existentialists had reduced human purpose to creation of subjective truth; science provided the last remnant of objective truth in Western thought.

Nature, then, was the answer; investigation of nature became the purpose.

The legacy of Western thought had relied on natural law—the idea of universal purposes discernible in the universe through the use of reason. Nature was seen not as a justification for behavior, but as a hint toward a broader pattern in creation: things were designed with a purpose, and it was the job of free human beings to act in accordance with right reason in achieving that purpose. What we ought to do was inherent in what is: a hammer was made for hammering, a pen for writing, and a human for reasoning. Human beings could reason about the good, and then shape the world around them to achieve it.

Now, however, a new form of natural law came to fruition: the belief that whatever occurred in nature was "natural," and therefore true. This was a far cry from the original "natural law"; it said that human beings were animals, and that their purpose was to act according to their instincts, not their reason.

But the newfound faith that science would take us to the stars and beyond was about to collapse. For while the ancients had counted on human reason to allow us to freely seek and find moral truths, while Judeo-Christian teachings had called on man to use reason to find God and free will to follow Him, science now undermined reason and will.

The first serious advocate of the position that human beings were no longer rational, free actors came from Sigmund Freud (1856–1939). Freud was a charlatan, a phenomenal publicist but a devastatingly terrible practicing psychologist. He was a quack who routinely prescribed measures damaging to patients, then wrote fictional papers bragging about his phenomenal results. In one 1896 lecture, he claimed that by uncovering childhood sexual trauma he had healed some eighteen patients; he later admitted he hadn't cured anyone. Freud himself stated, "I am actually not at all a man of science, not an observer, not an experimenter, not a thinker. I am by temperament nothing but a conquistador—an adventurer, if you want it translated—with all the curiosity, daring and tenacity characteristic of a man of this sort."[12]

But Freud's radical theories about human nature became world famous. He submitted that religion was but a form of "childhood neurosis" from which the world had to recover. He suggested that the roots of religion lay in an ancient event during which a group of prehistoric brothers had killed their father. Dreams were a form of wish fulfillment, behavior was a manifestation of unconscious desires; in general, people were governed by forces beyond their control. Mirroring Plato, Freud posited a tripartite soul—Plato suggested reason, spirit, and appetite, while Freud suggested superego (moral reason), ego (life experience militating between appetite and reason), and id (appetite). But where Plato suggested that man should work to ally spirit with reason to overcome appetite, Freud suggested that working to uncover unconscious forces shaping our id would be the best possible solution. In other words, Freud believed that we were all governed by forces we couldn't understand, absent psychoanalytic intervention.

Freud's heavy focus here was on sexual neurosis. And while Freud thought that sexual neurosis could be sublimated— energies rechanneled toward more fruitful pursuits—it was only a short step to rejecting that sublimation in favor of freeing us from neurosis through sexual profligacy. Thus Alfred Kinsey (1894–1956) entered the public eye, riding a wave of enthusiasm for promiscuity and excuse making for it. Kinsey was a zoologist at Indiana University fascinated with the supposed hypocrisy of repressed Americans. Kinsey believed, unlike Freud, that human beings could only be freed by throwing off the shackles of Judeo-Christian morality; he was contemptuous of Freud's theories and, according to biographer and coworker Wardell Pomeroy, "shocked by the moral judgments Freud constantly made."[13]

In 1948, Kinsey came out with his groundbreaking book *Sexual Behavior in the Human Male*; five years later he returned with *Sexual Behavior in the Human Female*. These supposedly rigorous studies found that 85 percent of men and 48 percent of women had had premarital sex, and half of men and four in ten women had cheated on their spouses. According to Kinsey, nearly seven in ten men had slept with prostitutes, 10 percent had been homosexual for a prolonged period of time, and 17 percent of males on farms had pursued sex with livestock. Kinsey also claimed that 95 percent of single women had had abortions, along with 25 percent of married women. Americans were, Kinsey argued, a rather bawdy lot.

The first book flew off the shelves, selling two hundred thousand copies in two months alone.

But the science Kinsey pursued was deeply flawed. As journalist Sue Ellin Browder explains, Kinsey's statistics weren't reflective of reality, because his sample wasn't reflective of reality: of his original 5,300 white male sample, at least 317 were sexually abused minors, "several hundred" male prostitutes, and hundreds were likely sex offenders in prison when they were interviewed. The interviewees were also self-selected, and those who opt into such studies tend to be more sexually profligate. Kinsey used similarly terrible methodology when surveying women. No wonder the chairman of the University of Chicago committee on statistics, W. Allen Wallis, scoffed at Kinsey's "entire method of collecting and presenting the statistics."[14]

But the reality of Kinsey's methodology mattered less than his implicit promise: human beings could be bettered by casting aside the vestiges of the old morality. And the best news of all was this: it was all *natural*. No more struggling to seek the natural law; no more utilizing reason to hem in biological urges. By becoming animal, we could become more free. If it felt good, not only should we do it, we had a biological *imperative* to do it. Forget striving for existential meaning—we could all find truth by *being ourselves*. This was Rousseau's argument for the noble savage taken to its biological extreme.

And the basis for that argument would only grow stronger in the scientific community. Scientists would soon argue that the capacity for free choice itself was no longer present—that we were automatons, slaves to our biology, robots deceived by the sophisticated outgrowth of our own neurocircuitry.

Harvard professor E. O. Wilson was perhaps the greatest advocate of this position: he posited that human beings had inescapable programming that made us behave in certain ways in response to our environment. Furthermore, through investigation of the interaction of that innate nature and the environment, we could fully predict human behavior. Culture was merely an outgrowth of that interaction: Darwinian evolution ruled the roost. Wilson called his theory of everything sociobiology. Sociobiology, he said, could provide the great "consilience" of science, merging neuroscience and evolutionary biology and physics—all of science—into a cohesive whole.

So man's capacity disappeared. Man's purpose seemed to disappear as well. If human beings could change nothing, being non-free actors, and if David Hume's distinction between what *is* and what *ought to be* remained valid—if you couldn't learn what was moral from nature itself—then human beings were left with nothing but hedonism. They were creatures of pleasures and pain, animals rooted in biology, responding to stimuli.

THE NEO-ENLIGHTENMENT

But many of the same scientists who promoted the mechanistic, materialist vision of human beings and the universe were unwilling—thankfully—to leave human beings utterly adrift. Instead, many of them clawed their way back to the roots of the Enlightenment. Just as Enlightenment thinkers had relied on the power of reason, they relied on the power of science. Supposedly, the human mind could once again reign supreme, after analyzing the world around it. This search would provide human beings with meaning: by investigating the nature of the universe, we would finally understand its unity. Wilson himself declares that his goal is to resume the Enlightenment quest: "when built from reality and reason alone, cleansed of superstition, all of knowledge might come together to form what in 1620 Francis Bacon, greatest of the Enlightenment's forerunners, termed the 'empire of man.'"[15]

Of course, as we have seen, the Enlightenment's reliance on reason unmoored from revelation—the assumption by its greatest thinkers that human beings could in fact derive *ought* from *is* and then impose the *ought*—led from the bloody streets of French Revolutionary Paris to the thumping jackboots of Hitler. Wilson's optimism would have sounded far better in 1789 than it does in 2018.

Nonetheless, neo-Enlightenment thinkers continue to trumpet a new purpose for mankind, discernible through science. As Wilson wrote:

Preferring a search for objective reality over revelation is another way of satisfying religious hunger. . . . It aims to save the spirit, not by surrender but by liberation of the human mind. Its central tenet, as Einstein knew, is the unification of knowledge. When we have unified enough certain knowledge, we will understand who we are and why we are here.[16]

Wilson rejects Aquinas and Kant; he rejects any attempt to create purpose or meaning on the back of transcendent and eternal values. Those values, he recognizes, depend largely on the notion of free will that modern science has apparently rejected.

Instead, Wilson proposes a new sort of faith: faith in science.

Now, we could easily ask at this point whether faith in science was not the faith that brought us eugenics and central planning. But Wilson has something else in mind: not the scientific manipulation of human beings, but the gradual emergence of workable values in tune with the nature that defines us all. Wilson believes that ethics are an outgrowth of evolution itself, in combination with environment; culture is an effect, not a cause. Wilson explains the way things *are*.

Wilson argues that the empiricist spots the value of an ethical system in its success: "ethics is conduct favored consistently enough throughout a society to be expressed as a code of principles." The rightness of an ethical system can be explained by its prevalence.

But what about the fact that awful ethical systems have dominated throughout human history? What about the fact that billions live under tyranny, or that the religious bigotry that alienated Wilson from the church originally now thrives across the globe? What about the fact that instead of the world gradually surrendering to the beauties of transnational liberalism, as Francis Fukuyama suggested it would, clashes of civilization have broken out anew, in accordance with the theories of Samuel Huntington? What about the fact that certain constants that Wilson full-throatedly rejects have marked human experience and human morality—including the commonality of religious practice, and its use as a basis for moral systems?

This is where Wilson makes his leap of faith: "The empiricist argument holds that if we explore the biological roots of moral behavior, and explain their material origins and biases, we should be able to fashion a wise and enduring ethical consensus."

Now, though, Wilson is using tools that are no longer at his disposal. Who decides what that "wise and enduring" consensus looks like? The vox populi—which worldview is "more widely *perceived* to be correct." This is fully relativistic—popularity cannot substitute for any reliable moral compass. And so Wilson slides back into Hegel: that which is right is imminent, or will change to become *more* right. Wilson obliterates David Hume's argument that we cannot learn what we *ought* to do from what *is* in nature—because there *is no ought*. There is only what is. And that can always change. According to Wilson, the evolution of human morality is not about human beings working to better the world, but about human beings acting as agents of information integration, who spit out updated morals on a regular basis. Morality becomes an "ensemble of many algorithms, whose interlocking activities guide the mind across a landscape of nuanced moods and choices."[17]

This obviously leaves some serious questions unanswered. First, how ought we to live? There is no *ought*—there is only how we *do* live. But that gives us no purpose after all. Human beings were not fashioned to find meaning in *being*. Wilson offers us no help there. Second, Wilson uses an awful lot of active verbs to describe the quest for meaning—"We are about to abandon natural selection, the process that created us, in order to direct our own evolution by volitional selection," he writes in *The Meaning of Human Existence*.[18] But "we" are a bundle of neurons; "direct" is an active verb when we, in truth, have no active role in defining what we do next. Can there truly be meaning when we cannot determine what we do next—if we are biological stones thrown through space, destined to land at a predetermined place and time?

In the end, Wilson retreats into the existentialism of Sartre, though he lacks Sartre's stirring faith in man's will: "We are, it seems, completely alone. And that in my opinion is a very good thing. It means we are completely free. . . . Laid before us are new options scarcely dreamed of in earlier ages." But this is untrue by Wilson's own lights. All of "our options" have been foreclosed by Wilson's scientism—they are not "ours," since we are just animals living without the freedom to have our own options, and they are not "options," since nature commands, it does not request. Those "options" are nature's path, laid before us, which we will unerringly tread, regardless of whether we believe we want to do so or not. When Wilson states, "We have enough intelligence, goodwill, generosity, and enterprise to turn Earth into a paradise both for ourselves and for the biosphere that gave us birth," he offers us no plausible reason what paradise constitutes, how we can actively pursue that paradise, or why we should do so, given that our lives matter approximately as much as the lives of the ants he originally studied. When Wilson states, "We need to understand ourselves in both evolutionary and psychological terms in order to plan a more rational, catastrophe-proof future," he strays from his own naturalistic, deterministic genealogy of morals, and begins preaching something close to the transcendental values he supposedly deplores.[19]

Other thinkers seem to embrace transcendent Enlightenment values more clearly—and antiscientifically. If the new science had foreclosed the possibility of free choice and will, advocates of scientism were willing to overlook that rather inconvenient fact. If the new science had called into question the possibility of universal human truths, advocates of scientism were willing to overlook that, too. Instead, these neo-Enlightenment thinkers returned to the premises of the Enlightenment in the name of science: the same Enlightenment that had brought about scientific progress, they argued, had ushered in an age of universal morality as well.

Take, for example, Harvard psychologist Steven Pinker. Pinker's book *Enlightenment Now* is a powerful ode to Enlightenment values. Where Wilson discards Kant as antiscientific, Pinker embraces Kant's call to "understand." He also endorses in glowing terms the power of reason: "The Enlightenment principle that we can apply reason and sympathy to enhance human flourishing may seem obvious, trite, old-fashioned. . . . I have come to realize that it is not."[20] And Pinker is obviously correct in celebrating in voluminous fashion the outgrowth of human reason—the material gains that are its products.

But Pinker does cheat just a bit. Most obviously, he seems to endorse versions of will and truth that science can't justify; these versions spring from a Judeo-Christian tradition he rejects. He simultaneously embraces Enlightenment ideas that have Judeo-Christian roots, and chops off those roots. Pinker treats the Enlightenment as a significant break from the thought that preceded it. That's not true, as we've seen. He also engages in the No True Scotsman fallacy—he labels Enlightenment thinkers like Rousseau, Herder, Schelling, and others members of a "counter-Enlightenment," ignoring their commonalities with fellow Enlightenment thinkers and casting them off into the outer darkness. In a four-hundred-page book about the Enlightenment, he never mentions the French Revolution—which, as we have seen, worshipped the Cult of Reason. Pinker wants to pluck the fruit of the Enlightenment without stepping in the manure. But the manure was heavily linked to precisely the worship of God-free reason that Pinker embraces. As Yoram Hazony observes, "In short, the principle advances that today's Enlightenment enthusiasts want to claim were 'set in motion' much earlier. And it isn't at all clear how helpful the Enlightenment was once it arrived."[21]

More important, however, Pinker never explains why reason ought to triumph; he assumes as self-evident the idea that material gain is the highest priority. He writes that human progress "requires only the convictions that life is better than death, health is better than sickness, abundance is better than want, freedom is better than coercion, happiness is better than suffering, and knowledge is better than superstition and ignorance." This is circular reasoning: if you assume that Pinker is right, it turns out that Pinker is right. But he *isn't* right, at least not for most human beings. It all depends on the meaning of happiness, which Pinker contrasts with suffering—as though all happiness can be got from a 98.6 degree temperature, a hearty meal, and a steady supply of sex. But that's not what happiness actually constitutes. Human beings keep showing that they need something more—man cannot live by quality of life indicators alone. Material human progress in the absence of spiritual fulfillment *isn't enough*. People need meaning.

And so Pinker seems to miss the central question of his own book. He acknowledges that the "appeal of regressive ideas is perennial," but can't seem to figure out why. If we are all material beings merely looking for material well-being, we should embrace the Enlightenment merely for its utilitarian purposes— but we don't because we aren't. He opens his book by retelling the story of a student who asked him precisely that question: "Why should I live?" According to Pinker, his answer went something like this:

> As a sentient being, you have the potential to flourish. You can refine your faculty of reason itself by learning and debating. You can seek explanations of the natural world through science, and insight into the human condition through the arts and humanities. You can make the most of your capacity for pleasure and satisfaction, which allowed your ancestors to thrive and thereby allowed you to exist. You can appreciate the beauty and richness of the natural and cultural world. As the heir to billions of years of life perpetuating itself, you can perpetuate life in return. . . . And because reason tells you that none of this is particular to you, you have the responsibility to provide to others what you expect for yourself.[22]

This isn't much of an answer. It offers a smorgasbord of choices and then suggests that the smorgasbord itself provides meaning. But *that wasn't the question*. The question was *why to choose from the smorgasbord in the first place.* Pinker has no answer to that question, because it requires a reliance on universal truths outside the realm of human reason. And his halfhearted attempt to build a morality on the supposed ethic of Kantian mutuality falls apart quickly. His statement that reason tells you all other human beings are human, and therefore you have a responsibility to treat them as you would treat yourself is effectively a *religious appeal*, not a reasoned argument. Why not simply take what you want? Why not declare your tribe or class superior? Why not reason that your genetic offspring can only survive if you gain an advantage over others, in accordance with the survival of the fittest?

Before we laugh off such suggestions, review again the history of the twentieth century.

Pinker isn't alone in his quest to revitalize the ideas of the Enlightenment. And some of his colleagues look for moral truths in the dictates of reason as well. Michael Shermer, a historian of science and editor of *Skeptic* magazine, argues that there are real moral values "out there to be discovered . . . in human social nature." He considers himself a moral realist. How can we find those values? Shermer says they are inherent in the exercise of reason. So, he states, we don't need God to tell us that the Holocaust was wrong—it simply was. Why? Because his morality places at its center the "survival and flourishing of sentient beings. We all want to survive and flourish. It's in our nature. It's what evolution designed us to desire."[23] Sam Harris, too, takes this view—he says that the primary value that makes life worth living and gives us meaning is "the well-being of conscious creatures."[24] Like Hobbes, who saw the key to human systems in our desire to seek pleasure and avoid pain, moral systems can be built on the basis of a utilitarian calculation about human survival and flourishing.

But again, we all define human flourishing differently. Harris acknowledges the inherent vagary in the term: "the concept of well-being is like the concept of physical health: it resists precise definition, and yet it is indispensable." But Harris assures us that "there is every reason to think that this question has a finite range of answers . . . the moral landscape—will increasingly be illuminated by science." But has it been? As Harris acknowledges, "Most of what constitutes human well-being at this moment escapes any narrow Darwinian calculus."[25]

Here is the truth: most of what constitutes human well-being at *any* moment will escape narrow Darwinian calculus, because most human beings are not driven simply by the dictates of procreation and survival and pain avoidance.

And focusing on the need for survival doesn't beget a workable morality, either. Take, for example, a simple thought experiment: You are the leader of a nation. That nation is more technologically advanced and more intellectually and culturally adaptive than its neighbors. Your nation is relatively small, and there are populations that live in your nation that consume disproportionate resources and refuse to integrate into your superior culture. You are surrounded by more populous and more barbarous nations. Thus, you have two options. First, you can wait for the inevitable demographic swamping of your nation—which, in the long run, will result in the collapse of humanity's survival, since your neighbors are less adaptable. Second, you can attack your neighbors, and take whatever measures are necessary in order to assure the long-term survival of your nation.

That *was* Hitler's case for the Holocaust, after all.

When the highest moral cause is material success, it looks a lot like having no morals at all.

IS THE NEO-ENLIGHTENMENT SUSTAINABLE?

The neo-Enlightenment view is that Enlightenment ideals would have come from anyone using reason, and just happened to spring up in a particular place and time. How strange, then, that Pinker and Shermer and Harris and *I* agree on nearly all the same values—values that arose in the Judeo-Christian West alone, that spread from there outward, and that relied on the words of revelation and the application of Greek teleology.

It isn't strange, of course. We all grew up in a West formulated on the basis of thousands of years of history. History isn't merely happenstance; movements don't merely wink into existence. To explain our current notions of individual rights, we must look to foundational ideas.

The neo-Enlightenment attempts to disown Judeo-Christian values and Greek teleology rest in historical ignorance. Neo-Enlightenment advocates tend to attribute every ill of the past several centuries to religious superstition and ancient mumbo-jumbo, failing to acknowledge that the values they hold dear rest on ancient foundations.

Neo-Enlightenment philosophers like to connect religion with slavery, overlooking that the abolitionist movement in the West was almost entirely led by religious Christians—and ignoring that the global movement against slavery was led by the West (slavery was only legally abolished in China in 1909, and slavery was only legally ended in Saudi Arabia in 1962). Even Enlightenment philosophers who opposed slavery did so because they were steeped in a Judeo-Christian tradition stemming from the basic notion of *imago dei* and natural rights. The French philosopher Diderot, a declared atheist, wrote this regarding slavery in his *Encyclopédie*: "This purchase of Negroes to reduce them into slavery is a negotiation that violates all religion, morals, natural law, and human rights."[26] This wasn't a scientific perspective. It was a moral one, steeped in an abolitionist ideal born centuries beforehand in Catholic Europe.

How about universal suffrage? Again, it wasn't science that supported that notion—it was a belief in the individual, born of the Judeo-Christian tradition and Greek reason. Yes, Elizabeth Cady Stanton wrote *The Woman's Bible* to challenge precisely the sexism she saw in the Bible—but in doing so, she cut herself off from influence with the suffrage movement, which reached success by leaving her behind and appealing to the better angels of the Christian nature (Frances Willard's Woman's Christian Temperance Union was far more instrumental in achieving the women's vote than Stanton). And naturally, even Stanton was groomed in a Christian society and inculcated Christian values.

The same holds true of the movement against Jim Crow. Martin Luther King Jr. quoted the Bible far more than he quoted David Hume—and with good reason. It was the prophet Isaiah's dream that animated King's: "I have a dream that one day every valley shall be exalted, and every hill and mountain shall be made low, the rough places will be made plain, and the crooked places will be made straight; 'and the glory of the Lord shall be revealed and all flesh shall see it together.'"

Yes, religious people have been on both sides of those movements. *Of course they have*, since we live in a world shaped by the Bible. But that's precisely the point: those arguments have taken place in a common context in which Biblical values are held up against other Biblical values, in which Greek teleological reason is held up against itself. The traditions of individual liberty didn't spring into being in the West miraculously, from nothing. They sprang from the tension between Jerusalem and Athens. Western civilization is a bridge suspended over the waters of chaos. Removing that tension collapses that bridge into the roiling river below.

Carving off the roots of the Western tree while hoping to maintain the integrity of the trunk amidst high winds is an exercise in wishful thinking. In December 2017, I discussed this issue precisely with Harris, who was arguing that the Bible was a rotten text filled with awful lessons: I told him, "The moral system by which you suggest that that portion of the Bible should be removed is built on the moral system of the Bible, developed over two thousand years." When Harris protested that his most considered view of ethics came from a broader framework of studies, I answered, "I'm not talking about your browsing in world literature. I'm talking about the fundamental moral precepts that you took to be moral from the time you were a child arise from a Western civilization predicated on Judeo-Christian notions of good and bad."[27]

Enlightenment ideals didn't arise in a vacuum, and treating

them as though they can survive and thrive without the water and oxygen that nourished them for thousands of years—revelation and reason, telos and purpose, free will and responsibility— isn't likely to sustain those ideals beyond those who read the neo-Enlightenment philosophers and scientists. The neo-Enlightenment isn't teachable; attempt to transplant it to the soil of other cultures, and it withers.

Don't get me wrong—I think what Harris and Pinker and Shermer are doing in reviving Enlightenment ideals is spectacular. I *agree* with a lot of Enlightenment ideals, particularly regarding individual liberty and natural rights, as we've discussed. But the new scientific Athenians will have to make common cause with the devotees of Jerusalem, rather than making war on them. The same holds true in reverse. For, as it turns out, there are larger philosophical threats to Western civilization that require our attention.

CHAPTER 9

THE RETURN TO PAGANISM

In 2015, I appeared on CNN HLN's *Dr. Drew Show*. The topic was ESPN's decision to award Caitlyn Jenner their Arthur Ashe Courage Award for his decision to announce his transgenderism. Caitlyn Jenner is, of course, a biological male. Several different people comprised the panel for Dr. Drew's show; one of them was Zoey Tur, a transgender female and biological male. The conversation began with a unanimous vote of approval for ESPN's decision . . . until I was asked about the situation. I explained that I didn't understand why society ought to engage in the mass delusion that Jenner was in fact a woman. Jenner may call himself a transwoman; Jenner may change his name. But Jenner is not, by any biological metric, a woman. And a society that refuses to acknowledge the biological differences between men and women is engaging in knowing falsehood.

This rather simple statement drew Tur's ire. Tur proceeded to berate and belittle me for my perspective, calling me an ignorant "little boy." I responded by reiterating that Jenner is a biological male, and that believing you are a member of the opposite sex is a mental disorder—that men cannot magically become women and women cannot magically become men. After Tur responded again with insults, I finally asked Tur, "What are your genetics, sir?"

The question wasn't meant as a provocation—it was meant to make a point. Biology matters. Facts matter. Reason matters.

But at this point, all hell broke loose. Tur grabbed me by the back of the neck on national television, and threatened to send me home in an ambulance (an odd offer, since you don't usually go home in an ambulance). Other members of the panel reacted with horror to my "insulting the pronouns."

Needless to say, none of this had to do with reason.

Unfortunately, reason is no longer in vogue. That's why when I visited Berkeley to speak, protesters outside chanted "SPEECH IS VIOLENCE!" It's why I—an Orthodox Jew, and the leading antagonist of the racist alt-right—have been routinely castigated as a Nazi. Subjectivity rules the day.

Reason, in fact, is insulting. Reason suggests that one person can know better than another, that one person's perspective can be more *correct* than someone else's. Reason is intolerant. Reason demands standards. Better to destroy reason than to abide by its dictates.

After the enormous human developments brought about by the exercise of reason, all this should seem bizarre. But the death of reason could have been predicted once reason alone failed to provide us with meaning. The existentialist philosophy of Jaspers, Heidegger, and Sartre left man alone at the edge of the cosmos—an odd conglomeration of stardust, sentient but purposeless, incapable of making sense of the chaotic universe around him. All logic could be deconstructed into interplay of social forces; all individual decision-making could be degraded to the level of reactionary biology.

None of this was new, of course. It was merely a return to a very old way of thinking—a pagan way of thinking. Where the Greeks had insisted on a telos discoverable in the universe by way of investigating nature and thereby piercing through to the Unmoved Mover's design, the post–World War II West discarded telos altogether. Where Judeo-Christian values had insisted on a unified master plan, an objective moral standard, a progression in history, and the inescapable importance of free choice, the post–World War II West substituted chaos and subjectivism.

For the Enlightenment thinkers, science had ripped man from his place at the center of the universe, but reason could restore him to the center of meaning. However, this was no longer true, thanks to the new knowledge of science. God was dead at the hands of man; now man was dead at his own hands. There was no grand design behind the confusion of everyday life. Human morality was just that: a construct created by some at the expense of others. History was not a story of progress, but a story of oppression and suffering—as Voltaire wrote in "Jeannot et Colin," "all ancient histories, as one of our wits has observed, are only fables that men have agreed to admit as true; with regard to modern history, it is a mere chaos, a confusion which it is impossible to make anything of."[1] And individual human beings had no power of choice—they were corks bobbing on the eddies of time.

The story of humanity was over; human beings were animals once again.

Unless.

Unless purveyors of Athens and Jerusalem had been wrong all along.

What if those purveyors of Athens and Jerusalem, those creators of the Constitution and the Magna Carta, those thinkers behind the scientific method and deductive reasoning—what if they had all pulled a fast one? What if, as it turned out, man was born free but was everywhere in chains *because of these systems of thought themselves?* What if objective truth was a trap? What if reason was a trap? What if the system of rights promoted by the Enlightenment was *actually* a cleverly disguised method for enshrining the power of the few at the expense of the many?

What if the system itself could be torn down?

And if the system *could* be torn down, *how* could it be torn down?

The answer, as it turns out, was simple enough: by rejection of all prevailing societal norms in favor of precisely the tribal paganism and animalistic passion that had preceded those norms. Only by going back to the beginning could humanity be built again from scratch. Everything had to be torn down in order to be built back up again.

BAITING THE BABBITTS

This was a bigger problem in the United States than it was in Europe. Europe had been devastated by war; Europe had discarded religion long ago. But in the United States, the post–World War II situation looked bright. Unlike in Europe, religious practice remained incredibly strong. As of 1950, about three-quarters of Americans were members of a church, synagogue, or mosque; in 1954, almost half of all Americans said they had attended church, synagogue, or mosque in the last seven days. Over nine in ten Americans identified as Christian.[2]

This didn't mean that America was full of dead-eyed androids praising Jesus and stumping for segregation and sexism. Jim Crow remained in full, evil force in the South; sexism remained a serious obstacle to women. But the 1950s and early 1960s saw the rise of a burgeoning black middle class—as Thomas Sowell points out, "from 1954 to 1964 . . . the number of blacks in professional, technical, and similar high-level positions more than doubled. In other kinds of occupations, the advance of blacks was even greater during the 1940s—when there was little or no civil rights policy—than during the 1950s when the civil rights revolution was in its heyday."[3] And the number of women in the workplace had been rising steadily for decades: in 1950, one in three women were in the workforce,[4] as compared to just 19 percent of working-age women fifty years earlier.[5] Across the board, American living standards changed radically for the better as the United States took global leadership.

Furthermore, America was hardly a cultural desert. The attempt to paint the American dream as an American nightmare had common currency on the American Left; Sinclair Lewis's *Babbitt* (1922) painted a businessman as an unfulfilled dreamer, coining the term *Babbitt* as an insult for everyday Americans. But in the aftermath of World War II, the American dream was still very much alive. And that dream was never merely a white picket fence, a dog, and two kids out in suburbia. It was a dream of cultural enrichment and common purpose. As Fred Siegel reports, between 1940 and 1955, local symphony orchestras increased 250 percent; in 1955, thirty-five million people paid to attend symphonies as opposed to fifteen million paying to attend baseball games. Even early television became part of the cultural education of the public: NBC presented a three-hour production of Laurence Olivier's *Richard III*; as of 1951, there were twenty-five thousand members of the Great Books discussion groups, with "50,000 Americans a year . . . buying collections of the writings of Plato, Aristotle, the Founding Fathers, and Hegel" at serious cost to themselves.[6]

But the American Left could not accept that a capitalistic America could produce a more cultured America—and a more tolerant America. Thus, the argument went, the growing wealth and culture of the American middle class was merely a ruse: deep down in their hearts, Americans were empty pretenders, Stepford wives and Babbitt husbands. They were shallow materialists who shunted human suffering to the back of the bus in favor of their vainglorious pursuit of wealth at all costs. They were repressives who hid pornography beneath the bed and petty jealousy in their hearts.

On the other hand, changing the system could bring about a new humanity: a humanity renewed in individual and communal purpose, and in individual and communal capacity. Human beings had been fooled into believing that they had purpose and capacity under the Judeo-Christian-supported Enlightenment system. But they could be disabused of that notion. They could be changed for better—if only the system itself could be reduced to rubble.

This argument had deep roots on the Marxist Left. Italian socialist Antonio Gramsci (1891–1937) had supposed in 1916 that the failure of World War I to usher in global Marxist revolution was a result of culture—that too many people had grown up under the repressive orthodoxy of capitalism. "Man is above all else mind, consciousness—that is, he is a product of history, not of nature. There is no other way of explaining why socialism has not come into existence already," he wrote.[7]

Gramsci died in an Italian prison under the regime of Mussolini, but his philosophy was picked up by the members of the so-called Frankfurt School, a group of German scholars expelled from Germany amidst the rise of the Nazi Party. Their leader, Max Horkheimer (1895–1973), preached the gospel of social change—and suggested that systems had to be deconstructed in order to make way for that social change. He explained that what he termed critical theory was "suspicious of the very categories of better, useful, appropriate, productive, and valuable, as those are understood in the present order."[8] The present order had to change, Horkheimer said, because "the wretchedness of our own time is connected with the structure of society."[9] And the way to change it was to tear it down. It is no coincidence that various forms of university study dedicated to various alleged victim groups—black studies, Jewish studies, LGBT studies—all find a home under the "critical studies" rubric.

Horkheimer and other members of the Frankfurt School were forced to leave Germany with the rise of the Nazis, but they made their way to the United States with the help of Edward R. Murrow, among others. Leading lights like Theodor Adorno (1903–1969) posited that American culture was replete with antirevolutionary materialism; Erich Fromm (1900–1980) suggested that the roots of totalitarianism could be found in the materialism he saw in the United States. Fromm stated that fascism would rise in the United States thanks to its devotion to capitalism. Individuals had been alienated from society by its consumerism, made into widgets. Indeed, we are not free—we only *think* we are, thanks to the lies of the Enlightenment and Western civilization. "We are proud that we are not subject to any external authority," Fromm writes, "that we are free to express our thoughts and feelings, and we take it for granted that this freedom almost automatically guarantees our individuality. *The right to express our thoughts*, however, *means something only if we are able to have thoughts of our own*." The powerlessness of Western man could only find solace in "compulsive conforming in the process of which the isolated individual becomes an automaton," or in "the authoritarian character." Without Marxism remolding, men became either Nazis or the trite little consumers of modern America—who, in turn, would become proto-fascists.[10]

This was a dire and deliberate misreading of the nature of American individualism, which rested on Judeo-Christian values and Greek reason. Fromm wasn't wrong that the replacement of individual and communal purpose with base materialism is a problem—but his diagnosis, the destruction of the American value system rather than its restoration, was dramatically off. Nazism didn't arise from consumerism. It arose from communal purpose overriding individual purpose, and individual capacity abandoned in favor of worship of the communal capacity of the state. Nazism, in other words, lay a lot closer to Marxism than capitalism did.

But Fromm and thinkers like him suggested that the solution to the supposedly inevitable slide from dull consumerist conformity to horrible fascism lay in complete rebellion. Only acts of rebellion could destroy the system within. Rebellion in sex; rebellion in art; rebellion in work; rebellion everywhere.

The leading advocate of that rebellion was Herbert Marcuse (1898–1979). Marcuse, one of the progenitors of the so-called New Left, preached that the prevailing order had to be torn out root and branch. In 1955, coincident with the rise of Kinsey's thought, Marcuse penned *Eros and Civilization*, in which he argued that repressive sexuality had damaged mankind, and that only freeing man of his Victorian mentality regarding sex could build a better world. Like Kinsey, Marcuse rejected Freud; instead, he posited a world of liberated *eros*, and called for "the concept of a non-repressive civilization, based on a fundamentally different experience of being, a fundamentally different relation between man and nature, and fundamentally different existential relations."[11] Capitalism had structured adults so that they fell into patterns of labor specialization—and that same logic held true for sex, where certain body parts were for certain things. But no more! Now, "the body in its entirety would become an object of cathexis, a thing to be enjoyed—an instrument of pleasure."[12] Everything would become happy and wonderful as human beings finally gloried in their total self-realization: "No longer employed as instruments for retaining men in alienated performances, the barriers against absolute gratification would become elements of human freedom. . . . This *sensuous* rationality contains its own moral laws."[13]

Unbridle Dionysian paganism, and the world would become free. No wonder Marcuse's popular slogan ran "Make love, not war." Students in Paris during the 1968 revolt carried banners reading MARX, MAO, AND MARCUSE.

But Marcuse's pagan revelry didn't stop with revolutionary sex. The capstone to his theory came in the form of censorship—what he called, in Orwellian fashion, "repressive tolerance." Marcuse suggested that certain forms of speech had to be barred so that they could not emerge victorious, toppling critical theory itself. According to Marcuse, "the objective of tolerance would call for intolerance toward prevailing policies, attitudes, opinions, and the extension of tolerance to policies, attitudes, and opinions which are outlawed or suppressed." Freedom, Marcuse said, was "serving the cause of oppression"; oppression, therefore, could serve the cause of freedom. Speech could be labeled violence—Marcuse called to "reexamine the issue of violence and the traditional distinction between violent and non-violent action"—and violence speech. In essence, "Liberating tolerance, then, would mean intolerance against movements from the Right and toleration of movements from the Left . . . it would extend to the stage of action as well as of discussion and propaganda, of deed as well as of word." The marketplace of ideas had to die, since it was "organized and delimited by those who determine the national and the individual interest." Minority groups had to be given special privileges to shut down opposition: "liberation of the Damned of the Earth presupposes suppression not only of their old but also of their new masters."[14] The roots of sexual liberation, victim politics, and political correctness had been laid.

The Left properly pointed out the widespread problems of racism and sexism in American society in the 1950s—and their diagnosis was to destroy the system utterly. That diagnosis was self-serving—since Marx, the Left had seen Western civilization as the problem, a hierarchy of property-owners seeking to suppress their supposed inferiors. Now, the Left claimed that all the ills of society could be laid at the feet of the system they so despised. And young Americans, living through the turbulent social change of the 1960s, resonated to that message. In the 1960s and 1970s, the counterculture, which saw America as a place replete with evil and suffering, became the dominant culture in academia and the media.

"I'M ON THE RIGHT TRACK, BABY"

If the system was to blame for all human shortcomings, then the answers could be found by pursuing *your* truth. Virtue, it turns out, was part of that old-style hierarchy that had kept humanity penned in for millennia. No, people merely had to "find themselves." This newfangled gloss on Rousseauian romanticism found ecstatic followers on the New Left. Where once conscience had reigned supreme, now self-fulfillment became the key to self-betterment.

The psychological theory of Abraham Maslow (1908–1970)

was hijacked to support this new journey within. Maslow said that human beings sought self-realization—not the pursuit of virtue through acting in accordance with an objective telos, but realization of what *you* truly want. Repression prevents us from realizing what we want and need—and such repression begins in childhood, "mostly as a response to parental and cultural disapprovals." We should seek our inner nature, which is "definitely not 'evil,' but is either what we adults in our culture call 'good,' or else it is neutral." By removing repression, we can unlock our own good.[15]

Dr. Benjamin Spock's (1903–1998) *Common Sense Book of Baby and Child Care* (1946), which sold fifty million copies between its publication and Spock's death in 1998, placed the same emphasis on self-esteem. Spock, a devotee of the New Left, had told parents to put aside the rigidity of old-school parenting, which could instill insecurity and anxiety. Instead, parents should follow their instincts and refrain from criticizing their children. Spock admitted that his initial draft of the book led many parents to believe that they had to bend over for their children. "Parents began to be afraid to impose on the child in any way," he said. Spock actually would change his book to emphasize parental standards in later editions.[16] But Spock did believe in a notion of natural man as inherently *good*. "John Dewey and Freud said that kids don't have to be disciplined into adulthood but can direct themselves toward adulthood by following their own will," Spock stated in 1972, while running for president on the People's Party ticket (his platform included free medical care, full withdrawal of all American troops from foreign countries, and a guaranteed minimum income).[17]

This was hot stuff in the 1960s and 1970s. Nathaniel Branden (1930–2014), famously Ayn Rand's paramour and an early objectivist, penned the bestselling *The Psychology of Self-Esteem*, in which he stated that the central human search was for self-esteem—and that self-esteem could be achieved only through rational appraisal. He attacked the doctrine of Original Sin, and argued that the will to understand could grant purpose.[18] Later, Branden would write that there was not a "single psychological problem—from anxiety and depression, to fear of intimacy or of success, to spouse battery or child molestation—that is not traceable to the problem of poor self-esteem."[19]

Now, Maslow and Spock and Branden may have argued that self-esteem still had to be earned—but that message was quickly shunted aside in favor of a simple headline version of their philosophy: elevating self-esteem had to be pursued at all costs. If fulfillment lay in self-esteem, then children had to be taught that they were special. Furthermore, if values and standards stood in the way of self-esteem, then those values and standards had to be obliterated for the sake of true self-realization. Politicians began to echo the idea that children were *owed* a culture of self-esteem; as Jesse Singal of *The Cut* writes, "The self-esteem craze changed how countless organizations were run, how an entire generation—millennials—was educated, and how that generation went on to perceive itself (quite favorably)." As Singal also points out, the social science to suggest that crime and suffering would be minimized with the maximization of self-esteem was junk—it turns out not that self-esteem makes people more high-achieving, but that more high-achieving people tend to have higher self-esteem *thanks to their achievements*.[20]

The true effect wasn't to create generations of more fulfilled human beings, though—it was to create generations of
more self-obsessed human beings. But society was quick to
embrace the self-esteem movement, the notion that everyone's
feelings were to be honored in order to prevent crucial loss of
self-esteem. Barney sang to countless school children, "Oh,
you are special, special, everyone is special / Everyone in his
or her own way." And as they grew, Lady Gaga would sing
to them, "Just love yourself and you're set / I'm on the right
track, baby / I was born this way." Where children had once
learned from *Pinocchio* to "always let your conscience be your
guide," now they were taught by *Frozen*, "no right, no wrong,
no rules for me / I'm free! / Let it go!" Or, most crudely,
Americans might hear that you and me baby ain't nothin' but
mammals who ought to do it like they do on the Discovery
Channel—not exactly the transcendental uplift of Psalms or
Beethoven. Natural law had become nature, and through reveling in their nature rather than channeling it, human beings
could finally find their bliss.

THE RISE OF INTERSECTIONALITY

For the advocates of the Frankfurt School, the point of focusing on self-esteem was obvious: if they focused instead on the
spread of material prosperity, they'd have to give up Marxism in favor of Judeo-Christian-values-supported capitalism.
By focusing on self-esteem, however, the New Left could kill
three birds with one stone: they could overturn reliance on

Judeo-Christian religion, Greek teleology, and capitalism. Religion, Greek teleology, and capitalism all have something in common: none of them cares particularly much about "your bliss." Religion suggests that your self-realization lies in consonance with God, and that any attempt to placate your ego through pursuit of personally defined happiness is bound to fail. Religion suggests that "your bliss" does not exist: only God's bliss does. Greek teleology is utterly unconcerned with your personal definition of self-realization; the only thing that counts is whether you are acting virtuously in accordance with right reason. And capitalism cares far less about how you're feeling than about your ability to create products and services someone else wants.

By calling self-realization the highest good, then, the New Left had cast out the specter of the roots of Western civilization and replaced them with a call to action. What was that call to action? Forming alliances directed at tearing down the system. The theory went like this: self-esteem is the key good. But self-esteem cannot be achieved while there are structural impediments to that self-esteem.

Those structural impediments came in the form of sexism, racism, and other forms of bigotry. Such bigotry didn't have to be expressed outwardly—the structures of society themselves were institutionally biased against victim groups. And members of those victim groups couldn't achieve self-realization so long as those institutions remained standing.

Second-wave feminists like Betty Friedan (1921–2006) characterized the role of American women as "the comfortable concentration camp." She argued, like other members of the

New Left, that women were being prevented from achieving true happiness by the informal expectations of society; in *The Feminine Mystique* (1963) she lamented, "a strange stirring, a sense of dissatisfaction, a yearning that women suffered in the middle of the twentieth century in the United States." What had led to this unspoken suffering? Quoting Maslow, among others, Friedan argued that women had sold themselves out thanks to societal pressures, turning themselves into "walking corpses."[21] Feminist author Simone de Beauvoir, author of *The Second Sex* and existentialist partner of Sartre, went so far as to say that society should *bar* women from becoming mothers: "No woman should be authorized to stay at home to raise her children. Society should be totally different. Women should not have that choice, precisely because if there is such a choice, too many women will make that one. It is a way of forcing women in a certain direction."[22]

Meanwhile, in the aftermath of the civil rights movement, which righteously fought against true institutionalized racism through legal structures, a new argument was made: that America was irredeemably racist, and that such racism could never be overcome. Malcolm X argued in 1963 that even the pursuit of civil rights legislation was foolhardy: it would "never solve our problems."[23] Black Panther honorary prime minister Stokely Carmichael, along with Charles Hamilton, wrote in 1967 in *Black Power: The Politics of Liberation*, that institutional racism went far too deep for anything but total systemic change to abrogate it. "Racism is both overt and covert," they wrote. "It takes two, closely related forms: individual whites acting against individual blacks, and acts by the total white community against the black community. We call these individual racism and institutional racism." Institutional racism is vague and difficult to target—but we can tell it by its fruits. Wherever there is disparity, there is obviously discrimination. When black Americans lack "proper food, shelter and medical facilities, and thousands more are destroyed and maimed physically, emotionally and intellectually because of conditions of poverty and discrimination in the black community, that is a function of institutional racism." White people may not be bombing churches anymore or stoning black families, but they are still "support[ing] political officials and institutions that would and do perpetuate institutionally racist policies." Thus, political disagreement is merely a guise for covert racism.[24]

The only way for members of these victimized groups to restore their self-esteem would come by banding together to tear down the system. Feminist Gloria Steinem wrote that women and other victimized groups could not actually achieve self-esteem in the current system; to achieve self-esteem, victims would have to bond "with others who share similar experiences (from groups of variously abled people to conferences of indigenous nations) bonding with others in shared power . . . and taking one's place in a circle of true selves."[25]

Professor Kimberlé Crenshaw of Columbia University came up with a term to describe this coalition of victims: *intersectionality*. According to Crenshaw, human beings are members of various groups: racial groups, gender groups, religious groups, sexual orientation groups. And we can describe their "lived realities" by referring to the intersection between those groups. Thus, a black female lesbian Muslim has a different lived reality than a white male heterosexual Christian. Furthermore, we can identify the level of difficulty someone has experienced in life simply by referencing the various groups of which she is a member. The more minority groups to which you are a member, the more you have been victimized; the more you have been victimized, the more your opinion about the innate institutional bigotry of the United States ought to carry weight.

The actual goal, as Crenshaw acknowledges, is to bully those who aren't members of these intersectional groups—to force them to "check their privilege." Crenshaw explains, "Acknowledging privilege is hard—particularly for those who also experience discrimination and exclusion." But acknowledge they must, or be accused of complicity in institutional racism.[26]

White citizens must recognize their white privilege or be cast out; males must recognize their "toxic masculinity"; identity politics becomes a path toward true justice. Repressive tolerance must be exercised against those who would fight the tribal notion of intersectionality. Those who refuse to abide by tribal dictates of intersectionality—people who insist that they are not victims of American society simply by dint of their skin color—are deemed sell-outs, Uncle Toms. Thus Clarence Thomas is not legitimately black because he doesn't vote Democrat; Nikki Haley isn't legitimately a woman because she is a pro-life Republican. According to Ta-Nehisi Coates, when black people call for individualistic thinking that strays from traditional Democratic ideology, that means supporting "white freedom":

"freedom without consequence, freedom without criticism, freedom to be proud and ignorant."[27]

VICTIMHOOD TRIUMPHANT

In order to promote discussions about intersectionality, systems of oppression must be curbed—including the speech of others. Discussions must end. Reason must be thrown out the window since, owing to our different life experiences, we cannot understand one another. Freedom—supposedly a tool of the white power structure—itself must be redefined so as to protect the self-realization of intersectional people.

Science, too, must take a backseat. Science might undercut the intersectional argument by providing evidence that not all suffering springs from institutional discrimination. Say, for example, that social science shows a high correlation between single motherhood and crime—and that single motherhood is especially predominant among American blacks. Or say that there are group differences in IQ, and that those differences may be at least partially heritable. Or say that men and women are biologically different, and that this difference explains differences in pay—since women choose different types of jobs than men and make different decisions with regard to the number of hours worked, their pay tends to be lower on average than that of men. Or say that gender is connected with sex, and that males who believe they are female are not in fact female.

These basic facts become subject to scrutiny since *science itself* is a construct of the system. That's the argument of Donna

Hughes in the *Women's Studies International Forum*, who explains, "The scientific method is a tool for the construction and justification of dominance in the world . . . the new methodological techniques were invented by men who were interested in explaining the inheritance of traits in order to support their political ideology of natural human superiority and inferiority."[28]

This sounds bizarre and foolish. That's because it is. Science has created vaccines that have saved millions; that's not a social construct, that's a fact. But this postmodern idea about science as an ethnocentric construct has quickly entered the mainstream. In 2018, a lawsuit by former Google employee James Damore for wrongful termination alleged that the company had distributed an official handout to all managers. That memo, meant to encourage "inclusion," suggested that "aspects of white dominant culture" could not be rewarded by managers. Those aspects included thinking in terms of "individual achievement," "meritocracy," "we are objective," and "colorblind racial frame." Instead, managers should seek to promote "noticing race/color and any racial patterns in treatment" as well as the concept that "everything is subjective."[29]

Most obviously, advocates of verifiable science have found themselves attacked for their supposed motives in discussing science at all. In January 2018, Steven Pinker discussed the problem of political radicalization, and particularly the newfound attraction by some college students to the alt-right. He stated that one of the reason for the alt-right's sudden upsurge had come as a result of attempts to silence discussion about science. He mentioned that if rational people cited basic facts—facts like "different ethnic groups commit violent crimes at different rates" or "men and women are not identical in their life priorities, in their sexuality, in their tastes and interests"—they were immediately called racist and sexist. Because the Left saw such facts as inherently debasing of self-esteem, they sought to quash discussion of those facts—with the result that people who wanted to talk about those facts were more likely to draw foolish inferences from them. As Pinker explained, "If you've never heard these facts before and you stumble across them or someone mentions them, it is possible to come to some extreme conclusions . . . you're never exposed to the ways of putting these facts into context so that they don't lead to racism and sexism." Pinker added, "If they were exposed, then the rationale for putting them into proper political and moral context could also be articulated, and I don't think you would have quite the extreme backlash."

For expressing his *opposition* to drawing extreme views from facts, and for expressing his support of discussing controversial facts, Pinker was accused of complicity in racism and sexism—he was actually accused of being a member of the alt-right for a speech *deriding the alt-right*. Professor Joshua Loftus of New York University (a self-reported member of the Democratic Socialists of America) said that Pinker's idea were indicative of a "pernicious problem . . . radical centrism of the likes of Pinker, Jon Haidt, Christina Hoff Sommers, Sam Harris, James Damore."[30] Jamelle Bouie of *Slate* magazine suggested that Pinker had embraced statements like "blacks cause crime" and "jews control the world."[31]

The same sort of ire has met Sam Harris, who dared to point out that IQ differentials between groups exist. He did not say they were entirely genetic; he did not draw any policy inferences from IQ studies (for the record, Harris was a Hillary Clinton supporter). Nonetheless, Ezra Klein's *Vox* chided him for citing studies, with scientists Eric Turkheimer, Kathryn Paige Harden, and Richard Nisbett suggesting that Harris had engaged in "pseudoscientific racialist speculation."[32] When confronted by Harris about this, Klein immediately retreated to the confines of identity politics: "These hypotheses about biological racial difference are now, and have always been, used to advance clear political agendas." Thus, these hypotheses must never be discussed, since they fall afoul of identity politics considerations. And even engaging in scientific discussion is a *form of identity politics*, according to Klein—citing studies and fighting back against attempts to censor those studies is merely engaging in a tribalism of white scientists.[33]

This pathetic illogic has even extended to the realm of scientific staffing. The National Science Foundation, a federal funding agency for science, says that it wants to pursue a "diverse STEM workforce"—not the best scientists of all races, but a specifically diverse group. To that end, the NSF spent millions funding projects on implicit bias research, one of the least-verified, most-hyped attempts to ferret out secret racism ever attempted, as well as $500,000 on studying intersectionality. Science departments around the country are seeking not those with the highest scores or the best credentials, but those with special "contributions to diversity." As Heather Mac Donald points out, the American Astronomical Society has now asked PhD programs to stop using the Graduate Record Exam (GRE) in physics for applicants, since too few women were doing well. The same is happening in medicine, where schools have been encouraged to stop using the Medical College Admission Test (MCAT) for ethnic minorities. The impact: "From 2013 to 2016, medical schools nationally admitted 57 percent of black applicants with a low MCAT of 24 to 26, but only 8 percent of whites and 6 percent of Asians with those same low scores, according to Claremont McKenna professor Frederick Lynch." How it helps patients to have less qualified but more ethnically diverse heart surgeons remains unexplained.[34]

We've seen this sort of antiscientific blatherskite rear its ugly head over and over. Former Treasury secretary Lawrence Summers lost his job as president of Harvard University when professors voted to oust him; Summers had the temerity to cite studies suggesting that there are more men who fall on both the higher and lower ends of the spectrum of test score distribution, thereby creating disparity in the distribution of men and women in particular science and mathematics jobs.[35] Jordan Peterson, professor at the University of Toronto, received a letter from his administration warning him that his refusal to use transgender pronouns was "contrary to the rights of those persons to equal treatment without discrimination based on their 'gender identity' and 'gender expression.'" The letter suggested that Peterson's insistence on using correct pronouns in accordance with biology had been "emotionally disturbing and painful" for some students.[36] Lindsay Shepherd, a graduate student at Wilfrid Laurier in Canada, was disciplined after showing a video of Peterson discussing the use of "made-up pronouns" in order to placate transgender people.[37] At Boise State, Professor Scott Yenor was called on the carpet for the great sin of writing a piece suggesting that radical feminism's insistence that gender was a social construct had paved the way for the transgender rights movement.[38] Students walked out on Evergreen State College's Professor Heather Heying when she pointed out that men are taller than women.[39] Heying's husband, Professor Bret Weinstein, lost his job at Evergreen when he refused to leave campus after black students demanded that white teachers not teach on a particular day; students called him a racist and led a takeover of campus buildings.[40] College speakers ranging from Charles Murray to Heather Mac Donald to Christina Hoff Sommers have been run off campus, usually following violent protests, for the sin of citing statistics.

Better false statistics and bad social science than to violate someone's sense of self-esteem.

This antiscientific, anti-reason nonsense is a return to the random chaos of the pagan—a belief in subjectivity above objectivity, a belief in lack of control over your own fate, a belief that reason itself is merely a reflection of power dynamics. The same scientific method, reliance on reason, and belief in individual worth that led to the greatest surge of wealth in human history are now under assault—all on behalf of the quest for self-realization and self-worth.

All of this is deeply damaging to precisely the people who are supposed to be freed by it. Intersectional thinking promotes a victim mentality entirely at odds with the pursuit of fulfillment and success. If you are told repeatedly that your self-esteem is threatened by the system and the structure, and that even statistics and science must not offend you—if you are taught that your bliss matters more than objective truth—you become weak and fragile, unable to cope in the real world. Social psychologist Jonathan Haidt of New York University points out that the most effective type of therapy for distorted thinking is cognitive behavioral therapy, in which people are taught to break chains of thought by using reason and evaluation—precisely the opposite of what our modern universities have been doing. "The recent collegiate trend of uncovering allegedly racist, sexist, classist, or otherwise discriminatory microaggressions doesn't *incidentally* teach students to focus on small or accidental slights," he writes. "Its *purpose* is to get students to focus on them and then relabel the people who have made such remarks as aggressors." This, Haidt concludes, makes society more censorious, and makes students more psychologically unstable: "The new protectiveness may be teaching students to think pathologically."[41]

Even worse, people who perceive themselves as victims are also more likely to become aggressors; as social psychologist Roy Baumeister explains, "Many violent people believe that their actions were justified by the offensive acts of the person who became their victim."[42] Which is precisely what we've seen from campus rioters and social media malcontents and the movement to use government force to shut down particular types of disapproved speech.

But, we are told, at least this new awareness of our intersectional problems will bring about a more *aware* world, and thus perhaps a better one. Not so. Focusing on right-able wrongs is worthwhile; blaming all disparities on discrimination leads to more political polarization and individual failure. Studies show that perceived discrimination is heavily connected with "lower grades, less academic motivation . . . and less persistence when encountering an academic challenge."[43] That's certainly a case for fighting discrimination. It's also a case for not exaggerating its extent, or silencing conversations in order to pander to sensitivities.

THE END OF PROGRESS

So, has the vision of the cultural Left provided fulfillment? It's provided solipsism, for certain. But it's also provided polarization. It's not merely that intersectionality has carved off individuals into racial groups, then pitted them against one another. Racial solidarity among members of the intersectional coalition has also driven reverse racial solidarity from the so-called alt-right—a group of racists who have sought to promote white pride. Leaders in this movement include the execrable Richard Spencer, Jared Taylor, and Vox Day—all of whom use IQ data to explain racial disparities, while claiming that the roots of Western civilization lie not in ideas, but in race. The alt-right remains a fringe movement, but their arguments have penetrated into more visible circles thanks to a reactionary tendency by some on the Right to embrace anyone who supposedly opposes political correctness.

The cultural Left's view of reality has driven anger and hatred—polls show that Americans are more divided than ever. That sense that the world is spinning out of control only feeds into intersectionality's attack on agency. Individual capacity has been abandoned in this worldview—individuals, after all, are mere creations of the systems into which they have been born. Collective purpose, too, has gone by the wayside—after all, it's the system keeping you down.

But tribal identity is alive and well.

Tribal identity cannot provide prosperity. But it can provide meaning.

The problem, of course, is that tribal identity also tears down the civilization that has granted us our freedoms and our rights, our prosperity and our health. But perhaps all those things are meaningless in the long run. So argues Yuval Noah Harari, lecturer at Hebrew University of Jerusalem and author of *Sapiens: A Brief History of Humankind*. Harari, unlike intersectional thinkers of the Left, is honest enough to admit the brutal, existential truth of a civilization unmoored from Judeo-Christian values and reason: he says we may have been happier in the Stone Age, and that attempts at meaning are merely ways for our brains to amuse themselves while we journey toward death. History doesn't progress; history is merely the movie *Groundhog Day*, albeit with nicer alarm clocks to wake you up every morning.[44] Perhaps we can only be truly happy by discarding truth and reality. "Do we really want to live in a world in which billions of people are immersed in fantasies, pursuing make-believe goals and obeying imaginary laws? Well, like it or not, that's the world we have been living in for thousands of years already," Harari argues.[45] Perhaps humanity will change itself beyond recognition through technology, and save itself from the rut. Perhaps not.

Harari is right about one thing: capitalism, it turns out, cannot fulfill the human longing for meaning, even if it betters our material condition. And so the fantasy of a new humanity promulgated by the Left continues to romance us. We cycle between attempting to fulfill that dream, suffering for that attempt, abandoning that attempt, and taking up the dream again. Our only alternative would be to return to the Judeo-Christian values and Greek reason that undergirded America's founding. It's not enough to make the case for the utility of the Enlightenment; the Enlightenment was the ground floor of the building, resting on certain foundational ideas and basic premises. We must shore up those ideas and premises if we hope to keep building skyward rather than adding weight to an already shaky superstructure.

Next, we turn to that task.

CONCLUSION:
HOW TO BUILD

America is struggling right now in a lot of ways. But its largest struggle is the struggle for our national soul. We are so *angry* at each other right now. That anger is palpable. Where did it come from? It came from the destruction of a common vision. We used to believe in the Founding vision, supported by a framework of personal virtue culled from Judeo-Christian morality. We used to see each other as brothers and sisters, not "the 1 percent vs. the 99 percent" or "the privileged vs. the victims." We weren't enemies. We were a community, forged in fire and tethered together by a set of values stretching back to the Garden of Eden—a community of individuals working to understand the value of each other as images of God, a community of individuals who believed in our own capacity to change ourselves and the world around us.

We can regain that. We *must* regain that. Our individual and communal happiness depends on us regaining the values we're losing all too quickly.

To do so will require boldness.

To do so will require sacrifice.

Perhaps the most polarizing and puzzling story in the Bible is the story of Abraham's binding of Isaac. It's a deceptively simple story: God tells Abraham to sacrifice his son, Abraham acquiesces without argument, Abraham takes Isaac to the top of a mountain to slaughter him, an angel intervenes and stops the killing, and Abraham substitutes a ram for Isaac rather than killing his son. But the story raises serious questions, obviously. Is God barbaric? Richard Dawkins says yes: "By the standards of modern morality, this disgraceful story is an example simultaneously of child abuse, bullying in two asymmetrical power relations, and the first recorded use of the Nuremberg defence: 'I was only obeying orders.'" Dawkins says that the story can't be an allegory for anything praiseworthy. And it can't teach anything moral: "what kind of morals could one derive from this appalling story?"[1]

And indeed, religious philosophers have argued over the meaning of this story for centuries. Kierkegaard suggested that Abraham's binding of Isaac represented the height of religious, personal faith over the ethical. Aquinas saw in Isaac a proto-Jesus figure.

But instead of questioning whether God was right or wrong in this scenario, or whether Abraham was right or wrong, let's focus instead on the request: to sacrifice one's child. Now, we know that Abraham has been willing to sacrifice himself in every way for God's honor: he has left his home in search of an unnamed place God has pledged to show him; he has separated from one of his wives, Hagar, and one of his sons, Ishmael, at God's behest; he has fought a war with kings; he has circumcised himself. But all of this amounts to a show of Abraham's commitment to his ideals.

Now God is asking Abraham to commit his own children to

his ideals—to consider putting his own son in danger of death for a higher purpose.

As a parent of two children, it's nearly impossible to imagine the horror with which Abraham must have greeted this commandment. Isn't it the job of every parent to keep their children safe from harm?

But in reality, this is what we are *all* asked to do, every day. We are asked to train our children to defend the good against the evil, the light against the darkness. Each day, we are asked to put our children in danger for the sake of a higher ideal. We may think that we are neutral participants in the world—and thanks to the sacrifices of our parents and grandparents, the cost of defending purposeful living has dropped dramatically. But make no mistake: we are still living in a fractious world, filled with people who target those who love individual freedom and Western virtue. That truth came home to us on 9/11; it is a truth that is convenient to forget.

What God asks of us, what our ancestors ask of us, and our civilization asks of us, is not only that we become defenders of valuable and eternal truths, but that we train our children to become defenders of those truths as well. Historically, this *has* meant putting our own children in direct danger. My own family history is replete with extended relatives murdered in Europe for their devotion to Judaism.

The easiest way to evade responsibility is to avoid teaching our children our values. If we merely let them choose their value system for themselves, we reason, then we put them in no danger; if we act as neutral arbiters, bubbling them off from the possibility of harm through vague shibboleths about tolerance (though we're never quite specific about just what we're willing to tolerate). We can leave our chosenness behind. In *Fiddler on the Roof*, Tevye complains, "I know, I know, we are Your chosen people. But once in a while, can't You choose someone else?"

The answer is obvious: we can opt out. All we have to do is stop teaching our children.

If we wish for our civilization to survive, however, we must be willing to teach our children. The only way to protect *their* children is to make warriors of our own children. We must make of our children messengers for the truths that *matter*. That comes with risk. And that is a risk we must be willing to take. As Ronald Reagan put it, "Freedom is never more than one generation away from extinction. We didn't pass it to our children in the bloodstream. It must be fought for, protected, and handed on for them to do the same, or one day we will spend our sunset years telling our children and our children's children what it was once like in the United States where men were free."[2]

My father is fond of saying that in life, there aren't six directions (east, west, north, south, up, and down). There are just two: forward and backward. Are we moving toward something, or away from it? Are we teaching our children to march forward, the banner of their civilization in hand, or to back slowly away from it, watching the shining city on the hill receding into the distance?

So, what do we teach our children? When I look at my four-year-old daughter and two-year-old son, what do I want them to know—what *must* they know to become defenders of the only civilization worth fighting for?

My wife and I will start by teaching our children four simple lessons.

1. Your Life Has Purpose. Life is not a bewildering, chaotic mess. It's a struggle, but it's a struggle *guided by a higher meaning*. You were designed to use your reason and your natural gifts—and to cultivate those assets toward fulfillment of a higher end. That end can be discovered by investigating the nature of the world, and by exploring the history of our civilization. That end includes defending the rights of the individual and the preciousness of individual lives; it includes acting with virtues including justice and mercy. It means restoring the foundations of your civilization, and building new and more beautiful structures atop those foundations. We care what you do; your long-dead ancestors care what you do; your children will care what you do; your God cares what you do.

2. You Can Do It. Forge forth and conquer. Build. Cultivate. You were given the ability to choose your path in life—and you were born into the freest civilization in the history of mankind. Make the most of it. You are not a victim. In a free society, you are responsible for your actions. Your successes are your accomplishments, but they are also the legacy of those who came before you and those who stand with you; your failures are purely your own. Look to your own house before blaming the society that bore you. And if society *is* acting to violate individual rights, it is your job to work to change it. You are a human being, made in the image of God, bound to the earth but with a soul that dreams of the eternal. There is no greater risk than that and no greater opportunity than that.

3. Your Civilization Is Unique. Recognize that what you have been given is unique in human history. Most human beings throughout time have lived in poverty and squalor, at serious risk of disease and death; most human beings throughout time have experienced more pure pain in their first few years than you will likely experience throughout your life. Most human beings have lived under the control of others, suffered tyranny and oppression. You have not. The freedom you enjoy, and morals in which you believe, are products of a unique civilization—the civilization of Dante and Shakespeare, the civilization of Bach and Beethoven, the civilization of the Bible and Aristotle. You did not create your freedoms or your definition of virtue, nor did they arise in a vacuum. Learn your history. Explore where the roots of your values lie: in Jerusalem and Athens. Be grateful for those roots. Then defend those roots, even as you grow to new heights.

　　4. We Are All Brothers and Sisters. We are not enemies if we share a common cause. And our common cause is a civilization replete with purpose, both communal and individual, a civilization that celebrates both individual and communal capacity. If we fight alongside one another rather than against one another, we are stronger. But we can only be stronger when we pull in the same direction, and when we share the same vision. We must share the same definition of liberty when it comes to politics, and, broadly speaking, the same definition of virtue when it comes to creating and maintaining social capital. As Abraham Lincoln said in his First Inaugural Address, "We are not enemies, but friends. We must not be enemies. Though passion may have strained it must not break our bonds of affection. The mystic chords of memory, stretching from every battlefield and patriot grave to every living heart and hearthstone all over this broad land, will yet swell the chorus of the Union, when again touched, as surely they will be, by the better angels of our nature."[3]

That's where our task starts. But that's not where it ends. As my daughter and son grow older, their questions will become harder. Good. That's what reason is designed to do: to question. And it will be our job to try to find answers for them, and to assure them that though we may not have all the answers, with effort, they can find answers that uphold the traditions of our history while exploring new horizons. We will teach our children that they stand on powerful, vital foundations built by hands not their own, and that they are protected by walls they, too, must defend. We will teach them that they must learn *why* the walls exist before tearing them down. We will say to them, as G. K. Chesterton did, "If you don't see the use of [that wall], I certainly won't let you clear it away. Go away and think. Then, when you can come back and tell me that you do see the use of it, I may allow you to destroy it."[4] We will do our best to teach them what made our civilization great—and what makes our civilization great still. It is our job to reconnect with both the word of God and with the philosophy of reason and individual liberty—two ideas that are, after all, inextricably intertwined.

I don't tend to be much of an emotional creature. But having kids changes that. One evening recently, at bedtime, my daughter turned to me and asked, "Daddy, will you always be my daddy?"

Surprised, I answered, "Of course, sweetheart."

"But," she clarified, "one day I'll be older. And *really* old people die. So will you still be there?"

I felt a catch in my throat—because, naturally, she's right. I don't like to think about death with regard to my own parents, let alone with respect to my children. And while I'm a believer in the afterlife, there's no real way to know. I don't know what comes after this. Nobody does.

I put my hand to her hair and stroked her head. "Yes, baby," I answered. "Mommy and I will always be there. We'll always be your mommy and daddy."

I turned out the light and left the room. Then I sat outside her door and thought about how much I loved her, and how one day she'd face all the tough questions we all face. And I thought about how I would answer those tough questions for myself: in the end, are we all orphans? Are we bound to lose all those we love, and live and die alone? Are we specks blinking in and out of existence, leaving no trace?

I don't think we are. I think that the history of Western civilization shows that our parents live on in us—that when we accept our past, when we learn the lessons they teach us, when we recognize their wisdom even as we develop our own, we become a link in the chain of history. Our parents never die so long as we keep the flame of their ideals alive, and pass that flame along to our children.

After I knew my daughter was asleep, I sneaked back into her room and kissed her head again. She was asleep; I know she probably didn't feel it. But maybe she did. And that maybe is all we can hope for, all we can strive for.

It is our job to carry on the tradition. It is our job to push the task forward.

If we do, then we will be truly deserving of God's blessing, and fit to proclaim liberty throughout all the land unto all the inhabitants thereof. We will choose life, so that we and our children may live.

ACKNOWLEDGMENTS

This book was the work of many years of thinking and just as many years of conversations about profound issues. All those conversations, discussions, and arguments have had an impact on my thinking—so I'd like to thank all my friends and opponents for helping me develop that thinking. As always, all faults or errors are mine and mine alone.

Thank you to my best friend, Jeremy Boreing, an unsung hero of the conservative movement who has been my partner in business and in the political foxhole. I can think of no one with whom I'd rather go into ideological battle. It's a privilege and a pleasure to do that every day.

Thank you to Caleb Robinson, the CEO of Forward Publishing, who helps steer the course with dignity and pragmatism. It's rare to find a man so dedicated to principle. I'm proud to be in business with him.

Thank you to Eric Nelson, editor of this book, who had to slog his way through this material several times and who helped me bring the starry sky down to earth—at least, as far as I was able.

Thank you to Frank Breeden, my agent, who understood that this was a passion project, and encouraged both the passion and the project.

Thank you to all the respected colleagues and thinkers who read the manuscript for this book and helped me improve it every step of the way, including Yoram Hazony, Yuval Levin, Matthew Continetti, John Podhoretz, Andrew Klavan, the execrable Michael Knowles, Rabbi David Wolpe, Eric Weinstein, David French, Dana Perino, and my friend and Talmudic study partner Rabbi Moshe Samuels. Their generosity has been unending.

Thank you to all the great folks I work with every day at Daily Wire, from our writers and editors to our producers. I simply couldn't do what I do without their incredible support—and they certainly have my gratitude.

Thank you to our broadcast partners at Westwood One, who have been groundbreaking in their approach to both the podcast and the radio show.

Thank you to our partners at Young America's Foundation, who help us bring our message to hundreds of thousands of young people on college campuses across America.

Thank you to my syndicators at Creators Syndicate, the editors of *National Review*, and the editors of *Newsweek*, all of whom allow me to reach readers across the political and cultural spectrum.

Most of all, thank you to all our listeners, watchers, readers, and social media followers: you inspire me to improve every day, and I hope to live up to your trust.

Finally, thank you to God, Creator of the heavens and the earth, Master of meaning and purpose, and Benevolent Father of human freedom.

Thank you.

NOTES

INTRODUCTION

1. "Achievements in Public Health, 1900–1999: Healthier Mothers and Babies," CDC.gov, October 1, 1999, https://www.cdc.gov/mmwr/preview/mmwrhtml/mm4838a2.htm.

2. "Exit polls," CNN.com, November 23, 2016, http://www.cnn.com/election/results/exit-polls.

3. Aaron Blake, "Nearly Half of Liberals Don't Even Like to Be around Trump Supporters," WashingtonPost.com, July 20, 2017, https://www.washingtonpost.com/news/the-fix/wp/2017/07/20/half-of-liberals-cant-even-stand-to-be-around-trump-supporters/?utm_term=.be6b213ac75c.

4. Clare Malone, "Americans Don't Trust Their Institutions Anymore," FiveThirtyEight.com, November 16, 2016, https://fivethirtyeight.com/features/americans-dont-trust-their-institutions-anymore/.

5. Jim Norman, "Americans' Confidence in Institutions Stays Low," Gallup.com, June 13, 2016, http://news.gallup.com/poll/192581/americans-confidence-institutions-stays-low.aspx.

6. Jeffrey M. Jones, "In U.S., Confidence in Police Lowest in 22 Years," Gallup.com, June 19, 2015, http://news.gallup.com/poll/183704/confidence-police-lowest-years.aspx?g_source=position2&g_medium=related&g_campaign=tiles.

7. Norman, "Americans' Confidence in Institutions Stays Low."

8. George Gao, "Americans Divided on How Much They Trust Their Neighbors," Pew Research, April 13, 2016, http://www.pewresearch.org/fact-tank/2016/04/13/americans-divided-on-how-much-they-trust-their-neighbors/.

9. Nathaniel Persily and Jon Cohen, "Americans Are Losing Faith in

Democracy—and in Each Other," WashingtonPost.com, October 14, 2016, https://www.washingtonpost.com/opinions/americans-are-losing-faith-in-democracy-and-in-each-other/2016/10/14/b35234ea-90c6-11e6-9c52-0b10449e33c4_story.html?utm_term=.4a67e7724901.

10. Josh Zumbrun, "Not Just the 1%: The Upper Middle Class Is Larger and Richer Than Ever," WSJ.com, June 21, 2016, https://blogs.wsj.com/economics/2016/06/21/not-just-the-1-the-upper-middle-class-is-larger-and-richer-than-ever/.

11. "Mobility, Measured," Economist.com, February 1, 2014, http://www.economist.com/news/united-states/21595437-america-no-less-socially-mobile-it-was-generation-ago-mobility-measured.

12. Ta-Nehisi Coates, "The Champion Barack Obama," TheAtlantic.com, January 31, 2014, https://www.theatlantic.com/politics/archive/2014/01/the-champion-barack-obama/283458/.

13. Ta-Nehisi Coates, "The First White President," Atlantic, October 2017, https://www.theatlantic.com/magazine/archive/2017/10/the-first-white-president-ta-nehisi-coates/537909/.

14. Ta-Nehisi Coates, Between the World and Me (New York: Spiegel and Grau ,2015), 111.

15. Thomas Chatterton Williams, "How Ta-Nehisi Coates Gives Whiteness Power," New York Times, October 6, 2017, https://www.nytimes.com/2017/10/06/opinion/ta-nehisi-coates-whiteness-power.html?smid=tw-share&_r=1&mtrref=www.nationalreview.com&assetType=opinion.

16. Frank Newport, "In US, 87% Approve of Black-White Intermarriage, vs. 4% in 1958," Gallup.com, July 25, 2013, http://news.gallup.com/poll/163697/approve-marriage-blacks-whites.aspx.

17. "Race Relations," Gallup.com, http://news.gallup.com/poll/1687/race-relations.aspx.

18. Mostafa El-Bermawy, "Your Filter Bubble Is Destroying Democracy," Wired.com, November 18, 2016, https://www.wired.com/2016/11/filter-bubble-destroying-democracy/.

19. Levi Boxell, Matthew Gentzkow, and Jesse M. Shapiro, "Is the Internet Causing Political Polarization? Evidence from Demographics," Brown.edu, March 2017, https://www.brown.edu/Research/Shapiro/pdfs/age-polars.pdf.

20. Jonah Engel Bromwich, "Social Media Is Not Contributing Significantly to Political Polarization, Paper Says," NYTimes.com, April 13, 2017, https://www.nytimes.com/2017/04/13/us/political-polarization-internet.html?mtrref=www.google.com.

21. Jonah Goldberg, The Suicide of the West (New York: Crown Forum, 2018), 8.

22. Steven Pinker, Enlightenment Now: The Case for Reason, Science, Humanism, and Progress (New York: Penguin Random House, 2018).

23. ADL's Task Force on Harassment and Journalism, *Anti-Semitic Targeting of Journalists during the 2016 Presidential Campaign*, ADL.org, October 19, 2016, https://www.adl.org/sites/default/files/documents/assets/pdf/press-center /CR_4862_Journalism-Task-Force_v2.pdf.

CHAPTER 1: THE PURSUIT OF HAPPINESS

1. William Kristol, "It's All about Him," *New York Times*, February 25, 2008, http://www.nytimes.com/2008/02/25/opinion/25kristol.html.

2. Eli Stokols, "Unapologetic, Trump Promises to Make America Rich," Politico.com, May 26, 2016, http://www.politico.com/story/2016/05/ unapologetic-trump-promises-to-make-america-rich-223632.

3. Dana Milbank, "Americans' Optimism Is Dying," *Washington Post*, August 12, 2014, https://www.washingtonpost.com/opinions/dana-milbank -americans-optimism-is-dying/2014/08/12/f81808d8-224c-11e4-8593 -da634b334390_story.html?utm_term=.5f205324fd19.

4. Shira Schoenberg, "Poll: Young Americans Fearful about Future of America, Overwhelmingly Support Hillary Clinton," MassLive.com, October 26, 2016, http://www.masslive.com/politics/index.ssf/2016/10/young _americans_fearful_about.html.

5. "US Suicide Rate Surges, Particularly among White People," BBC.com, April 22, 2016, http://www.bbc.com/news/world-us-canada-36116166.

6. Ecclesiastes 2:1 (Torah Mitzion).

7. Deuteronomy 28:47–48 (NIV).

8. Ecclesiastes 3:22 (NIV).

9. Ethics of the Fathers 2:15.

10. Aristotle, *Nicomachean Ethics* 1101a.

11. George Washington, Letter to the Protestant Episcopal Church, August 19, 1789, https://founders.archives.gov/documents/Washington/05-03-02-0289.

12. Charles Krauthammer, "A Note to Readers," *Washington Post*, June 8, 2018.

13. Viktor Frankl, *Man's Search for Meaning* (Boston: Beacon Press, 2017), 80 (emphasis mine).

14. Steve Taylor, PhD, "A Sense of Purpose Means a Longer Life," PsychologyToday.com, November 12, 2014, https://www.psychologytoday.com/ blog/out-the-darkness/201411/sense-purpose-means-longer-life.

15. Dhruv Khullar, MD, "Finding Purpose for a Good Life. But Also a Healthy One," *New York Times*, January 1, 2018, https://www.nytimes .com/2018/01/01/upshot/finding-purpose-for-a-good-life-but-also-a -healthy-one.html?smid=tw-nytimes&smtyp=cur.

16. Psalms 8:5 (NIV).

17. "George Washington's Rules of Civility," NPR.org, May 11, 2003, http:// www.npr.org/templates/story/story.php?storyId=1248919.

18. Brett and Kate McKay, "The Virtuous Life: Wrap Up," ArtOfManliness

.com, June 1, 2008, http://www.artofmanliness.com/2008/06/01/the-virtuous-life-wrap-up/.

19. Frankl, *Man's Search for Meaning*, 69.

20. *Seneca's Letters*, Book II, Letter XLVIII.

21. Ecclesiastes 4:9–10.

22. Jonathan Haidt, *The Happiness Hypothesis: Finding Modern Truth in Ancient Wisdom* (New York: Basic Books, 2006), 133.

23. Liz Mineo, "Good Genes Are Nice, but Joy Is Better," *Harvard Gazette*, April 11, 2017, https://news.harvard.edu/gazette/story/2017/04/over-nearly-80-years-harvard-study-has-been-showing-how-to-live-a-healthy-and-happy-life/.

24. "Political Scientist: Does Diversity Really Work?," NPR.org, August 15, 2007, http://www.npr.org/templates/story/story.php?storyId=12802663.

25. From John Adams to Massachusetts Militia, October 11, 1798, https://founders.archives.gov/documents/Adams/99-02-02-3102.

CHAPTER 2: FROM THE MOUNTAINTOP

1. H. W. F. Saggs, *Civilization before Greece and Rome* (New Haven, CT: Yale University Press, 1989), 268.

2. Jordan B. Peterson, *Maps of Meaning: The Architecture of Belief* (New York: Routledge, 1999).

3. Jonathan Sacks, "The Wilderness and the Word," RabbiSacks.org, May 31, 2008, http://rabbisacks.org/covenant-conversation-5768-bemidbar-the-wilderness-and-the-word-2/.

4. Tammi J. Schneider, *An Introduction to Ancient Mesopotamian Religion* (Grand Rapids, MI: William B. Eerdmans, 2011), 103.

5. Exodus 20:2–3 (NIV).

6. Exodus 33:19–20 (NIV).

7. Deuteronomy 32:4 (NIV).

8. Talmud Bavli, Bava Metzia 59b.

9. Deuteronomy 12:2–3.

10. Saggs, *Civilization before Greece and Rome*, 268.

11. Leviticus 11:45.

12. Talmud Bavli, Eruvin 100b.

13. Gerald A. Press, *The Development of the Idea of History in Antiquity* (Kingston, ON: McGill-Queen's University Press, 1982), 7.

14. Albert Kirk Grayson, *Babylonian Historical-Literary Texts* (Toronto, ON: University of Toronto Press, 1975).

15. Arnold Krupat, *Ethnocriticism: Ethnography, History, Literature* (Berkeley: University of California Press, 1992), 38.

16. Masao Abe, *Buddhism and Interfaith Dialogue* (Houndmills, Basingstoke, England: Macmillan, 1995), 60.

17. Genesis 9:13–15.

18. Deuteronomy 4:34 (NIV).

19. Paul Johnson, *A History of the Jews* (New York: Harper & Row, 1987), 2.

20. Virginia Schomp, *The Ancient Egyptians* (New York: Marshall Cavendish, 2008), 41.

21. "Religion and Power: Divine Kingship in the Ancient World and Beyond," Uchicago.edu, February 23–24, 2007, https://oi.uchicago.edu/research/symposia /religion-and-power-divine-kingship-ancient-world-and-beyond-0.

22. "The Code of Hammurabi," http://avalon.law.yale.edu/ancient/ham-frame.asp.

23. Genesis 6:2–3.

24. Genesis 4:6–7.

25. Deuteronomy 30:15–20 (NIV).

26. Exodus 24:7.

27. Ecclesiastes 12:13

28. Ecclesiastes 3:12, 22

29. Exodus 32:12–13.

30. Genesis 12:3.

31. Richard Tarnas, *The Passion of the Western Mind* (New York: Ballantine Books, 1991), 99.

32. Matt Lewis, "Obama Loves Martin Luther King's Great Quote—But He Uses It Incorrectly," TheDailyBeast.com, January 16, 2017, https://www .thedailybeast.com/obama-loves-martin-luther-kings-great-quotebut-he -uses-it-incorrectly.

33. Deuteronomy 17:14–20.

34. Judges 8:23.

35. 1 Samuel 8:10–18.

CHAPTER 3: FROM THE DUST

1. Daniel Walker Howe, "Classical Education in America," *Wilson Quarterly*, Spring 2011, https://wilsonquarterly.com/quarterly/spring-2011-the-city -bounces-back-four-portraits/classical-education-in-america/.

2. Ashley Thorne, "The Drive to Put Western Civ Back in the College Curriculum," *New York Post*, March 29, 2016, https://nypost.com/2016/03/29 /the-drive-to-put-western-civ-back-in-the-college-curriculum/.

3. Edward W. Said, *Orientalism* (New York: Vintage Books, 1979).

4. Charlotte Allen, "Confucius and the Scholars," TheAtlantic.com, April 1999, https://www.theatlantic.com/magazine/archive/1999/04/confucius -and-the-scholars/377530/.

5. Chris Bodenner, "The Surprising Revolt at the Most Liberal College in the Country," TheAtlantic.com, November 2, 2017, https://www.theatlantic .com/education/archive/2017/11/the-surprising-revolt-at-reed/544682/.

6. Walter Kerr, *Tragedy and Comedy* (New York: Da Capo Press, 1985), 146.

7. Plato, *The Republic* (New York: Basic Books, 1968), 514a–520a.

8. W. K. C. Guthrie, *A History of Greek Philosophy* (Cambridge: Cambridge University Press, 1965), 415.

9. Plato, *The Republic*, 353c–353e.

10. Guthrie, *A History of Greek Philosophy*, 415.

11. Aristotle, *Nichomachean Ethics* (Chicago: University of Chicago Press, 2011), 1098a.

12. Jonathan Haidt, *The Happiness Hypothesis: Finding Modern Truth in Ancient Wisdom* (New York: Basic Books, 2006), 163–65.

13. Leo Strauss, *Natural Right and History* (Chicago: University of Chicago Press, 1953), 162.

14. Richard Tarnas, *The Passion of the Western Mind* (New York: Ballantine Books, 1991), 47.

15. Ibid., 46.

16. Alasdair MacIntyre, *After Virtue* (Notre Dame, IN: University of Notre Dame Press, 2007), 135.

17. Will Durant, *The Story of Philosophy* (New York: Pocket Books, 1926), 39.

18. Plato, *The Republic*, 473c–d.

19. Karl Popper, *The Open Society and Its Enemies* (Princeton, NJ: Princeton University Press, 1994), 85–87 (italics in original).

20. Matthew J. Franck, "Fr. Barron and Prof. Popper—and Popper's Critics," FirstThings.com, June 20, 2013, https://www.firstthings.com/blogs/first-thoughts/2013/06/fr-barron-and-prof-popper-and-poppers-critics.

21. Aristotle, *Politics of Aristotle*, trans. Benjamin Jowett (New York: Colonial Press, 1899), Book II, Chapter V, http://classics.mit.edu/Aristotle/politics.2.two.html.

22. Cicero, *De Re Publica* (Cambridge, MA: Loeb Classical Library, Harvard University Press, 2000), 211.

23. Ibid., 203.

24. Mogens Herman Hansen, "Democratic Freedom and the Concept of Freedom in Plato and Aristotle," *Greek, Roman, and Byzantine Studies* 50 (2010): 1–27.

CHAPTER 4: COMING TOGETHER

1. Naomi Pasachoff and Robert J. Littman, *A Concise History of the Jewish People* (Lanham, MD: Rowman & Littlefield, 2005), 67.

2. Jonathan Sacks, *The Great Partnership: Science, Religion, and the Search for Meaning* (New York: Schocken Books, 2011), 83.

3. Richard Tarnas, *The Passion of the Western Mind* (New York: Ballantine Books, 1991), 103.

4. Romans 10:4–13 (NIV).

5. Linda Zagzebski and Timothy D. Miller, eds., *Readings in Philosophy of Religion* (Hoboken, NJ: Blackwell, 1999), 488.

6. Johannes Quasten, Walter Burghardt, and Thomas Lawler, eds., *Ancient*

Christian Writers: The Works of the Fathers in Translation (Mahwah, NJ: Paulist Press, 1982), 59.

7. Ernest L. Fortin, "St. Augustine," in *History of Political Philosophy*, 3rd ed., ed. Leo Strauss and Joseph Crowley (Chicago: University of Chicago Press, 1987), 196.

8. St. Augustine, *The City of God*, trans. William Babcock (New York: New City Press, 2012), 55.

9. St. Augustine, *The Letters of St. Augustine*, trans. J. G. Cunningham (Loschberg, Germany: Jazzybee Verlag, 2015), 180.

10. Rodney Stark, *The Rise of Christianity: A Sociologist Reconsiders History* (Princeton, NJ: Princeton University Press, 1996), 5–6.

11. Ibid., 83–84.

12. Karen Osman, *The Italian Renaissance* (New York: Lucent Books, 1996), 20.

13. Andrew Fleming West, "The Seven Liberal Arts," in *Alcuin and the Rise of the Christian Schools* (New York: Charles Scribner's Sons, 1912), http://classicalsubjects.com/resources/TheSevenLiberalArts.pdf.

14. Rodney Stark, *How the West Won: The Neglected Story of the Triumph of Modernity* (Wilmington, DE: ISI Books, 2014).

15. Ibid., 124–36.

16. Tarnas, *The Passion of the Western Mind*, 175.

17. Thomas E. Woods Jr., "The Catholic Church and the Creation of the University," LewRockwell.com, May 16, 2005, https://www.catholiceducation.org/en/education/catholic-contributions/the-catholic-church-and-the-creation-of-the-university.html.

18. Michael W. Tkacz, "St. Augustine's Appropriation and Transformation of Aristotelian *Eudaimonia*," in *The Reception of Aristotle's Ethics*, ed. Jon Miller (Cambridge: Cambridge University Press, 2012), 67.

19. Thomas P. Rausch, *Reconciling Faith and Reason: Apologists, Evangelists, and Theologians in a Divided Church* (Collegeville, MN: Liturgical Press, 2000), 12.

20. Edward Feser, *The Last Superstition* (South Bend, IN: St. Augustine's Press, 2008), 91–96.

21. St. Thomas Aquinas, *Summa Theologica*, vol. 1, 418.

22. Edward Feser, *Aquinas: A Beginner's Guide* (Oxford, UK: Oneworld, 2009), 39.

23. Fortin, "St. Thomas Aquinas," in *History of Political Philosophy*, 252.

24. Stark, *How the West Won*, 170.

25. Peter Karl Koritansky, *Thomas Aquinas and the Philosophy of Punishment* (Washington, DC: Catholic University of America Press, 2012), 81–86.

CHAPTER 5: ENDOWED BY THEIR CREATORS

1. Rodney Stark, *How the West Won: The Neglected Story of the Triumph of Modernity* (Wilmington, DE: ISI Books, 2014), 175–77.

2. Steph Solis, "Copernicus and the Church: What the History Books Don't Say," CSMonitor.com, February 19, 2013, https://www.csmonitor.com/Technology /2013/0219/Copernicus-and-the-Church-What-the-history-books-don-t-say.

3. Joseph-Nicolas Robert-Fleury, "Vatican Admits Galileo Was Right," NewScientist.com, November 7, 1992, https://www.newscientist.com/article /mg13618460.600-vatican-admits-galileo-was-right-/.

4. Del Ratzsch, "The Religious Roots of Science," in Melville Y. Stewart, *Science and Religion in Dialogue*, vol. 1 (Hoboken, NJ: Wiley-Blackwell 2009), 59.

5. Stark, *How the West Won*, 317.

6. Ratzsch, "The Religious Roots of Science," 59.

7. Isaac Newton, Keynes Ms. 7, King's College, Cambridge UK, http:// www.newtonproject.ox.ac.uk/view/texts/normalized/THEM00007.

8. Will Durant, *The Story of Philosophy* (New York: Pocket Books, 1926), 129.

9. B. H. G. Wormald, *Francis Bacon: History, Politics & Science* (Cambridge: Cambridge University Press, 1993), 262.

10. Durant, *The Story of Philosophy*, 122.

11. Francis Bacon, "Atheism," in *Lord Bacon's Essays*, ed. James R. Boyed (New York and Chicago: A. S. Barnes, 1867), 133.

12. Francis Bacon, *Novum Organum*, ed. Joseph Devey (New York: P. F. Collier, 1902; originally published 1620), CXXIX, http://oll.libertyfund.org /titles/bacon-novum-organum.

13. Richard Kennington, "René Descartes," in *History of Political Philosophy*, 3rd ed., ed. Leo Strauss and Joseph Crowley (Chicago: University of Chicago Press, 1987), 422.

14. René Descartes, *Discourse on Method* (Harvard Classics, 1909–1914), part IV, http://www.bartleby.com/34/1/4.html.

15. Annabel Brett, "Introduction," in Marsilius of Padua, *The Defender of the Peace*, trans. Annabel Brett (Cambridge, MA: Cambridge University Press, 2005).

16. Niccolò Machiavelli, *The Prince*, trans. W. K. Marriott (Italy, 1532; Project Gutenberg, 2006), https://www.gutenberg.org/files/1232/1232-h/1232-h.htm.

17. Niccolò Machiavelli, *Discourses on Livy*, trans. Julia Conaway Bondanella and Peter Bondanella (New York: Oxford University Press, 1997).

18. Joseph Loconte, "How Martin Luther Advanced Freedom," *Wall Street Journal*, October 26, 2017.

19. Duncan B. Forrester, "Martin Luther and John Calvin," in *History of Political Philosophy*, 335.

20. Richard H. Cox, "Hugo Grotius," in *History of Political Philosophy*, 389.

21. David Novak, *Natural Law in Judaism* (Cambridge: Cambridge University Press, 1998), 156.

22. Thomas Hobbes, *Leviathan* (Oxford, UK: Clarendon Press, 1947; reprinted from the 1651 ed.), 47.

23. Laurence Berns, "Thomas Hobbes," in *History of Political Philosophy*, 396–419.

24. John Locke, *Two Treatises of Government*, 3rd ed. (New York: Cambridge University Press, 1988), Book 1, Sec. 30.

25. Ibid., Book 2, Sec. 57.

26. Ibid., Book 2, Sec. 222.

27. Adam Smith, *An Inquiry into the Nature and Causes of the Wealth of Nations* (London: Methuen, 1776), Book IV, Chapter 9, Sec. 50.

28. Thomas Jefferson, "To Henry Lee," May 8, 1825, in *The Works of Thomas Jefferson*, ed. Paul Leicester Ford, vol. 10, *Federal Edition* (New York: G. P. Putnam's Sons, 1904–1905), 342–43.

29. Michael Pakaluk, "Aristotle, Natural Law, and the Founders," NLNRAC .org, http://www.nlnrac.org/classical/aristotle#_ednref3.

30. Pauline Maier, "The Strange History of 'All Men Are Created Equal,'" *Washington and Lee Law Review* 56, no. 3 (June 1, 1999): 873–88, https://scholarlycommons.law.wlu.edu/cgi/viewcontent.cgi?article=1547&context =wlulr.

31. Thomas G. West, *The Political Theory of the American Founding* (Cambridge: Cambridge University Press, 2017), 30–31.

32. John Locke, *An Essay Concerning Human Understanding* (London: William Tegg, 1849), 168–69.

33. Harry V. Jaffa, "Aristotle and Locke in the American Founding," *Claremont Review of Books* 1, no. 2 (Winter 2001), http://www.claremont.org/crb/article/aristotle-and-locke-in-the-american-founding/.

34. "From John Adams to Massachusetts Militia, October 11, 1798," https://founders.archives.gov/documents/Adams/99-02-02-3102.

35. George Washington, "First Inaugural Address," April 30, 1789, https://www.archives.gov/exhibits/american_originals/inaugtxt.html.

36. Thomas Jefferson, "A Bill for Establishing Religious Freedom, 18 June 1779," https://founders.archives.gov/documents/Jefferson/01-02-02-0132-0004-0082.

37. John Adams, *The Works of John Adams*, vol. 6 (Boston: Charles C. Little and James Brown, 1851), 448, 519.

38. Thomas Jefferson, Letter to James Madison, 27 April 1809, https://founders.archives.gov/documents/Jefferson/03-01-02-0140.

39. Alexis de Tocqueville, "On the Use that the Americans Make of Association in Civil Life," in *Democracy in America*, ed. and trans. Harvey Mansfield and Delba Winthrop (Chicago: University of Chicago Press, 2000), http://www.press.uchicago.edu/Misc/Chicago/805328.html.

40. James Madison, *Federalist No. 51*, The Avalon Project, http://avalon.law .yale.edu/18th_century/fed51.asp.

41. Peter C. Myers, "Frederick Douglass's America: Race, Justice, and the Promise of the Founding," Heritage.org, January 11, 2011, https://www .heritage.org/political-process/report/frederick-douglasss-america-race -justice-and-the-promise-the-founding.

42. Ibid.

CHAPTER 6: KILLING PURPOSE, KILLING CAPACITY

1. Niccolò Machiavelli, *The Prince*, trans. W. K. Marriott (Italy, 1532; Project Gutenberg, 2006), https://www.gutenberg.org/files/1232/1232-h/1232-h.htm.

2. Harvey C. Mansfield, *Machiavelli's Virtue* (Chicago: University of Chicago Press, 1966), 11.

3. Thomas Hobbes, *Leviathan* (Oxford, UK: Clarendon Press, 1947; reprinted from the 1651 ed.), 196–97.

4. Ibid., 47.

5. Ibid., 63.

6. Will Durant, *The Story of Philosophy* (New York: Pocket Books, 1926), 152.

7. Baruch Spinoza, *Spinoza: Complete Works*, ed. Michael L. Morgan, trans. Samuel Shirley (Indianapolis, IN: Hackett, 2002), 504.

8. Ibid., 456.

9. Durant, *The Story of Philosophy*, 175–76.

10. Ibid., 189–96.

11. Voltaire, *A Philosophical Dictionary, from the French*, vol. 3 (London: John and Henry L. Hunt, 1824), 155–56.

12. Voltaire, *The Works of Voltaire: A Philosophical Dictionary*, vol. 12 (Paris: E. R. DuMont, 1901), 18.

13. Graham Gargett, "Voltaire and the Bible," in *The Cambridge Companion to Voltaire*, ed. Nicholas Cronk (New York: Cambridge University Press, 2009), 196–99.

14. Voltaire, *Candide or Optimism*, ed. and trans. Theo Cuffe (New York: Penguin Books, 2005), 4.

15. Voltaire, "The Nature of Pleasure," in John Morley, ed., *The Works of Voltaire: A Contemporary Version*, trans. William F. Fleming, vol. 10 (New York: E. R. DuMont, 1901), 243–44.

16. Immanuel Kant, "What Is Enlightenment?," trans. Mary C. Smith, http://www.columbia.edu/acis/ets/CCREAD/etscc/kant.html.

17. *The Cambridge Companion to Kant*, ed. Paul Guyer (Cambridge: Cambridge University Press, 1992), 1.

18. Durant, *The Story of Philosophy*, 265–77.

19. Immanuel Kant, *Grounding for the Metaphysics of Morals*, trans. James W. Ellington (Indianapolis, IN: Hackett, 1994), 2:421.

20. Ross Harrison, "Bentham," in *The Philosophers: Introducing Great Western Thinkers*, ed. Ted Honderich (New York: Oxford University Press, 1999), 128.

21. Vickie B. Sullivan, *Machiavelli, Hobbes, & the Formation of a Liberal Republicanism in England* (Cambridge: Cambridge University Press, 2004), 93–95.

22. Richard Kennington, "René Descartes," in *History of Political Philosophy*, 3rd ed., ed. Leo Strauss and Joseph Crowley (Chicago: University of Chicago Press, 1987), 421–39.

23. Benedict de Spinoza, *On the Improvement of the Understanding/The Ethics/Correspondence*, trans. R. H. M. Elwes (New York: Dover, 1955), 390.

24. David Hume, "Moral Distinctions Not Derived from Reason," in *Ethical Theory: An Anthology*, ed. Russ Shafer-Landau (Hoboken, NJ: Wiley-Blackwell, 2012), 10–11.

25. Mary Ann Glendon, *The Forum and the Tower: How Scholars and Politicians Have Imagined the World, from Plato to Eleanor Roosevelt* (New York: Oxford University Press, 2011), 122.

26. Daniel C. Dennett, *Darwin's Dangerous Idea* (New York: Simon & Schuster Paperbacks, 1995), 521.

27. Jason Farago, "Who's Afraid of the Marquis de Sade?," BBC.com, October 6, 2014, http://www.bbc.com/culture/story/20141006-marquis-de-sade-still-shocking.

28. Fyodor Dostoyevsky, *The Brothers Karamazov*, trans. Constance Garnett (New York: Barnes & Noble Classics, 2004), 234–40.

29. Fyodor Dostoyevsky, *Notes from the Underground* (Ebook).

30. Friedrich Nietzsche, *The Complete Works of Friedrich Nietzsche*, vol. 11: *Thus Spake Zarathustra*, ed. Oscar Levy (New York: Macmillan, 1911), 335.

31. Ibid., 146.

32. Ibid., 351.

CHAPTER 7: THE REMAKING OF THE WORLD

1. Phillip Nicholas Furbank, *Diderot: A Critical Biography* (London: Faber and Faber, 2011), 354.

2. Jonah Goldberg, *The Suicide of the West* (New York: Crown Forum, 2018), 153.

3. Thomas Carlyle, *The French Revolution: A History* (London: Chapman and Hall, 1857), 300.

4. Mona Ozouf, *Festivals and the French Revolution* (Cambridge, MA: Harvard University Press, 1988), 98.

5. Ibid., 28.

6. "February 5, 1794 (17 Pluviose, An II): Robespierre's Report on the Principles of Political Morality," in *The French Revolution*, ed. Paul H. Beik (New York: Harper & Row, 1970), 280–83.

7. Jessica Riskin, *The Restless Clock* (Chicago: University of Chicago Press, 2016), 160.

8. Lester G. Crocker, *Diderot's Chaotic Order* (Princeton, NJ: Princeton University Press, 1974), 100.

9. "Declaration of the Rights of Man—1789," The Avalon Project, http://avalon.law.yale.edu/18th_century/rightsof.asp.

10. Raymond Jonas, *France and the Cult of the Sacred Heart* (Berkeley: University of California Press, 2000), 74.

11. David P. Jordan, *The Revolutionary Career of Maximilien Robespierre* (Chicago: University of Chicago Press, 1989), 33.

12. James Miller, *Rousseau: Dreamer of Democracy* (New Haven, CT: Yale University Press, 1984), 163–64.

13. Edmund Burke, *Reflections on the Revolution in France* (New York: Oxford University Press, 1999), 8–9.

14. Ibid., 79–80.

15. Russell Kirk, *The Conservative Mind* (Chicago: Regnery Books, 1986), 29.

16. William Rogers Brubaker, "The French Revolution and the Invention of Citizenship," *French Politics and Society* 7, no. 3 (Summer 1989): 30–49, https://www.sscnet.ucla.edu/soc/faculty/brubaker/Publications/04_The_French_Revolution_and_the_Invention_of_Citizenship.pdf.

17. Alan Forrest, "L'armée de l'an II: la levée en masse et la création d'un mythe républicain," August 23, 1793, http://journals.openedition.org/ahrf/1385#bodyftn15.

18. Donald Stoker, *Clausewitz* (New York: Oxford University Press, 2014), 19.

19. Yoram Hazony, *The Virtue of Nationalism* (New York: Hachette Book Group, 2018), 24–25.

20. Goldberg, *The Suicide of the West*, 313.

21. Pierre Hasner, "Georg W. F. Hegel," in *History of Political Philosophy*, 3rd ed., ed. Leo Strauss and Joseph Crowley (Chicago: University of Chicago Press, 1987), 733–58.

22. Harrison Fluss, "Hegel on Bastille Day," *Jacobin*, July 14, 2016, https://www.jacobinmag.com/2016/07/hegel-bastille-day-burke-french-revolution.

23. Sean Monahan, "Reading Paine from the Left," Jacobinmag.com, March 6, 2015, https://www.jacobinmag.com/2015/03/thomas-paine-american-revolution-common-sense/.

24. Henry Heller, "Marx, the French Revolution, and the Spectre of the Bourgeoisie," *Science and Society* 74, no. 2 (April 2010): 184–214.

25. Jon Elster, *Making Sense of Marx* (New York: Cambridge University Press, 1985), 168.

26. Karl Marx and Friedrich Engels, *The Communist Manifesto* (Chicago: Haymarket Books, 2005), 152.

27. Karl Marx, *The German Ideology* (Moscow, 1932; Marxist Internet Archive, accessed 2018), https://www.marxists.org/archive/marx/works/1845/german-ideology/ch01d.htm. Written in 1845.

28. Marx and Engels, *The Communist Manifesto*, 67–68.

29. Karl Marx, *Critique of Hegel's "Philosophy of Right"* (Cambridge: Cambridge University Press, 1970), 131.

30. Marx and Engels, *The Communist Manifesto*, 71.

31. Peter McPhee, ed., *A Companion to the French Revolution*, (Malden, MA: John Wiley & Sons, 2013), 346–47.

32. Carl K. Y. Shaw, "Hegel's Theory of Modern Bureaucracy," *The American Political Science Review* 86, no. 2 (June 1992): 381–89.

33. Martin Slattery, *Key Ideas in Sociology* (Cheltenham, UK: Nelson Thornes, 2003), 28.

34. Mary Pickering, *Auguste Comte: An Intellectual Biography*, vol. 1 (New York: Cambridge University Press, 1992), 187–88.

35. Robert Horwitz, "John Dewey," in *History of Political Philosophy*, 851–69.

36. Ronald J. Pestritto, "Progressivism and America's Tradition of Natural Law and Natural Rights," NLNRAC.org, http://www.nlnrac.org/critics/american-progressivism#_edn1.

37. John R. Shook and James A. Good, *John Dewey's Philosophy of Spirit, with the 1897 Lecture on Hegel* (New York: Fordham University Press, 2010), 29.

38. Ronald J. Pestritto, *Woodrow Wilson and the Roots of Modern Liberalism* (Lanham, MD: Rowman & Littlefield, 2005).

39. As quoted in Ronald J. Pestritto, "Woodrow Wilson and the Rejection of the Founders' Principles," Hillsdale.edu, https://online.hillsdale.edu/document.doc?id=313.

40. *Woodrow Wilson: The Essential Political Writings*, ed. Ronald J. Pestritto (Lanham, MD: Rowman & Littlefield, 2005), 184.

41. Manuel Borutta, "Enemies at the Gate: The Moabit Klostersturm and the Kulturkampf: Germany," in *Culture Wars: Secular-Catholic Conflict in Nineteenth-Century Europe*, ed. Christopher Clark and Wolfram Kaiser (New York: Cambridge University Press, 2003), 227.

42. Woodrow Wilson, "The Study of Administration," *Political Science Quarterly* 2, no. 2 (June 1887): 197–222, http://www.iupui.edu/~spea1/V502/Orosz/Units/Sections/u1s5/Woodrow_Wilson_Study_of_Administration_1887_jstor.pdf.

43. Richard Wagner, "Judaism in Music," trans. William Ashton Ellis, in *Sämtliche Schriften und Dichtungen*, vol. 5, pp. 66–85, http://jrbooksonline.com/PDF_Books/JudaismInMusic.pdf.

44. Isabel V. Hull, *The Entourage of Kaiser Wilhelm II: 1888–1918* (Cambridge: Cambridge University Press, 1982), 74.

45. Ian Kershaw, *Hitler: 1889–1936* (New York: W. W. Norton, 1998), 43, 135.

46. Yvonne Sherratt, *Hitler's Philosophers* (New Haven, CT: Yale University Press, 2013), 120–21.

47. George Orwell, *Orwell*, vol. 2: *My Country Right or Left, 1940–1943*, ed. Sonia Orwell and Ian Angus (Boston: Nonpareil Books, 1968), 14.

48. Karl Marx, "The Victory of the Counter-Revolution in Vienna," trans. Marx-Engels Institute, *Neue Rheinische Zeitung No. 136*, November 1848, https://www.marxists.org/archive/marx/works/1848/11/06.htm.

49. Marx and Engels, *The Communist Manifesto*, 89.

50. V. I. Lenin, "The State and Revolution," in *Princeton Readings in Political Thought*, ed. Mitchell Cohen and Nicole Fermon (Princeton, NJ: Princeton University Press, 1996), 541.

51. Richard Pipes, *The Russian Revolution* (New York: Vintage Books, 1990), 820.

52. Anne Applebaum, *Red Famine: Stalin's War on Ukraine* (New York: Doubleday, 2017).

53. Lee Edwards, "The Legacy of Mao Zedong Is Mass Murder," Heritage.org, February 2, 2010, https://www.heritage.org/asia/commentary/the-legacy -mao-zedong-mass-murder.

54. Jacques Steinberg, "Times Should Lose Pulitzer from 30's, Consultant Says," NYTimes.com, October 23, 2003, https://www.nytimes.com/2003/10/23/us /times-should-lose-pulitzer-from-30-s-consultant-says.html.

55. Jonah Goldberg, *Liberal Fascism: The Secret History of the American Left, from Mussolini to the Politics of Change* (New York: Crown Forum, 2009), 102–3.

56. Ben Shapiro, "NYT Op-Ed: 'For All Its Flaws, the Communist Revolution Taught Chinese Women to Dream Big," DailyWire.com, September 26, 2017, https://www.dailywire.com/news/21547/nyt-op-ed-all-its-flaws-communist -revolution-ben-shapiro.

57. Thomas L. Friedman, "Our One-Party Democracy," *New York Times*, September 8, 2009, https://www.nytimes.com/2009/09/09/opinion/09friedman .html.

58. David Filipov, "For Russians, Stalin Is the 'Most Outstanding' Figure in World History, Followed by Putin," WashingtonPost.com, June 26, 2017, https://www.washingtonpost.com/news/worldviews/wp/2017/06/26/for -russians-stalin-is-the-most-outstanding-figure-in-world-history-putin-is -next/?noredirect=on&utm_term=.279839e59134.

59. Svetlana Alexievich, *Secondhand Time: The Last of the Soviets* (New York: Random House, 2017), 176–86.

60. Meg Sullivan, "FDR's Policies Prolonged Depression by 7 Years, UCLA Economists Calculate," UCLA.edu, August 10, 2004, http://newsroom.ucla .edu/releases/FDR-s-Policies-Prolonged-Depression-5409.

61. Burton Folsom, *New Deal or Raw Deal?: How FDR's Economic Legacy Has Damaged America* (New York: Threshold Editions, 2008), 105.

62. Sullivan, "FDR's Policies Prolonged Depression by 7 years, UCLA Economists Calculate."

63. Thomas C. Leonard, *Illiberal Reformers: Race, Eugenics and American Economics in the Progressive Era* (Princeton, NJ: Princeton University Press, 2016), xiii.

64. "T. Roosevelt Letter to C. Davenport about 'Degenerates Reproducing,'" DNA Learning Center, January 3, 1913, https://www.dnalc.org/view/11219 -T-Roosevelt-letter-to-C-Davenport-about-degenerates-reproducing-.html.

65. Paul Rahe, "Progressive Racism," NationalReview.com, April 11, 2013, https://www.nationalreview.com/2013/04/progressive-racism-paul-rahe/.

66. *Buck v. Bell* (1927), 274 US 200.

67. Edward J. Larson, *Sex, Race, and Science* (Baltimore: Johns Hopkins University Press, 1996), 28.

68. Rachel Gur-Arie, "Eugenical Sterilization in the United States (1922), by Harry Laughlin," ASU.edu, August 12, 2015, https://embryo.asu.edu/pages/eugenical-sterilization-united-states-1922-harry-h-laughlin.

69. Paul A. Lombardo, *Three Generations, No Imbeciles* (Baltimore: Johns Hopkins University Press, 2008), 239.

70. Jennifer Latson, "What Margaret Sanger Really Said about Eugenics and Race," Time.com, October 14, 2016, http://time.com/4081760/margaret-sanger-history-eugenics/.

71. Margaret Sanger, "My Way to Peace," January 17, 1932, https://www.nyu.edu/projects/sanger/webedition/app/documents/show.php?sangerDoc=129037.xml.

72. "Eugenics and Birth Control," PBS.org, http://www.pbs.org/wgbh/americanexperience/features/pill-eugenics-and-birth-control/.

73. "Nomination Database: Margaret Sanger," NobelPrize.org, https://www.nobelprize.org/nomination/archive/show_people.php?id=8093.

CHAPTER 8: AFTER THE FIRE

1. Yvonne Sherratt, *Hitler's Philosophers* (New Haven, CT: Yale University Press, 2013), 16.

2. Hugh McLeod and Werner Ustorf, eds., *The Decline of Christendom in Western Europe, 1750–2000* (New York: Cambridge University Press, 2003).

3. Søren Kierkegaard, "Subjectivity Is Truth," in *Concluding Unscientific Postscript to the Philosophical Fragments*, trans. Louis Pojman, 1844, http://philosophyfaculty.ucsd.edu/faculty/rarneson/Courses/kierkegaardphillreading.pdf.

4. Walter Kaufmann, *Existentialism from Dostoevsky to Sartre* (Cleveland: Meridian Books, 1968), 18.

5. Friedrich Wilhelm Nietzsche, *Beyond Good and Evil: Prelude to a Philosophy of the Future*, trans. Helen Zimmern (New York: Macmillan, 1907), 155.

6. Kaufmann, *Existentialism from Dostoevsky to Sartre*, 33–34.

7. Herman Philipse, *Heidegger's Philosophy of Being: A Critical Interpretation* (Princeton, NJ: Princeton University Press, 1998), 259.

8. Mark A. Ralkowski, *Heidegger's Platonism* (London: Continuum Books, 2009), 100.

9. Martin Heidegger, "The Self-Assertion of the German University," trans. W. S. Lewis, in *The Heidegger Controversy: A Critical Reader*, ed. R. Wolin (Cambridge, MA: MIT Press, 1993), 29–39.

10. Jean-Paul Sartre, *Essays in Existentialism* (New York: Citadel Press, 1993), 41.

11. Max Roser, "Life Expectancy," OurWorldInData.org, https://ourworldindata.org/life-expectancy.

12. Kyle Smith, "Sigmund Fraud," NationalReview.com, December 19, 2017, https://www.nationalreview.com/2017/12/sigmund-freud-fake-charlatan-liar/.

13. Wardell B. Pomeroy, *Dr. Kinsey and the Institute for Sex Research* (New Haven, CT: Yale University Press, 1982), 68.

14. Sue Ellin Browder, "Kinsey's Secret: The Phony Science of the Sexual Revolution," CrisisMagazine.com, May 28, 2012, https://www.crisismagazine.com/2012/kinseys-secret-the-phony-science-of-the-sexual-revolution.

15. Edward O. Wilson, *The Meaning of Human Existence* (New York: Liveright, 2014), 38.

16. E. O. Wilson, *Consilience: The Unity of Knowledge* (New York: First Vintage Books/Random House, 1999), 7.

17. Edward O. Wilson, "The Biological Basis of Morality," *Atlantic*, April 1998, https://www.theatlantic.com/magazine/archive/1998/04/the-biological-basis-of-morality/377087/.

18. Wilson, *The Meaning of Human Existence*, 14.

19. Ibid., 173–80.

20. Steven Pinker, *Enlightenment Now: The Case for Reason, Science, Humanism and Progress* (New York: Viking, 2018), 4.

21. Yoram Hazony, "The Dark Side of the Enlightenment," *Wall Street Journal*, April 6, 2018, https://www.wsj.com/articles/the-dark-side-of-the-enlightenment-1523050206.

22. Pinker, *Enlightenment Now*, 3–4.

23. Michael Shermer, "How Do We Know Right from Wrong without God or Religion," BigThink.com, March 4, 2018, http://bigthink.com/videos/michael-shermer-how-we-know-right-from-wrong-without-god-or-religion.

24. Sam Harris, *The Moral Landscape* (New York: Free Press, 2010).

25. Ibid., 12–13.

26. Marvin Perry, *Sources of the Western Tradition*, vol. 2: *From the Renaissance to the Present* (Boston: Wadsworth Cengage Learning, 2014), 85.

27. "Waking Up with Sam Harris: Episode #112," https://www.youtube.com/watch?v=yTWCl32j8jM.

CHAPTER 9: THE RETURN TO PAGANISM

1. Voltaire, "Jeannot and Colin," in *The Oxford Magazine*, volume I (1768), 190

2. Frank Newport, "Five Key Findings on Religion in the US," Gallup.com, December 23, 2016, http://news.gallup.com/poll/200186/five-key-findings-religion.aspx.

3. Thomas E. Woods Jr., "Race, Inequality, and the Market," FEE.org, October 1, 2002, https://fee.org/articles/race-inequality-and-the-market/.

4. "Changes in Women's Labor Force Participation in the 20th Century," U.S. Bureau of Labor Statistics, February 16, 2000, https://www.bls.gov/opub/ted/2000/feb/wk3/art03.htm.

5. Donald M. Fisk, "American Labor in the 20th Century," U.S. Bureau of Labor Statistics, January 30, 2003, https://www.bls.gov/opub/mlr/cwc/american-labor-in-the-20th-century.pdf.

6. Fred Siegel, *The Revolt against the Masses* (New York: Encounter Books, 2013), 112–13.

7. Giuseppe Fiori, *Antonio Gramsci: Life of a Revolutionary* (New York: Schocken Books, 1973), 103.

8. Max Horkheimer, *Critical Theory: Selected Essays* (New York: Continuum, 2002), 207.

9. Rolf Wiggershaus, *The Frankfurt School: Its History, Theories, and Political Significance* (Cambridge, MA: MIT Press, 1995), 135.

10. Erich Fromm, *Escape from Freedom* (New York: Henry Holt, 1941), 240.

11. Herbert Marcuse, *Eros and Civilization* (Boston: Beacon Press, 1974), 5.

12. Christopher Holman, *Politics as Radical Creation* (Toronto, ON: University of Toronto Press, 2013), 44.

13. Marcuse, *Eros and Civilization*, 227–28.

14. Herbert Marcuse, "Repressive Tolerance" in Robert Paul Wolff, Barrington Moore Jr., and Herbert Marcuse, *A Critique of Pure Tolerance* (Boston, 1965; Marcuse.org, 2015), https://www.marcuse.org/herbert/pubs/60spubs /65repressivetolerance.htm.

15. Abraham H. Maslow, *Toward a Psychology of Being* (Start Publishing LLC, 2012).

16. Lisa Hammel, "Dr. Spock as a Father—No Mollycoddler," *New York Times*, November 8, 1968, https://archive.nytimes.com/www.nytimes.com /books/98/05/17/specials/spock-father.html?_r=1.

17. Eric Pace, "Benjamin Spock, World's Pediatrician, Dies at 94," *New York Times*, March 17, 1998, https://archive.nytimes.com/www.nytimes.com /books/98/05/17/specials/spock-obit.html.

18. Nathaniel Branden, *The Psychology of Self-Esteem* (Los Angeles: Nash, 2001), 114.

19. Steven C. Ward, *Modernizing the Mind* (Westport, CT: Praeger, 2002), 102.

20. Jesse Singal, "How the Self-Esteem Craze Took Over America," TheCut .com, May 30, 2017, https://www.thecut.com/2017/05/self-esteem-grit-do -they-really-help.html.

21. Christina Hoff Sommers, "Reconsiderations: Betty Friedan's 'The Feminine Mystique,'" NYSun.com, September 17, 2008, https://www.nysun.com/arts /reconsiderations-betty-friedans-the-feminine/86003/.

22. Betty Friedan, *It Changed My Life* (Cambridge, MA: Harvard University Press, 1998), 397.

23. Malcolm X, "Racial Separation," BlackPast.org, October 11, 1963, http:// www.blackpast.org/1963-malcolm-x-racial-separation.

24. Kwame Ture and Charles V. Hamilton, *Black Power: The Politics of Liberation in America* (New York: Vintage Books, 1992), 4–5.

25. Gloria Steinem, *Revolution from Within* (Boston: Little, Brown, 1992), 44–45.

26. Kimberlé Crenshaw, "Why Intersectionality Can't Wait," *Washington Post*, September 24, 2015, https://www.washingtonpost.com/news/in-theory/wp /2015/09/24/why-intersectionality-cant-wait/?noredirect=on&utm_term =.179ecf062277.

27. Ta-Nehisi Coates, "I'm Not Black, I'm Kanye," *Atlantic*, May 7, 2018, https://www.theatlantic.com/entertainment/archive/2018/05/im-not-black-im-kanye/559763/.

28. Donna M. Hughes, "Significant Differences: The Construction of Knowledge, Objectivity, and Dominance," *Women's Studies International Forum* 18, no. 4 (July–August 1995): 395–406, https://www.sciencedirect.com/science/article/abs/pii/027753959580031J.

29. Allum Bokhari, "Lawsuit: Google Instructed Managers That 'Individual Achievement' and 'Objectivity' Were Examples of 'White Dominant Culture,'" Breitbart.com, April 18, 2018, http://www.breitbart.com/tech/2018/04/18/lawsuit-google-instructed-managers-that-individual-achievement-and-objectivity-were-examples-of-white-dominant-culture/.

30. Joshua Loftus, "Steven Pinker's Radical Centrism and the 'Alt-right,'" Medium.com, January 11, 2018, https://medium.com/@joftius/steven-pinkers-radical-centrism-and-the-alt-right-b261fde5a24f.

31. Twitter, January 9, 2018, https://twitter.com/jbouie/status/950794932066947072?lang=en.

32. Eric Turkheimer, Kathryn Paige Harden, and Richard E. Nisbett, "Charles Murray Is Once Again Peddling Junk Science about Race and IQ," Vox.com, May 18, 2017, https://www.vox.com/the-big-idea/2017/5/18/15655638/charles-murray-race-iq-sam-harris-science-free-speech.

33. Ezra Klein, "The Sam Harris Debate," Vox.com, April 9, 2018, https://www.vox.com/2018/4/9/17210248/sam-harris-ezra-klein-charles-murray-transcript-podcast.

34. Heather Mac Donald, "How Identity Politics Is Harming the Sciences," City-Journal.org, Spring 2018, https://www.city-journal.org/html/how-identity-politics-harming-sciences-15826.html.

35. Lawrence H. Summers, "Remarks at NBER Conference on Diversifying the Science & Engineering Workforce," Office of the President of Harvard University, January 14, 2005, https://web.archive.org/web/20080130023006/http://www.president.harvard.edu/speeches/2005/nber.html.

36. Tom Yun, "U of T Letter Asks Jordan Peterson to Respect Pronouns, Stop Making Statements," TheVarsity.ca, October 24, 2016, https://thevarsity.ca/2016/10/24/u-of-t-letter-asks-jordan-peterson-to-respect-pronouns-stop-making-statements/.

37. Laura Booth, "Who Is Lindsay Shepherd?" TheRecord.com, December 12, 2017, https://www.therecord.com/news-story/7992232-who-is-lindsay-shepherd-/.

38. Ben Shapiro, "The Purge: Scott Yenor and the Witch Hunt at Boise State," WeeklyStandard.com, October 18, 2017, https://www.weeklystandard.com/ben-shapiro/the-purge-scott-yenor-and-the-witch-hunt-at-boise-state.

39. John Sexton, "Professor Notes Men Are Taller Than Women on Average, SJWs Storm Out Angrily," HotAir.com, March 14, 2018, https://hotair.com

/archives/2018/03/14/professor-points-men-taller-women-average-sjws-storm-angrily/.

40. Nick Roll, "Evergreen Professor Receives $500,000 Settlement," InsideHigherEd.com, September 18, 2017, https://www.insidehighered.com/quicktakes/2017/09/18/evergreen-professor-receives-500000-settlement.

41. Greg Lukianoff and Jonathan Haidt, "The Coddling of the American Mind," TheAtlantic.com, September 2015, https://www.theatlantic.com/magazine/archive/2015/09/the-coddling-of-the-american-mind/399356/.

42. Roy Baumeister, *Evil: Inside Human Violence and Cruelty* (New York: Holt Paperbacks, 1999), 45.

43. Melinda D. Anderson, "How the Stress of Racism Affects Learning," TheAtlantic.com, October 11, 2016, http://www.theatlantic.com/education/archive/2016/10/how-the-stress-of-racism-affects-learning/503567/.

44. Yuval Noah Harari, *Sapiens: A Brief History of Humankind* (New York: HarperCollins, 2015).

45. Yuval Noah Harari, "The Meaning of Life in a World without Work," *Guardian*, May 8, 2017, https://www.theguardian.com/technology/2017/may/08/virtual-reality-religion-robots-sapiens-book.

CONCLUSION: HOW TO BUILD

1. Richard Dawkins, *The God Delusion* (Boston: Houghton Mifflin, 2008), 275.

2. Ronald Reagan, Phoenix Chamber of Commerce, March 30, 1961, https://archive.org/details/RonaldReagan-EncroachingControl.

3. Abraham Lincoln, First Inaugural Address, March 4, 1861, http://avalon.law.yale.edu/19th_century/lincoln1.asp.

4. G. K. Chesterton, *The Thing* (London, 1929; Martin Ward's Home Page, 2010), http://www.gkc.org.uk/gkc/books/The_Thing.txt.

INDEX

Abel, 32
abolitionism, 94, 179, 180
abortion, 167
Abraham, 24, 29, 35, 55, 212–13
Achilles, 42
Adam, 32, 45
Adams, John, 14, 88, 92
Adorno, Theodor, 189–90
Akkad, 31
Alexievich, Svetlana, 153
Al-Farabi, 67
allegory of the cave, 42, 58
alt-right, xvi, 184, 202–3, 208
Alzheimer's, 9
American Astronomical Society, 204
American dream, 187–88
American Enlightenment, 121–23, 127
American exceptionalism, 131
Amos, 180
Anaxagoras, 46
Anti-Defamation League, xxiii
Antigone, 42
Antiochus IV, 57
anti-Semitism, xxiii, 146–48
Apsu, 23
Aquinas, Thomas, 67–71, 74–75, 90, 170, 212

Arab world, 65–66
Aristotle, 5–7, 14, 42–45, 48, 50–53, 55, 66–67, 69–71, 76–77, 80, 82–83, 87–88, 90, 102, 106–7, 162, 188, 216
Aryanism, 146
astronomy, 68–69
atheism, 10, 100, 104–5, 114–15, 123, 133, 140, 180
Augustine, Saint, 59–61, 63–64, 69–71, 88
Augustus Caesar, emperor of Rome, 31
Austria, 130, 149
autocracy, 152

Babbitt (Lewis), 187–88
Babeuf, Gracchus, 134
Babylonians, 28
Bach, Johann S., 216
Bacon, Francis, 77–79, 107, 111, 165, 170
Bacon, Kevin, 16
Bacon, Roger, 69
Baumeister, Roy, 207
Beauvoir, Simone de, 198
Becket, Thomas, 63
Beethoven, Ludwig van, 216
Benedict, Saint, 64

Bentham, Jeremy, 110

Bible, 5, 7, 9–10, 20, 24, 27–31, 34,
36–37, 47, 65, 81, 87–89, 101,
103, 106, 123, 133, 160, 180–82,
212, 216

Bill for Establishing Religious
Freedom in Virginia, 91

Bismarck, Otto von, 145–46

Black Lives Matter, xix

Black Panther Party, 198

Black Power (Carmichael and
Hamilton), 198

blacks, xiv, xvi–xvii, 93–94, 187, 189,
198–201, 203, 206

Blackstone, 123

Bloom, Allan, 50

Boethius, 64

Boniface VIII, Pope, 74

Boreing, Jeremy, xx

Bouie, Jamelle, 203

Branden, Nathaniel, 195

Brandt, Karl, 156

Breitbart News, xxii

Britain, 121, 127

Brookhiser, Richard, 11

Brothers Karamazov, The
(Dostoyevsky), 116

Browder, Sue Ellin, 168

Brubaker, William Rogers, 129

Buck v. Bell, 155–56

Buddhism, 29

bureaucracy, 139–44, 153, 156

Burke, Edmund, 127–28

Byzantine Empire, 63

Cain, 32

Calvin, John, 75, 82, 100

Candide (Voltaire), 107

capacity, death of, 111–15. *See also*
communal or collective capacity;
individual capacity

capitalism, xviii, xxiii, 135–36, 154,
188–91, 197, 209–10

Carmichael, Stokely, 198

categorical imperative, 109–10, 118

Catholic Church, 61, 63, 65–66, 71,
74–76, 79–83, 100–101, 123,
125–26, 180

Chamberlain, Houston Stewart, 147

Chase, Stuart, 151

checks and balances, 50, 53, 85, 87

Chesterton, G. K., 217

children
as property of state, 142
sacrifice of, 212–13
training, to defend eternal truths,
213–19

China, 150, 152, 179

choice, 21, 32–33, 168, 174, 185

chosen people, 20, 29–30, 56, 214

Christianity, 21, 57–71, 127, 180, 187

church-state separation, 71, 97–98

Cicero, 50–51, 64, 87, 88

citizenship, 49–50, 56–57, 60, 80, 86,
97–98, 129, 142

City of God, City of Man and, 60–61,
63, 79

civic virtue, 14–15

civil rights movement, 187, 198

class antagonisms, 133–34, 137–38,
141, 207

classics, 39–41

Clausewitz, Carl von, 130

Clement of Alexandria, 58

Clement VI, Pope, 80

Click, Melissa, xix

Clinton, Hillary, xiii, xxii, 204

Cloots, Anacharsis, 123

Coates, Ta-Nehisi, xvi, 200

cognitive behavioral therapy, 206–7

Cole, Harold L., 154

collectivism, xxv, 124–25. *See also*
communal or collective capacity;
communal or collective purpose
Founding Fathers and, 87
individual vs., 10, 15, 16

Marx and, 136–38
nationalism and, 133
redistribution and, 144–45,
    149–56
common cause, 216–17
common good, 15
*Common Sense Book of Baby and Child
    Care* (Spock), 194
Common Sense (Paine), 134
communal or collective capacity, 9,
    15–18, 33
    America and, 97, 144, 190–91
    Athens and, 52, 53
    bureaucracy and, 153
    Catholic Church and, 65, 70–71
    Communism and, 152
    Founding Fathers and, 92–93
    Judaism and, 36
    nationalism and, 133
    teaching children about, 216–17
communal or collective moral
    purpose, 9, 13–18, 33
    America and, 98, 144, 190
    Athens and, 52–53
    bureaucracy and, 153
    Catholic Church and, 70–72
    Christianity and, 65
    Communism and, 152
    cultural Left and, 208
    Founding Fathers and, 92
    Judaism and, 20, 35–36
communism, 134–36, 147–53, 162
Communist Manifesto, The (Marx and
    Engels), 135–36, 137, 149
communitarianism, 52–53
community, 46, 49, 52–53, 143, 211
community of faith, 36
Comte, Auguste, 140–41, 143, 159, 161
Condorcet, Nicolas de, 122
Confucius, 40
Constantine, emperor of Rome, 62
Copernicus, Nicolaus, 69, 75–76
Counter-Enlightenment, 175

Crenshaw, Kimberlé, 199, 200
critical theory, 189–90
Cult of Reason, 123–24, 175
Cultural Revolution, 151
Cut, The (Singal), 195

Daily Wire, 1
Damore, James, 202, 203
Dante, 216
Dark Ages, 63–64
Darwin, Charles, 13, 69, 114–15,
    141–44, 159, 169, 178
David, Jacques-Louis, 123, 126
Dawkins, Richard, 103, 212
Day, Vox, 208
Declaration of Independence, xxv,
    87–88, 94, 125, 131, 144
Declaration of the Rights of Man, 125
Deism, 79, 106
democracy, xiv, 41, 48–51, 65, 80,
    141–42, 149–50, 152
Democracy in America (Tocqueville), 93
Democratic National Convention
    (2012), 16
Democratic Socialists of America, 203
Democrats, xiii, xiv, 3, 200
Democritus, 43–44
Dennett, Daniel, 115
Depression, xv, 154
De revolutionibus (Copernicus), 75
Descartes, René, 78–79, 112, 162
Deuteronomy, 25, 33
Dewey, John, 141–44, 152, 155, 194
dictatorship of the proletariat, 149
Diderot, Denis, 122, 124, 180
Diocletian, emperor of Rome, 62
Discourses on Livy (Machiavelli), 80
Donatists, 61
Dostoyevsky, Fyodor, 115–17
Douglass, Frederick, 94
Down's syndrome, 154
Dr. Drew Show, 183
Dreamers, 3

Dred Scott decision, 94
Du Bois, W. E. B., 152
Duranty, Walter, 151
Durkheim, Emile, 13
duties, 10, 84, 90, 124

Earth, movement of, 75
East, othering of, 40
Eastern Empire, 62–63
Eastern religions, 23
Ecclesiastes, 5, 13, 34
education, 65, 66, 137, 142
ego, 166
Egypt, ancient, 22–23, 31, 64, 101
*Eighteenth Brumaire of Louis
　　Napoleon, The* (Marx), 135
Einstein, Albert, 170
El-Bermanwy, Mostafa, xvii
elections
　　1972, 194
　　2008, 3–4
　　2016, xiii, xxii–xxiii, 4
Eliezer, Rabbi, 25
Elijah, 25
Emancipation Proclamation, xxv
Encyclopédie (Diderot), 122, 180
Engels, Friedrich, 135, 137
Enlightenment, xviii, 70, 74, 76,
　　98–100, 105–11, 121. *See
　　also* Founding Fathers; neo-
　　Enlightenment *and specific
　　individuals*
　　American, 121–23, 127
　　bureaucracy and, 139
　　dark side of, 116–18, 121
　　European, 122–23, 126–27,
　　　159–60
　　Jerusalem and Athens and, 121,
　　　181–82, 210
　　neo-Enlightenment vs., 174–75
　　postwar era and, 159–64
　　reason and, 185–86
　　W.W II and, 156–57

Enlightenment Now (Pinker), xviii, 174
equality, 32, 84, 88–89, 126, 128
Eros and Civilization (Marcuse), 191
ESPN Ashe Courage Award, 183
"Essay Concerning Human
　　Understanding" (Locke), 89–90
ethics, 6, 48, 49, 77–78, 160–61,
　　171–72, 181
eugenics, 154–56, 159
evolution, 114, 169, 171, 173, 177. *See
　　also* Darwin, Charles
existentialism, 160–65, 173, 184–85
Exodus, 24–25, 64
expertise, 142–43

Facebook, xvii
faith, 58–59, 65–69, 81–82, 171
fascism, 190–91
Federalist Papers, 91
　　No. 51, 93
Feminine Mystique (Friedan), 198
feminism, 197–99
Festival of Reason, 123
Fichte, Johann, 132
Fiddler on the Roof (musical), 214
final causes, 45, 79, 102
First Amendment, xx
Fortin, Ernest, 69
*Foundations of the Nineteenth Century,
　　The* (Chamberlain), 147
Founding Fathers, 2–3, 11, 17, 39, 51,
　　86–95, 99, 143, 144, 188, 209, 211
France, 63, 130–131
　　coup of 1851, 134–35
　　Revolution of 1789, 122–35, 139,
　　　140, 170, 175
Franciscans, 75
Frankfurt School, 189–90, 196
Frankl, Viktor, 8, 11–12
Franklin, Benjamin, 11
freedom, xii, xxiv, 17, 41–42, 53, 79,
　　85, 100, 108, 112, 122, 136, 150,
　　190, 192, 200–201, 214–16

freedom of religion, 101, 104, 125
freedom of speech, 104, 125, 201, 207
free markets, 86, 135
free will, 32–33, 70, 99, 111, 112, 116,
    165, 171, 181
Freud, Sigmund, 166–67, 191, 194
Friedan, Betty, 197–98
Friedman, Thomas, 152
Fromm, Erich, 190, 191
Frozen (film), 196
Fukuyama, Francis, 171

Galerius, emperor of Rome, 62
Galileo Galilei, 75–76
Gandhi, Mohandas, 156
gender equality, xii, 201
general will, 113, 122, 124–25,
    128–29, 138, 143–44
Genesis, 9–10, 24, 32, 35, 84
Germany, 63, 145–47
    Nazi, 147–48, 155–57, 189–91
Gideon, 36
Glendon, Mary Ann, 113
Glorious Revolution, 122
God. *See also* Unmoved Mover
    Abraham and Isaac and, 212
    antimaterialistic, 25–26
    Aquinas and, 67–68
    Christianity and, 58–59
    covenant with, 33
    Darwin and, 114–15
    Descartes and, 79
    death of, 117–18, 185
    Dostoyevsky and, 115–16
    Galileo and, 76
    humans in image of, 10, 32–34
    Judaism and unified, 20–28
    Kierkegaard and, 161
    Moses vs. Aristotle and, 55–56
    progress and, 28–31
    proofs of existence of, 67–68,
        104–5
gods, 22, 25–26, 29, 31–32

Goldberg, Jonah, xviii, 151
Golden Rule, 110
Gospels, 57, 59
grace, 21, 58–59
Gramsci, Antonio, 189
Grand Designer, 46
"Grand Inquisitor" (Dostoyevsky),
    115–16
Great Leap Forward, 151
Greece (Athens), xxiv–xxvii, 5,
    17–18, 22, 28–29, 39–58, 64,
    65–69, 89, 91, 180, 181, 209–10
Gregory VII, Pope, 63
Grotius, Hugo, 82–83
Groundhog Day (film), 209
gulags, 150

Hagar, 212
Haidt, Jonathan, 13, 45, 203, 207
Haley, Nikki, 200
Hamilton, Charles, 198
Hammurabi, 9, 31, 40
Hanukkah, 57
happiness, 1–9
    Aristotle and, 53
    Catholic Church and, 70
    capacity and, 6, 9
    communal capacity and, 15–17
    communal purpose and, 13–17
    Diderot on, 124
    Divine meaning underlying, 17
    Founding Fathers and, 89–95
    four elements of, 17–18
    Greeks and, 5–7, 49, 53–54
    Hebrew Bible and, 5–7
    individual capacity and, 11–13
    individual purpose and, 9–13, 17
    Judaism and four elements of,
        33–37
    maximizing, 106
    moral purpose and, 5–9
    need to regain individual and
        communal, 211–12

happiness (*cont.*)
  Nietzsche and, 119
  politics and, 3–4
  pursuit of, 2, 4–5, 17–18
  Stone Age and, 209
  Washington on, 7–8
Harari, Yuval Noah, 209–10
Harden, Kathryn Paige, 204
Harrington, 88
Harris, Sam, 177–79, 181–82,
    203–4
Hasmonean dynasty, 57
Hazony, Yoram, 131, 175
Hebrew language, 25, 47
hedonism, xxv, 10, 107, 169
Hegel, Georg, 133, 137, 139, 141, 143,
    159, 161, 172, 188
Heidegger, Martin, 148, 162, 184
heliocentric solar system, 69
Hemings, Sally, 94
Henry II, king of England, 63
Henry IV, Holy Roman emperor, 63
Heraclitus, 46
Herder, 175
Heying, Heather, 206
Hinduism, 28
Hispanics, xiv
history, 99
  end of progress and, 209–10
  Enlightenment and, 185
  God of Abraham and, 55
  Marx and, 136
  pagans and circular movement of,
      28–29
  progress of, 20, 28–31, 35–36,
      55, 132
  state and, 130–31
Hitler, Adolf, 147, 149, 155, 159, 179
Hobbes, Thomas, 83–85, 88, 102–5,
    110, 112, 125, 177
Holmes, Oliver Wendell, 155
Holocaust, 8, 11–12, 156–57, 179, 213
Holy Roman Empire, 63

homosexuality, 167
Horkheimer, Max, 189–90
Horwitz, Robert, 141
Hughes, Donna, 201–2
Hugh of Saint-Victor, 66
humanism, xviii, 101, 154
human nature, xviii, 108, 113, 127,
    136, 166, 168–69
human rights, xxiv, 41, 82–85, 140
Hume, David, 104–5, 112–13, 169,
    172, 180
Huntington, Samuel, 171

id, 166
identity politics, 200, 204
idols, 23, 26, 27
Iliad, The (Homer), 29
immigrants, xxvi, 3
imperialism, 131, 133
individual capacity, 9, 11–13, 17, 33
  America and, 97, 190–91
  Athens and, 42, 52
  Catholic Church and, 70
  Christianity and, 65
  cultural Left and, 208
  evolutionary biology and, 169
  Founding Fathers and, 91–92
  Judaism and, 34, 42
  nationalism and, 133, 144
  need to regain, 211
  teaching children about, 215–16
individualism, 16, 190–91, 200, 206
  bureaucracy and, 138–39
  collectivism and, 138, 144
  existentialism and, 163–64
  Hegel and, 132
  Luther and, 81–82
  polis and, 56–57
  rise of, 83–87
individual moral purpose, 9–11, 15, 18
  America and, 98, 190–91
  Athens and, 52
  Catholic Church and, 70

Christianity and, 65
communal capacity and, 18
Founding Fathers and, 91, 144
Judaism and, 20, 33–34
teaching children about, 215
individual rights, 84, 87, 98–99, 122, 124–25, 133, 139–40, 143
individual will, xxiv, 125
intersectionality, 196–209
IQ differences, 201, 203, 208
Isaac, 29, 212
Ishmael, 212
Islamic civilization, 65
"is-ought" distinction, 105, 169–70, 172
Israel, 29, 35, 101
Italy, fascist, 189

Jackson, Jesse, 39
Jacob, 29
Jaffa, Harry, 90
Japanese Americans, internment of, 157
Jaspers, Karl, 162, 184
"Jeannot et Colin" (Voltaire), 185
Jefferson, Thomas, 2–3, 87–89, 91–94, 143
Jenner, Caitlyn, 183–84
Jeremiah, Rabbi, 25
Jesus Christ, 58–60, 67, 70, 212
"Jewishness in Music" (Wagner), 146
Jewish Temple, 57
destruction of, 62
Jim Crow, xiv, xvii, 180, 187
John, king of England, 160
Johnson, Paul, 30–31
Jonas, Raymond, 126
Joshua, Rabbi, 25
Judaism (Jerusalem), xxiv–xxvi, 17–18, 20–37, 41, 43, 51–52, 55–58, 62, 66–70, 146, 213
Judea, 57
Julian, emperor of Rome, 61–62
Julian calendar, 69

Jung, Georg, 145
justice, 49, 86, 91, 124

Kaganovich, Lazar, 16
Kant, Immanuel, xxiv, 108–10, 118, 159, 161, 170, 174, 177
Kennedy, John F., 164
Kepler, Johannes, 76–77
Kerr, Walter, 42
Kershaw, Ian, 148
KGB, 152
Khullar, Dr. Dhruv, 9
Kierkegaard, Søren, 160–61, 212
King, Martin Luther, Jr., xxv, 35, 180
Kinsey, Alfred, 167–69, 191
Klein, Ezra, 203–4
Krauthammer, Charles, 8
Ku Klux Klan, xxii
Kulturkampf, 145

labor, 135–37, 151
Lady Gaga, 196
laissez-faire, 153
Laughlin, Harry, 155–56
Left, 73, 152, 188–93, 202–3, 208–10. See also New Left
Leibniz, Gottfried Wilhelm, 106–7
Lenin, Vladimir, 149–50
Leonard, Thomas, 154
"Letter from Birmingham Jail" (King), xxv
Levada Center, 153
Leviathan, 84, 112, 125
Levites, 36
Leviticus, 30
Lewis, Sinclair, 187–88
LGBT studies, 189
liberal arts, 64–65
Liberal Fascism (Goldberg), 151
liberalism, xviii
classical, 79–83, 99–100
transnational, 171
libertarianism, 104, 108

libertinism, 10

liberty, 41, 92, 94, 143. *See also*
    freedom
    French Revolution and, 123,
        125–28

Lincoln, Abraham, xxv, 216–17

Livy, 88

Locke, John, 84–90, 122–23, 143, 160

Loconte, Joseph, 81

Loftus, Joshua, 203

Logos, 46–47, 58

Luther, Martin, 75, 81–82, 88, 100

Lynch, Frederick, 205

Maccabees, 57

Mac Donald, Heather, 204, 206

Machiavelli, Niccolò, 80–83, 101–2,
        111–12

MacIntyre, Alasdair, 48–49

Madison, James, 92–94

Magna Carta, xxv, 160, 186

Maher, Bill, 106

Maimonides, 27, 67

Malcolm X, 198

Mansfield, Harvey, 101

Man's Search for Meaning (Frankl), 8

Mao Tse-tung, 151, 162, 192

Marcuse, Herbert, 191–93

Marduk, 23, 31

Marsilius of Padua, 79–80

Marx, Karl, 129, 134–38, 141, 148–50,
        159, 162–64, 189–93, 196

Maslow, Abraham, 193–94, 195, 198

Mason, George, 88

materialism, 98, 107, 115–18, 124,
        141, 175, 178–79, 190, 196
    redistributionist, 133, 144

mathematics, 47–48, 76, 83

Mauzi, Robert, 124

Meaning of Human Existence, The
        (Wilson), 173

Medical College Admission Test
        (MCAT), 205

Mein Kampf (Hitler), 148

Mendelssohn, Felix, 146

meritocracy, 129

Mesopotamia, 22–23, 31

Messiah, 59–60

Middle Ages, 64–65, 71

Milan, Edict of, 62

military draft, 129–30

millennials, 195

minorities, 192–93, 199–200, 204–5

"Model Eugenical Sterilization Law"
        (Laughlin), 155–56

monarchy, 36, 65

monasteries, 64–65, 70

monotheism, 27, 46, 104

Montesquieu, 85, 123

morality, xxiii
    Christianity and, 61–62
    Darwinian evolution and, 114
    Enlightenment and, 185
    French Revolution, 127–28
    God's expectations for man and,
        26–28
    Greek virtue and, 45–46
    Judaism and, 24–25, , 28–29
    Kinsey and, 167–68
    Marx and, 137
    neo-Enlightenment and, 171–74,
        177–78, 181
    Nietzsche and, 118–19
    Paine and, 134
    reason alone and, 105–11, 113,
        117–18
    religion and, 171
    scientific materialism and, 115–17
    subjectivity and, xxv–xxvi, 118,
        161–62

moral minimum, 131

moral purpose
    communal, 13–17
    Divine meaning and, 18
    faith and, 65
    happiness and, 5–9, 17–18

individual, 9–13, 20
    Judaism and, 20
moral realism, 177
moral relativism, 100–105, 124,
    128, 172
moral truth, 161–62, 165
Morgenthau, Henry, 154
Moses, 24, 29, 36, 40, 54–55, 101, 103
Murray, Charles, 206
Murrow, Edward R., 189–90
Muslims, 65, 67
Mussolini, Benito, 189

Napoleon Bonaparte, 124, 127, 131
Naram-Sin of Akkad, 31
Nathan, Rabbi, 25
nationalism, xxvi, 128–33, 138
    romantic, 144–49, 156
National Science Foundation
    (NSF), 204
national self-determination, 131
nation-state, 129, 131
Native Americans, 22, 28
natural law, 43–48, 50–52, 54, 56, 82,
    84–88, 164–69, 180, 196
natural liberty, 86
natural rights, 74, 82–87, 110, 143, 180
natural selection, 114, 172
Nazis, xxii, xxiv–xxv, 147–49,
    155–57, 162, 184, 189–91
NBC, 188
neo-Enlightenment, 169–82, 209–10
New Deal, 151
New Left, 191–94, 196–98
New Testament, 70, 103
Newton, Isaac, 76–77
New York Times, 9, 151, 152
    Magazine, xvi
Nicaea, First Council of, 62
Nicene Creed, 62
Nicholas of Cusa, 75
Nietzsche, Friedrich, 117–19, 159,
    161–62

9/11, 213
Nisbett, Richard, 204
Noah, 29
Noahide Laws, 28, 83
nonaggression principle, 125
North Korea, 150–51
Notes from the Underground
    (Dostoyevsky), 116
Notre Dame Cathedral, 123
nous (universal logic), 46
Novum Organum (Bacon), 78
Nuremberg trials, 156

Obama, Barack, xvi, 3–4, 35
Obama, Michelle, 3–4
objectivism, 194–95
Ohanian, Lee E., 154
Old Testament, 103
Olivier, Laurence, 188
On the Origin of Species (Darwin), 114
Oresme, Nicole, 75
Orientalism (Said), 40
Original Sin, 195
Orwell, George, 148, 192

paganism, 22, 26–27, 61–62,
    185–96, 206
Paine, Thomas, 133–35
pantheism, 23
Panthéon, 126
papal plenitude of power, 79
Paris revolt of 1968, 192
passion, 112–15, 117, 123, 186
patriotism, 133
Paul, 59
Paul III, Pope, 75
People's Party, 194
perfectibility, 119, 122, 136
Peterson, Jordan, 205
Philip IV, king of France, 74
Pinker, Steven, xviii, 174–77, 179,
    182, 202–3
Pinocchio (film), 196

Pipes, Richard, 150
planetary motion, 76
Plan for the Scientific Work Necessary to Reorganize Society (Comte), 141
Planned Parenthood, 156
Plato, 42–44, 48–50, 52–54, 58, 71, 82, 88, 109, 162, 166, 188
polarization, 207, 208, 212
polis, 48–49, 53–54, 56–57, 60, 83
political correctness, 193, 208
Polynesia, 22
polyphonic music, 64
polytheism, 22–23, 27, 31, 46, 104
Pomeroy, Wardell, 167
Popper, Karl, 49–50
positivism, 105
postmodernism, 202
poverty, xi, xxiv, 41, 61
pragmatism, 143–44
Prince, The (Machiavelli), 80, 101
privacy, 104
progress, 28–31, 68–69, 99, 131–33, 175, 185
     end of, 208–10
Progressivism, xxvi, 141–44, 154, 156
proletariat, 138, 149
Prometheus, 42
property, 84–86, 89, 113, 134, 136–37, 193
prostitution, 167
Protestant Episcopal Church, 7
Prussia, 132, 145
Psychology of Self-Esteem, The (Branden), 195
public schools, prayer in, 97
Puritans, 16
purpose, 104–5, 181
pursuit of happiness, 2–5, 7–13, 17, 89–94, 98
Putin, Vladimir, 153
Putnam, Robert, 14
Pythagoras, 47–48

quadrivarium, 64

race science, 154
racism, 193, 197–99, 203–4, 207–8
Ra (god), 31
Rand, Ayn, 194–95
Reagan, Ronald, 214
reason, xii–xiii, xix, 37
     Aquinas and, 67–71
     Augustine and, 70
     Bible and, 37
     Christianity, 59–60, 65
     Darwin and, 114–15
     death of, 184
     democracy and, 65
     Dostoyevsky and, 116
     Enlightenment and, 98, 100–111, 185
     Founding Fathers and, 87–92
     Greeks and, 41–45, 52, 56, 59–60
     Grotius and, 82
     happiness and, 7, 17–18
     individual capacity and, 12
     intersectionality and, 201
     Judaism and, 27, 37, 56
     Locke and, 84
     Luther and, 81–82
     morality and, 105–11, 117–18
     neo-Enlightenment and, 170, 175–79, 181
     Nietzsche and, 117–18
     paganism and, 206–7
     passion and, 111–15, 123
     postwar and, 160–61
     scholasticism, 66
     science and, 65
     trap of, 186
     virtue-free, 122
rebellion, 191
redistributionism, 133, 144–45
Red Terror, 150
Reflections on the Revolution in France (Burke), 127–28

religion, xiv, xv
   Comte and, 140–41
   empowering nature of, 41
   Founding Fathers and, 90
   Freud and, 166
   intersectionality and, 196–97
   Marx and, 137
   neo-Enlightenment and, 179,
      180–81
   postwar era and, 160, 187
   rejection of, 98
religious fundamentalism, 100
Renaissance, 74, 101
repression, 192, 194, 200
Republic, The (Cicero), 50–51
Republic, The (Plato), 44
Republicans, xiii, 3, 200
revelation, 28, 37, 56, 59, 69, 170, 179, 181
revolution, 136, 149
Richard III (Shakespeare), 188
rights. *See also* freedom; human rights;
   individual rights; natural rights
   duties and, 10, 90
   to liberty, 84, 88–89
   to life, 84, 89
   to property, 84–86, 89
Robespierre, Maximilien, 124, 126
romanticism, 193. *See also*
   nationalism, romantic
Rome, ancient, 22, 31, 55, 60–64
Romulus Augustus, Emperor of
   Rome, 63
Roosevelt, Franklin D., 151, 153–54
Roosevelt, Teddy, 155
Rousseau, Jean-Jacques, 108, 113,
   122, 125–26, 128, 136, 139, 144,
   168, 175, 193
Russia, post-communist, 152
Russian Revolution, 149–50. *See also*
   Soviet Union

Sabbath, 2
Sacks, Rabbi Jonathan, 23, 55

Sade, Marquis de, 115
Saggs, Henry William Frederick,
   22, 26
Said, Edward, 40
salvation, 62
Samuel, 36
Sanders, Bernie, 150
Sanger, Margaret, 156
Sapiens (Harari), 209
Sartre, Jean-Paul, 162–64, 173,
   184, 198
Saudi Arabia, 179
Schelling, 175
scholasticism, 66, 69–70
science, xviii–xix, xxiv–xxv, 34, 43,
   47–48, 53, 65, 68–69, 74–79
   bureaucracy and, 140
   Darwinian evolution and, 115
   intersectionality and, 201–5
   morality and, 116–17
   neo-Enlightenment and, 169–79
   postwar era and, 164–69
   religion and, 75–77
scientific determinism, 117
scientific governance, 157, 164
scientific materialism, xxvi, 12, 118
scientific method, 48, 69, 78, 141, 186,
   201, 206
scientific positivism, 140
scientific progressivism, 144–45
scientism, 161, 173–74
Secondhand Time (Alexievich), 153
Second Sex, The (de Beauvoir), 198
self-esteem, 195–97, 199, 206
self-realization, 162, 193–98, 206
Seneca, 13, 64
sexism, 193, 197, 203, 207
Sexual Behavior in the Human Female
   (Kinsey), 167
Sexual Behavior in the Human Male
   (Kinsey), 167
sexuality, 167–68, 191–93
Shakespeare, William, 216

Shepherd, Lindsay, 205
Shermer, Michael, 177, 179, 182
Siegel, Fred, 188
Sinai, revelation at, 20, 25, 33
Singal, Jesse, 195
Skeptic, 177
Slate, 203
slavery, xvii, xxiv, 29, 86, 94,
     179–80
Smith, Adam, xxiii, 86
Social Contract, The (Rousseau), 126
social contract theory, 143
socialism, 134, 149, 189
social leveling, 133–38
social science, 141, 154, 195, 201
sociobiology, 169
sociology, 154
Socrates, 42, 49
Sodom and Gomorrah, 24
Solomon, 5–6, 13, 34
Solon, 40
Sommers, Christina Hoff, 203, 206
soul, tripartite, 166
sovereignty, 84
Soviet Union (USSR), xxv, 150–52,
     156–57, 162
Sowell, Thomas, 187
speech, as violence, 184, 192
Spencer, Herbert, 143
Spencer, Richard, xvi, xxiii, 208
Spinoza, Baruch, 102–4, 112
Spock, Dr. Benjamin, 194–95
Stalin, Joseph, 16, 150, 152–53, 157,
     159
Stanton, Elizabeth Cady, 180
Stark, Rodney, 61
state, 17, 36–37, 50–51, 71, 80,
     84, 104, 110, 112–13, 122,
     125, 129–30, 132, 137, 139,
     142
state of nature, 83–84, 86
Steinem, Gloria, 199
STEM, diversity and, 204–5

sterilization, compulsory, 155–56
Stoics, 44, 48, 52–53, 104, 108
Strauss, Leo, 46, 50
subjectivism, 118, 124, 161–62, 165,
     185, 206
suffrage, 180
suicide, 4, 13
Suicide of the West (Goldberg), xviii
Summers, Lawrence, 205
superego, 166
survival of the fittest, 143, 177

Talmud, 25, 27
Tarfon, Rabbi, 6
Tarnas, Richard, 46, 58
taxes, 137
Taylor, Jared, 208
Taylor, Steve, 8
technology, xvii–xviii, 74–75
telos and teleology, 44–46, 52–53,
     77, 79, 82, 98–99, 102–3, 106,
     111–12, 127, 132, 137, 161, 179,
     181, 185, 194, 197
     critics of, 100–105, 113–15, 119,
          144, 180–81
temperance, 91
Ten Commandments, 23, 26, 97
Tertullian, 59
theocracy, 37, 80
Theodosius, emperor of Rome, 63
Thirty Years' War, 82
Thomas, Clarence, 200
Thomism, 67, 76. *See also* Aquinas,
     Thomas
Thus Spake Zarathustra (Nietzsche),
     118
Tiamat (goddess), 23
Time, 15
Tocqueville, Alexis de, 93, 139
tolerance, 121, 214
     repressive, 192
tolerance, repressive, 192, 200
Tolstoy, Leo, xxiv

Torah, 25, 36, 56, 103
totalitarianism, 190
toxic masculinity, 200
transgenderism, 183–84, 206
tribalism, 128, 186, 200, 209
trivium, 64
Trojan War, 29
Trump, Donald, xiii, xvi, xxii, 3–4
truth, 34–35, 42, 48, 162, 165, 168,
    186, 206
Tur, Zoey, 183–84
Turkheimer, Eric, 204
Twitter, xxiii
tyranny, 16, 34, 36, 56, 108, 128,
    131, 171

Ukraine, 151
U.S. Congress, xiv, 155
U.S. Constitution, 85, 91, 92, 94, 131,
    144, 186
U.S. Senate, 123
U.S. Supreme Court, 40, 155
universalism, 58, 161
universality, 34, 56, 94
universe, 22, 24, 34, 46–48, 52
universities, 66
Unmoved Mover, 46, 68, 104, 105,
    185
utilitarianism, 118, 177
utopianism, xxv, 16, 49–50, 53, 119,
    122–23, 128
    bureaucracy and, 139–44
    leveling and, 133–38
    nationalism and, 128–33

values. *See also* morality
    neo-Enlightenment and, 170–71
    self-esteem and, 195
    training children to defend,
        213–19
Venezuela, xxv
victim mentality, 193, 197–207
violence, 192, 207

Virginia Declaration of Rights,
    88–89
virtù, 80, 101, 111, 124
virtue, 45–49, 52–54, 80, 83–84,
    87, 89–90, 99, 101, 122,
    193–94, 211
volkisch movement, 147
Voltaire, 10, 106–8, 110, 122, 126,
    185
Vox, 204

Wagner, Cosima, 147
Wagner, Richard, 146–47, 148
Wallis, W. Allen, 168
war, 41, 64–65, 132
    total, 129–30
War and Peace (Tolstoy), xxiv
Washington, George, 7, 11, 90
Washington Post, 8
Weber, Max, 140
Weimar Republic, 148
Weinstein, Bret, 206
Westphalia, Treaty of, xxv, 101, 131
"What Is Enlightenment?" (Kant),
    108
white pride, 208
white privilege, 200
white supremacy, xxii, 41
Wilhelm II, kaiser of Germany, 147
Willard, Frances, 180
William of Ockham, 75, 77
Williams, Thomas Chatterton, xvi
will to power, 117–19, 161
Wilson, E. O., 169–73
Wilson, Woodrow, 143–44, 146, 155
Wired.com, xvii
Woman's Bible, The (Stanton), 180
Woman's Christian Temperance
    Union, 180
women's rights, xv, 93–94, 180, 187,
    201, 204–5
Women's Studies International Forum
    (Hughes), 202

Woods, Thomas E., Jr., 66
World War I, 146–49, 157, 159–60, 164, 189
World War II, 152–53, 156–57, 159, 160, 164

Yenor, Scott, 206
yetzer (will), 47

Yiannopoulos, Milo, xxii–xiii
Yisrael (struggle with God), 25
Young America's Foundation, xx

zeitgeist, 132
Zinoviev, Grigory, 150

ABOUT THE AUTHOR

Ben Shapiro is editor in chief of the *Daily Wire* and host of *The Ben Shapiro Show*, the top conservative podcast and fastest-growing radio show in the nation. A *New York Times* bestselling author, Shapiro is a graduate of Harvard Law School and the nation's most requested campus speaker.